100

The Archaeology of Ancient Peru and the Work of Max Uhle

Dorothy Menzel

The Archaeology of Ancient Peru and the Work of Max Uhle

Dorothy Menzel

R. H. Lowie Museum
of Anthropology
University of California,
Berkeley

This book was prepared in conjunction with an exhibition at the R. H. Lowie Museum of Anthropology, University of California, Berkeley, in 1977. Dr. Menzel completed the manuscript in 1974. The project was supported by a grant from the National Endowment for the Arts in Washington, D.C.

Printing of the book was supported entirely by two separate donations from Mr. and Mrs. Thomas J. Ready, Jr., Pebble Beach, California.

Cover illustration: Carved ceremonial digging board, purchased by Uhle from an Indian at Ocucaje, Ica Valley, who had found it in the vicinity. 4-4663.

Contents

1

Introduction

"Peru" is the name the Spaniards gave to the great empire of the Incas, which flourished at their arrival in 1532. The Inca name for their realm was *Tawantinsuyu*. The term was tantamount to "civilized world" in the same sense in which the ancient Romans used the words to describe their empire. The civilized world of the Incas included all the highland and coastal regions of the country now called Peru, as well as modern Ecuador, Bolivia, western Argentina, the northern half of Chile, and probably parts of the tropical forest lands to the east of the Andean highlands (map 1). Its north to south length covered 36° of latitude. The term "ancient Peru" refers to *Tawantinsuyu*.

Before the German archaeologist Max Uhle began his explorations of ancient Peru in 1895, the only known history of *Tawantinsuyu* was that recorded by some of the Spanish clerics, secretaries, administrators and soldiers who were eye witnesses to the Spanish conquest, or who took part in the subsequent Spanish domination. Eventually a few native chroniclers and chroniclers of mixed Inca and Spanish ancestry joined their number. These accounts were fragmentary, specialized, and of uneven value. Much of Inca life and the workings of the Inca Empire went unrecorded, and there was even less record of the peoples conquered by the Incas. No orally transmitted records exist for the time before about 1350, and any such data predating about 1430 are heavily obscured by mythical history. It was the archaeological field work of Max Uhle that made it possible to enlarge our understanding of the nature and operations of the Inca Empire, and to begin to trace the history of the peoples of *Tawantinsuyu* back in time.

The purpose of this study is to assess the nature of Uhle's contribution to Andean culture history, which he made during the period 1899 to 1905 while working for the University of California under the sponsorship of Mrs. Phoebe Apperson Hearst.[1]* The collections made by Uhle during this period are deposited in the Robert H. Lowie Museum of Anthropology, together with Uhle's field catalogs, letters addressed to Mrs. Hearst, and some photographs. He also made other field notes and maps, which did not accompany his collections. The work Uhle

*See endnotes

did during 1896-1897 for the University of Pennsylvania formed in many ways the foundation for his subsequent work, and therefore references to this earlier work are also included here. For a more complete account of Uhle's career and scientific contribution, see Rowe, 1954.

Uhle came to the field of Andean archaeology with three important advantages. He had a concept of history, the idea that cultures change through time. He had studied the chronicles, and knew that at the time of the Spanish conquest some ruined sites were already ancient. Also, he had studied records of remains that were known to be associated with the Inca culture at the time of the Spanish conquest, and those of a ruin known to have been ancient at the time of the Spanish conquest. The latter ruin was Tiahuanaco, a site just south of Lake Titicaca.[2] Thus, at the outset Uhle recognized two distinct styles of archaeological remains, representing two different periods in the Andean past, and he knew which was the earlier and which was the later.

The recognition of the differences in style and age between the two culture units had more far-reaching effects than Uhle had anticipated. Both Inca-style remains and some resembling the style of Tiahuanaco were styles of empires which embraced large parts of the Andean area. Wherever an example of a particular imperial style was found, it indicated contemporaneity with the same kinds of objects found elsewhere, thus making it possible to cross-date styles and histories of different areas. Archaeological remains unrelated to the styles of the empires could be dated with reference to the widespread styles. This circumstance made it possible for Uhle to establish a chronological framework of style change through time applicable to the entire realm of ancient Peru.

Uhle achieved this chronological framework primarily through a purely stylistic argument. He argued that any style that pre-dated that of the Inca Empire would lack features of the imperial Inca style, and equally, any style that pre-dated what he called "Tiahuanaco" would lack features of that style. Archaeological remains that dated between his "Tiahuanaco" and Inca styles could be dated roughly by a process of stylistic seriation, in which those styles most similar to the "Tiahuanaco" style were presumed to be nearer to it in time, and those less similar to it later in time.[3] Uhle was able to support his seriational argument by evidence consisting of the relationship of burials to a sequence of stages of construction of the Temple of Pachacamac on the central coast of Peru. The earlier burials were covered by an extension of the structure.

Most of Uhle's field work after his visit to the site of Tiahuanaco was concerned with the discovery of remains relatable to the Inca Empire, to an empire with remains relatable to those of Tiahuanaco (the Huari Empire), and to the time between the two empires. He also uncovered remains datable to the years shortly after the Spanish conquest. At one estimate, this period covers some 1000 years, from about 540 A.D. to about 1570 A.D. (cf. chronological table).

In terms of culture history, the period from the Huari Empire to the Colonial Period is complex and eventful. Neither Uhle nor later archaeologists have yet succeeded in exploring the full potential of the available evidence. Both for this reason, and because this time period was covered by the largest part of Uhle's field work, it is the main subject of discussion in the chapters that follow.

Uhle's early experience with small collections of unusual objects in European museums also had channeled his interests into the search for the home and origin of two quite different, even less known art styles of ancient Peru. One was a beautiful style of pottery painted in many colors, now known as the "Nasca" style. The other was a style of pottery painted in red, white, and sometimes black, remarkable for its life-like representations both in painted and sculptured forms. This style is now known by the name of "Moche." Uhle succeeded in discovering the home areas of both these styles, the former in the Nasca and Ica Valleys on the south coast, the latter in the Moche Valley on the north coast. It was one of Uhle's great contributions to isolate these styles and associated remains, and to demonstrate that they predated the remains of the Huari Empire (cf. chronological table).

Uhle also discovered several additional, until then unsuspected, early cultures, including remnants of the "Lima" and "White-on-Red" styles and associated remains on the central coast, the "Paracas" culture of the south coast, and much more ancient remains of fishing cultures on the coast north of Lima (cf. chronological table). Although Uhle realized the relative antiquity of his finds, he did not have the necessary data to estimate their actual age. We now know that the earliest remains found by him belong to a fishing community at the mouth of the Supe Valley north of Lima, datable to

before 1500 B.C.[4] All the "pre-Tiahuanaco" remains of Uhle's discoveries form parts of independent histories which are being studied by specialists in these cultures, and which are subjects of continued explorations.

The culture history represented by the collections Uhle made between 1896 and 1905 is summarized graphically in the chronological table. This table is organized in terms of the information available at the present, after many archaeologists went on to build on Uhle's pioneer work. It is a great tribute to Uhle's achievement that the basic chronological framework of Andean culture history outlined by him continued to prove itself valid.

Columns 1-6 and 11-21 in the chronological table represent Uhle's collections from particular coastal valleys or highland basins. The shaded areas cover the time span represented by the objects collected in each region. Most of the collection represented by column 12 was made for the University of Pennsylvania. Columns 7, 8 and 9 represent the chronological framework in terms of Uhle's findings which are discussed in the chapters that follow. Column 10 lists some of the major events that are discernible in the archaeological record, and which explain subsequent events affecting larger areas.

Column 8 represents time in terms of our own calendar years, at 100 year intervals. Except for historical dates beginning about 1440 A.D., absolute dates in terms of our calendar are little better than rough estimates, based on a relatively unreliable chemical dating system of samples of organic matter (radiocarbon dating). Several alternative choices of correlations between radiocarbon years and our calendar years are available. The scale shown here represents a selection of one of these.[5]

In talking about culture history, it is essential to know with maximum precision what events are contemporary, what events are not, and how those that are not contemporary follow one another in time. It is not nearly as important to be able to correlate these events with our own calendar years. In order to bypass the inaccuracies inherent in the radiocarbon dating process, John H. Rowe devised a way of dealing with relative time without reference to a calendar. He proposed that a sequence of style changes in one small area form a master sequence, and that we discuss events in the culture history of other areas by cross-dating them with particular events and styles in the area of the master sequence.[6] In this way it is possible to deal with contemporary, earlier, or later events without committing ourselves to a particular date in our calendar. Even if it should be necessary to change our estimate of the calendar dates, the periods of relative time will remain unaffected.

Rowe chose the archaeological sequence of the Ica

Valley on the south coast of modern Peru for the master sequence. This was because Uhle's most thorough archaeological record for the longest period of time concerned the archaeology of the valley of Ica. Where a gap existed in the Ica record, it was covered by a collection from the neighboring area of Nasca, which had a closely related style history during that period. Rowe and his students have added extensive field work in the Ica Valley and neighboring valleys between 1954 and 1969 to fill in additional gaps in the Ica master sequence.

The episodes of style change in the archaeology of Ica took place in a succession of intervals of time. The episodes can therefore be translated into time periods, as shown in column 9 on the chronological table. For each major stylistic episode there is a style term in the Ica sequence, which is matched by a period term in the column for relative chronology. Gradual changes in distinctive style traditions can also be differentiated as subdivisions of a particular style. These style subdivisions are called "phases." The Ica style phases are translated into "epochs," that is, subdivisions of periods, when we are speaking of styles in areas other than Ica. If we say an event somewhere else took place in Epoch 6 of a period, for example, we mean that it took place at the time of Phase 6 of a particular style of Ica.

Three of the periods of relative time in column 9 of the chronological table are called "horizons," because of a traditional way of referring to archaeological peculiarities that could be observed during the periods. Sometime during the "horizons" it was possible to see a much wider spread of similar traits than during the other intervals of time. These three periods have been named Early Horizon, Middle Horizon, and Late Horizon.

In the Late Horizon the occurrence of similar objects over a very large area is known to reflect the history of the Inca Empire. The capital of the Inca Empire was the city of Cuzco in the south-central highlands of modern Peru. A centralized government at Cuzco imposed similar customs over the entire area of *Tawantinsuyu,* and contributed to the mingling of different art styles.

The pattern of archaeological remains during a part of the Middle Horizon is so similar to that of the Late Horizon, that it has led to the inference that it also reflects the existence of an empire. The capital of this empire was near the present city of Ayacucho in the highlands northwest of Cuzco, probably at the site called Huari, about 35 kilometers (22 miles) north of Ayacucho. The Huari Empire shared some aspects of its religious art with a neighboring state to the south which may also have been an empire, and which was contemporary with the Huari Empire. Its capital was at the site of Tiahuanaco. The realm of the Huari Empire covered most of modern highland and coastal Peru, except only the southernmost area around Lake Titicaca and the adjoining coast.

The pattern of archaeological remains during the Early Horizon has been less throughly explored, and it is not possible at present to make inferences concerning its political structure. However, it is clear that the wide spread of similar style traits was closely linked to a great religious center in the northern highlands, at the site of Chavín, east of the upper reaches of the Santa Valley.

During the times of the empires and the time when the religious center of Chavín was active and influential, the culture traits of Cuzco, Huari and Chavín, respectively, were widely distributed. Although regional differences existed during these periods, archaeological remains identical or nearly identical to those of the capitals were also found in farflung areas. With the collapse of the empires and the end of Chavín as a center of influence, direct communication with outlying areas ceased, as did the close resemblances of selected objects over large areas. However, the customs of art and culture established in the times of union did not stop abruptly. Instead, one sees gradual modifications in the traditions, with each community developing different modifications. Regional differences increased with time, until it is no longer possible to see the common culture base without tracing the history of each tradition independently.

Since the relative chronology is based on style changes in the master sequence of Ica, it is important to select those episodes of style change at Ica which are the most easily observable and most sharply marked. The sharpest stylistic demarcations at Ica do not necessarily occur at the beginnings or ends of the empires or other power units. This means that the existence of the empires or other kinds of power units is not synonymous with the term "horizon." The beginning or end of a horizon or other period depends on convenient style divisions at Ica, divisions that are not necessarily correlated with major cultural events elsewhere.

Thus, the Late Horizon begins with the earliest evidence of Inca influence in the archaeological record of Ica. Presumably this influence coincided with the Inca conquest of Ica. One historical account by Miguel Cabello Valboa, which is the most reasonable, tells us that the Ica Valley was incorporated into the Inca Empire about 1476, as part of the final campaign of the conquest of the Peruvian coast. According to Cabello the imperial expansion from the Incas' home at Cuzco began about 1438, and the entire northern part of the coast was conquered about 1462.[7] This means that the Inca Empire had its origins before the Late Horizon, early in the last epoch of the preceding period.

The Middle Horizon begins with style changes in the art of the valley of Ica (Phase 9 of the Nasca style). The expansion movement of the Huari Empire did not begin until about 50 years later (Middle Horizon Epoch 1B). The beginning of the Early Horizon is dated by the beginning of Chavín influence at Ica, but the creation and growth of the great temple of Chavín predated this time, and thus it dates to the preceding period.

The ends of the horizons are even less apt to coincide with the ends of the expansion movements, since the latter do not normally mark major style changes in the different localities. Such a coincidence occurs at Ica only at the end of the Late Horizon, when a major style change coincides with the end of Inca rule at Ica.

The "intermediate" periods between the "horizon" periods are times of relatively greater regional isolation. However, this does not preclude, as we shall see, the wide spread of influences or rules by regional governments at various times in the complex culture history of the area.

One other repeated phenomenon should be noted. Each of three empires, that is, the Huari Empire, the Inca Empire and the Spanish Empire, went through an initial period of conquest, and, after the conquest was accomplished, a major administrative reorganization. While innovations of various kinds can be discovered in the archaeological records for the respective initial conquest period of conquest, and, after the conquest was accomplished, a major administrative reorganization. While in administrative reorganizations. These reorganizations had the documented or inferable purpose of tightening the central control of the imperial governments over the conquered peoples. The times of the imperial reorganizations are shown on the chronological table, because they mark especially noticeable changes in the archaeological record.

The period before the Early Horizon is called "Initial Period." Its beginning is marked by the first use of pottery in the Ica Valley. Uhle found no remains predating the late part of the Initial Period.

Since Uhle did most of his field work for the University of California on the coast of Peru, this is the area that has received most attention. However, he made small but important collections at the Inca capital of Cuzco and its environs (chronological table, column 21). He also made a small but important collection in the northern highlands at an important center near the modern town of Huamachuco (chronological table, column 20).

Most of Uhle's field work on the coast was carried out between the Moche Valley in the north and the area of Chala in the south. He also collected a few objects from the Pacasmayo Valley north of Moche. This stretch of coast includes most of the area where those coastal cultures developed that had a significant influence on Andean culture history in general. Some of the reasons for this circumstance are discussed in the succeeding chapters. For the purpose of this study, the area from Paramonga (Fortaleza River) to Asia, just south of the Mala River, is called the "central coast." The "north coast" and "south coast" adjoin this central area (map 2, a & b).

The chapters that follow begin with examples of remains of the Inca Empire, and proceed roughly back in time in succeeding chapters. Chapter 2 deals with some of Uhle's discoveries of imperial Inca remains. Chapters 3 and 4 deal with remains that reflect the effects of Inca rule on some of the conquered peoples.

Chapter 4 is divided into four sections, each of which deals with archaeological remains of the coast from Pachacamac north for the period of the Middle Horizon and later. The first section (A) begins with geographical background data for this part of the coast. Sections B, C and D deal with sites where Uhle did some of his most valuable work, namely the ruins of Chimu Capac (Supe Valley), Moche and Ancón. The discussions of these three sites concern primarily the remains of the Huari Empire and its aftermath.

Chapter 5 deals with archaeological remains of the Huari Empire and its aftermath on the coast south of Pachacamac. It begins by furnishing geographical background data on this part of the coast.

Chapter 6 deals with cultural remains from the site of Moche which predate the Huari Empire and have a bearing on the archaeology of the Huari Empire and its aftermath. They constitute a small sample of the kinds of information that additional studies of Uhle's collections can reveal.

From the Early Horizon to the Middle Horizon, religious art played an important part in Andean culture history. Religious movements were central to the expansion of Chavín culture in the Early Horizon, as well as to the Huari expansion in the Middle Horizon. Religious depictions were also important in the art of the north and south coast during the Early Intermediate Period. The tracing of religious history is therefore a useful way of beginning a study of the culture history of these periods.

Even though religious art declined in use after the Middle Horizon, religion continued to form a central role in the lives of the peoples of the Andes. Chroniclers described the religion of the Incas and of some of the peoples the Incas had conquered, and told of the important part it played in their lives. The religious traditions of the Inca Empire survive to the present, and have been described by many obervers.

Religious beliefs and practices reflected in the art and archaeology of the Huari Empire are so similar to those of the Incas that it is evident that Inca religion was in the main a direct continuation of Huari religion. It is possible to infer much of the meaning of Huari religious art through its resemblances to religious concepts of the Incas. On the north coast, where native religious traditions have been recorded to the present, it is also possible to infer the meaning of some of the pre-Huari religious art from modern beliefs and concepts.

2

The Inca Empire: The Capital and Standardized Inca Practices

Toward the end of his field work for the University of California in 1905, Uhle worked in the area of Cuzco, the capital of the Inca Empire.[8] Rowe points out that Uhle found archaeological work in the highlands more difficult than on the coast, and therefore did not get a comparable record. However, though small and largely lacking in association data, his collections and notes have some importance, because they furnish samples of imperial Inca remains and reflect the operations of the Inca Empire at the capital.

Cuzco was a special kind of city.[9] Although it resembled most of our cities with its large, dense population and many public and private buildings, the resemblance stopped there. It was a sacred city built on a single plan under the direction of the first Inca Emperor, Pachakuti. The outline of the city was in the shape of a puma (mountain lion). The tail of the puma was the downvalley side, outlined by the confluence of two small canalized rivers. As a single river below Cuzco they flowed southeast through a 30 kilometer (18 mile) long valley into the great Vilcanota-Urubamba River east of Cuzco. The head of the puma-shaped capital was formed by the outline of the fortification walls of a great, precipitous fortress, called Sacsahuaman, located on a hill bordering the city at the head of the valley. Within the immediate confines of the city lived only the rulers and nobility, their families and their retainers. The city contained beautiful and elaborate public buildings, including three great temples, and the palaces of different rulers in the succession. A large plaza between the "legs" of the puma on the southwestern side of the city was the site of the many important public ceremonies that formed a great part of the activities of Cuzco.[10]

The larger metropolitan area of Cuzco extended about seven miles down the valley from the core city. In the valley and on the mountain slopes on either side of it were scattered residences of Inca and provincial nobles and their retainers and of government servants, as well as large areas of store houses and extensive terraced fields.

Large storage areas reflected an important aspect of Inca government, not only at Cuzco, but at all provincial capitals and lesser government establishments of the empire.[11] The Inca government was highly centralized. In some ways the Incas governed the entire empire the way only military services are operated under our system of government. People were drafted for all manners of services, and a special class of civil servants was supported by the state. Raw materials were collected for the government and distributed to craftsmen to be made into finished goods which were turned in. These finished goods were used for relief purposes, sacrifices, and "gifts" to reward loyal service. The most valuable gifts consisted of fine textiles and objects of gold and silver.[12] Both the raw materials and the finished products required government storage facilities.

Since draft services for the government pervaded most aspects of life under the Inca government, non-government trade was carried on only on a restricted, local, or limited regional basis. The wider distribution of goods took place under government control. The archaeological record reflects this practice.

Uhle collected three large jars at Cuzco, of the standardized kind probably made to government specifications (figs. 1, 2).[13] Fragments of large vessels of this kind are found in particular concentration around major government storage compounds at the capital, as well as at some other areas of major administrative centers or provincial capitals of the empire.[14] Such vessels probably served to store government supplies in large quantities.

Uhle also collected smaller vessels and fragments of vessels near the city of Cuzco, including objects from a small excavation at the fortress of Sacsahuaman. It is not known at present whether all the pottery collected by Uhle was the kind made for the government by civil servants, or whether some was made as private enterprise. Manufacture independent of government control also existed. In addition to pottery, Uhle collected construction tools, metal pins, other small metal objects, and stone bowls.

Uhle's collection contains objects that were probably government gifts to provincials. For example, the burial of a distinguished person of the Ica Valley who was not a member of the nobility, probably a high-ranking civil servant, contained two fine, standard Cuzco Inca-style vessels (figs. 3A, B). The appearance of the clay and pigments of these vessels indicates that they were not manufactured at Ica but in the highlands. Their manufacture is like that of vessels found at the Inca capital. Other "Inca-style" vessels from Ica are of local manufacture, as seen by peculiarities of clay, pigments and shape and design details. These latter vessels are found in a different pattern of associations from the imports.

Ica graves with contents indicative of the burials of civil servants also contained carved wooden cups, some or all of which may have been made to Inca government specifications. They follow a standardized style, and are like Inca wooden cups from the highlands. Wooden cups of this kind were symbols of moderate rank and distinction in the Inca Empire (fig. 4).[15] These cups probably also represent government gifts.

Uhle collected a standardized Inca tunic from the lower Acarí Valley (area of Chaviña) on the south coast (fig. 5). This tunic and its significance are discussed by Rowe.[16] Nearly identical tunics have been found in different parts of the Inca Empire. Uhle found the fragment of another one at the site of Olivar in the Pativilca Valley north of Lima.

Rowe points out that these tunics, like the wooden drinking cups, were probably government gifts to persons of moderate rank. One of Uhle's finds is a small modeled bottle from the valley of Ica, which depicts a seated man wearing the same kind of tunic (fig. 6). The man is seen drinking from a cup. Around his head the standard long headband of Inca men's dress is wound in several twists. The individual depicted in this pottery portrayal probably represents another privileged non-noble of the same class as the individuals in the civil servants' burials.

3

The Effects of the Inca Conquest on a Province: Ica Society Under the Incas and Before

Max Uhle is one of very few archaeologists who have recorded buried, unlooted tombs of nobles of ancient Peru, and the only place where he succeeded in doing so was Ica. This circumstance gives a special importance to the archaeology of Ica, as perhaps the best record for showing the relationships between different social classes in a non-Inca nation prior to the Spanish conquest. Uhle excavated seven tombs of Ica nobles which had not been looted after the arrival of the Spaniards. In our relative chronology, one of these tombs dates to Epoch 3A of the Late Intermediate Period (ca. 1050-1100 A.D.), one dates to Epoch 6 of the same period (ca. 1350-1400 A.D.), and five date to the later part of the Late Horizon, after the reorganization of the Inca Empire (ca. 1485-1534 A.D.). Tombs of all kinds of nobles are deep. Those of Epoch 6 and later have formal entry ways and structures suggesting dwellings, with provisions made for re-entry.

Uhle also excavated some 20 burials of Ica commoners of the Late Intermediate Period and Late Horizon. Burials of commoners are shallow, unstructured interments in the sand, without provisions for re-entry. The comparison of burials of different kinds of nobles and commoners of Ica, together with studies of other kinds of remains, makes it possible to reconstruct some of the class relationships or social structure of Ica society. A sample of this reconstruction is presented here. The record Uhle was able to make on the basis of his excavations bears out the meager historical accounts that exist on this subject, but it also provides much additional information not found in the written records.

The sum of the Late Horizon association patterns suggests that the Incas ruled at Ica through a high-ranking nobility entitled to the use of gold, and through a special class of individuals who were probably civil servants. The presumed civil servants were kept segregated from the rest of the native community. They were probably under direct Inca control, independent of the local nobility.

Inca rule brought profound social division to what had been a single unified culture, with considerable gaps between social strata. Ica art, particularly as observed in pottery, became a symbol of this divisive stratification. The lower strata of Ica society reacted by collecting and imitating antiques of the earlier Ica tradition, a time when Ica was free from foreign domination.

It is not possible to present here all the evidence on which this summary is based. Instead, we will examine the tomb of an Ica noble under the Incas, with comments on how it reflects Inca rule and Ica society, and how the data from it are related to others gathered from monuments and documents. In order to understand the impact that Inca rule had on Ica, we will make comparisons with the unlooted tomb of an Ica 6 noble, and with other contemporary remains of independent Ica.

The valley of Ica and the neighboring Pisco Valley to the north were occupied in pre-Inca times by an independent nation. National independence of Ica probably began in Middle Horizon Epoch 3, between the 8th and 9th centuries A.D., after the fall of the Huari Empire.[17] The Ica nation had considerable prestige abroad, prestige that rested on its art and culture. Its fine ornamental pottery, intricately woven textiles, gold and silver dinner ware and perhaps other products were widely imitated and sometimes traded over large stretches of the coast and highlands. History records, however, that Ica offered no resistance to the Inca conquest nor to an earlier Inca raid of the coast, unlike its neighbors north of Pisco.[18] The archaeological record also indicates that the Ica nation was not concerned with warlike pursuits, and that its wide influence abroad was not the result of the threat of force, but rather of the admiration its products called forth in other nations.

Ica society was stratified. It had a class of very distinguished nobles who were set apart from the rest of society by their wealth, as well as in a number of other ways. Spanish chroniclers record the existence of noble classes for many nations under *Tawantinsuyu,* ancient nobilities that antedated the time of the Inca Empire. In the archaeological record class differences are most clearly expressed by differences in residences and in the structure and contents of burials.

In late pre-Conquest times, noble families of the coast lived in large, elaborate residences of adobe construction, with covered terraces and a large courtyard where great feasts were given.[19] Remnants of such residences still survived some years ago on the arid valley borders and sandy elevations within the cultivated plain in different parts of Ica, as well as in other coastal valleys. The beauty, comfort and luxury of such residences can be seen and felt today at Puruchucu near Lima, where a small villa of a distinguished personage of late pre-Spanish times has been reconstructed.

The historian Cieza de León reports that the nobles of the coast were much feared and respected by their subjects, and surrounded themselves with great pomp. They had many wives, chosen from among the most beautiful women, and they were always accompanied by their jesters, dancers and musicians. Whenever the lord ate, many people attended and partook of his beer, somewhat as at the court of Louis XIV of France in the 17th and early 18th centuries. Attendants guarded the gates to make sure that only welcome or qualified guests appeared. The nobles were very hospitable to strangers, including the Spaniards, until the abuses of the latter changed this custom.[20]

In many of the coastal valleys, the noble families had their own cemeteries near their residences, or farther out along the valley borders. These places were held sacred and called by the Inca term for a sacred place, wak'a. These cemeteries contained great, deep, elaborate tombs with closed entrances. Cieza reports that such cemeteries, with their dead and their rotted and weathered clothing, could be seen in all the coastal valleys at the time of his travels between 1547 and 1550, after the Spaniards had engaged in large-scale looting of tombs. According to Cieza, it was customary in some of the coastal areas to open these tombs from time to time to renew the clothing and food for the dead.[21] The archaeological evidence collected by Uhle shows that another re-entry ritual, one not mentioned by Cieza, also took place before the Ica tombs were permanently closed.

The nature of the burials reflects the ideals of happiness for this world and the next of those who lived and died there. Cieza reports that it was generally believed that the souls of the dead lived eternally in another world, leading a happy life. In that other world the nobles continued to give their great feasts. In order to ensure that the nobility would have all they needed for this purpose, the noble dead were buried with their most beloved and beautiful wives, their most valued servants, sometimes their best friends, all their most precious possessions, their arms, personal ornaments, symbols of rank, and an abundance of food and drink. Some servants, retainers and women who would not fit into the tombs, nevertheless joined their lord in death in separate, simple burials. Such sacrifices were made in the belief that those buried together would not be parted, but would

be united in that other world and continue to be happy and feast, which was their greatest delight.[22]

Unfortunately for our better understanding of the history of ancient Peru, tombs of nobles, with their wealth of fine art and luxury objects, have been the main targets of treasure seekers since the arrival of the Spaniards, and they continue to be sought by looters working for collectors and dealers in antiquities. The people of the coast soon came to realize that their tombs were the chief targets for feverish looting by the invaders, and they closed them permanently, concealing all surface indications of their location. While this act did not stop the looting, it made the tombs harder to find, and looters had to acquire mining rights entitling them to search for hidden tombs.

Uhle discovered a section of a buried cemetery of nobles like those described by Cieza more or less accidentally in 1901. This section was part of the huge cemetery of the capital of Ica before the Spanish conquest. The old capital, known as Old Ica, is now in ruins, and lies some six miles down the valley from the present town. To this day the remnants of large adobe constructions can be seen at Old Ica, many of them once public buildings rather than private residences. The cemetery was located on one of the sandy elevations described by Cieza, some 800 yards south of the capital.

The tombs of the nobles found by Uhle were much as Cieza had described them. They were deep and large, excavated through approximately 12 feet of drift sand into the clay subsoil of the valley. The main grave chamber of each tomb was a rectangular room cut into the hard, moist clay. These chambers were evidently meant to be dwellings for the dead, for they were provided with lattice roofs of poles and thatch. The standard size of the chambers found by Uhle varied from about 6 feet by 6 feet in area and 3 feet in depth to 14 feet by 9 feet in area and 7 feet in depth. The chambers contained several dead, sometimes up to 12 or more. One or two large entry steps, and in one tomb a zigzagged access way about 18 feet long, were built to make entry into the deep chambers easier and perhaps more ornate.

One, two or three large burial posts had once stood beside the tombs as grave markers. They were made of tree trunks of very hard wood of the ''guarango'' or ''algarrobo,'' a desert tree botanically related to the mesquite tree of the southwestern United States (Prosopis chilensis). These markers originally stood upright in the ground, from 6 to 8 feet tall, with a carved and painted face at the top. When Uhle discovered them the burial posts had been cut down and hidden face down 4 to 6 feet below the surface, with the evident purpose of concealing the location of the tombs. The upright stumps of the posts remained at the spots where the posts had once stood. Uhle reports having seen upright grave posts still in place marking graves of this kind in another cemetery.[23] Burial posts are not described by Cieza; their use was apparently a particular custom of the people of Ica.

The dating of the Late Horizon tombs to the later time of the Inca Empire is based on the styles of the pottery in the tombs. The burial accompaniments show that Uhle did not find the tombs of the wealthiest or highest ranking nobles, but only those of nobles of a moderate degree of rank and wealth. Historians like Cieza report how Spaniards mining for precious metals and stones found much richer tombs at Ica, indicating burials of persons of much greater wealth and pomp.

Four of the tombs excavated by Uhle belong to a nobility entitled to the possession of gold.[24] Under the Inca system, the right to use gold had to be bestowed by the imperial government, and the privilege was granted only to individuals who held a relatively high degree of rank. Gold was the most highly valued metal. Any additional distinctions in social standing had to be expressed through increasing degrees of wealth and artistry of possessions, including more and finer objects of precious metals and stones, beautiful garments, artistic pottery and other articles of luxury, beautiful women, titles to land revenues, government office, and other symbols and devices bestowing power and privilege. Ultimately all privilege existed solely at the discretion of the Inca emperor.

In one of the tombs of the "gold nobles" of Ica (tomb Td-8) Uhle found a wooden stool (*tiyana;* fig. 7). Stools were seats denoting distinction, and were one of the emblems of rank under the Incas. Different heights and degrees of ornamentation and different materials of construction of these seats represented different degrees of rank. The stool found in tomb Td-8 is plate-shaped, oval, of plain, unadorned hard wood and with 4-inch high supports. According to the chronicler Guaman Poma, such seats represented the rank of administrator of 100 taxpayers (*pachak kamachikoq*) in the Inca system of hierarchy.[25]

A brief explanation of the system of rank and privilege under the Incas helps to understand the social setting of the people buried in the Ica tombs. The Incas created a new system of hereditary aristocracy for their empire, with a higher Inca class and a lower "curaca" (*kuraka*) class. The Inca class included all blood relatives of the Inca emperors, who formed a single dynasty, as well as some families from neighboring highland nations who spoke the same language as the Incas. The lower

kuraka class of the aristocracy was formed by rulers and nobles of formerly independent nations conquered by the Incas, and their descendants. Members of both classes of nobility held office in an elaborate imperial administrative hierarchy, in which jobs were matched to degrees of rank, or vice versa. For administrative purposes, the empire was divided into four quarters, and the quarters were subdivided into provinces. Many of the provinces corresponded to native states and ethnic groups existing at the time of the Inca conquest. The post of provincial governor was usually, though not necessarily, held by an Inca noble of the higher class of aristocracy. The officials under him, however, belonged to the *kuraka* class of the native hereditary nobility of the provinces.[26]

Five ranks of hereditary nobles of the *kuraka* class have been recorded in historical accounts. These ranks were associated with government offices of administrators of certain numbers of heads of household or taxpayers, including administrators of 10,000, 5,000, 1,000, 500 and 100 taxpayers, respectively. Lower administrative offices were filled by two ranks of foremen who did not belong to the *kuraka* class in the Inca system, and who were appointed by the *kurakas*. These foremen were chiefs of 50 and 10 taxpayers, respectively.[27]

Thus, if Guaman Poma's account of the ranks represented by different kinds of seats is correct, the rank of the principal individual buried in tomb Td-8 would correspond to the lowest rank of *kuraka*. Cieza's account lends rough support to Guaman Poma's more detailed description. Cieza reports that in the district of Cuzco, where nobles of the higher Inca class had their original home, important dead were buried seated on their stools, and that these stools were very ornate.[28]

The tomb containing the wooden seat evidently had been concealed prematurely and the grave posts cut down very soon after the original interment, as it showed none of the kinds of disturbances apparent in other tombs, where there is evidence of re-entry. The most likely explanation for this unusual circumstance is that the burial had taken place shortly before the arrival of the Spaniards, and the tomb was hidden to protect it from looters. Thanks to this exceptional situation, this tomb gives the only picture of the original burial arrangement of a noble's tomb.

Uhle describes three principal mummy bales placed in a row in the eastern half of the large chamber, facing three large, empty burial urns that stood in the western corner of the entrance into the tomb. The mummy bales consisted of layers of leaves held together by shrouds and ropes, with an adult dead in the center of each bale. These individuals were seated, with knees tightly drawn up, arms folded over the knees, and heads inclined forward. Partly due to the moisture in the clay, the clothing and other perishables were badly rotted and the bodies disintegrated in the process of removal from the grave chamber and could not be preserved. We may suppose that one of these principal dead was the *kuraka* himself, and the other two were favorite wives or perhaps a favorite wife and a close friend. Uhle does not comment on the sex or age of the dead.

Behind the principal personages stood two groups of tall, elaborately carved implements of wood, sheathed in gold and silver, and decorated with red and gold resin paint. Red and gold was a favorite color combination for ornamentation under the Inca Empire, and may have had special symbolic significance. Due to the poor preservation conditions in tomb Td-8, only remnants of the wooden parts of these objects were preserved (figs. 8A, B). However, similar wooden carvings which had been buried in dry sand in other, shallower graves, not of the nobility, were better preserved, and are shown here as examples of the complete objects (figs. 9, 10). The carvings from non-noble burials are less elaborately painted and lack gold or silver sheathing.

The ornate carvings were never used as tools. They were much enlarged forms of two kinds of digging tools used in agricultural work on the coast. One of these resembles a spade (fig. 10). The other has a unique shape (fig. 9). The remnants of four ceremonial "spades" and three examples of the other kind of digging board have been preserved from tomb Td-8. The real digging tools are of various much smaller sizes, quite plain, and are found in abundance in the habitation refuse of the agricultural settlements of the valley. Uhle found many. Their use as digging tools has been depicted in drawings made by the chronicler Guaman Poma.[29]

The ornate appearance, great size, and ceremonial placement of the wooden boards in tombs like Td-8 indicate that the boards were used as symbols of prestige, prestige that was related to agricultural production. Their sheathing in precious metals shows that the prestige was also related to high social standing in general. To this day one of the most distinguished compliments one man can pay another in native Andean society, which survives in the highlands, is to say that "he stands well in his field," meaning, that he is a fine farmer.[30] The burials from Ica suggest that in ancient Ica, also, one of the highest compliments that could be paid to a man was to extol his standing as a farmer, or as a fine manager of agricultural lands.

The most common ornamentation of the great digging boards in the tombs consists of carvings of sea birds eating fish. In ancient Peru, as today, one of the great sources of wealth was the abundance of sea life near the coast, particularly the great schools of anchovies. The anchovies are small fish that furnish the food for a great abundance and variety of larger food fish, as well as for sea birds like cormorants and pelicans. In ancient times the heads of anchovies were used on some parts of the coast south of Lima as fertilizer and buried with grains of corn (maize), which thrived on this treatment.[31] The droppings ("guano") of the sea birds that nested on isolated promontories and offshore islands were used as fertilizer on the coast north of Lima.[32] We can see, then, that the sea birds and anchovies had an important relationship to agricultural production, a relationship that may be reflected in the ornamental carvings and other art forms of the coast. These artistic depictions have a long tradition in this area, spanning most or all of the history of independent Ica.

Other common ornaments on the ceremonial digging tools from the graves of the Inca occupation period at Ica consist of carvings of animals and little men in various kinds of dress and poses, usually standing, either singly or in a row. Triangular blocks of steps were often carved along the side of long handles. Occasionally other kinds of birds and geometric ornaments were added to the carvings, sometimes in very intricate patterns.[33] Carving the three-dimensional ornaments in this very hard wood must have been a long and difficult process, requiring a high degree of skill.

Between the ceremonial digging tools and the three principal dead in the tomb stood 35 pottery vessels. Uhle recorded no food remains from these vessels. However, it is very likely that at least some of them had once contained food, for such remains have been recorded in pottery vessels from other burials. Examples are bowls filled with peanuts, beans or corn ears. In other parts of the coast food bowls filled with some of the great variety of other foods consumed by the coast peoples have been recorded. Bowls from other burials at Ica also sometimes contained alpaca wool and cotton yarns for weaving. Presumably the bottles and jars contained liquids which had long since disappeared, probably mainly the beer made of maize and sometimes other grains, which was drunk in great quantities at the feasts.

In front of the mummy bales, at the base of the lowest entrance step into the tomb, stood three nearly empty funerary urns. They were placed one in another. Perhaps each of these urns belonged to one of the three principal dead. In all the tombs of nobles funerary urns of this kind were found in about the same position at the entrance into the burial chamber. The only objects found in the urns in tomb Td-8 are a fragmentary pottery vessel and a gold ornament. These objects were not found within the central urn, but were hidden between the walls of the outer and middle urns, where they had apparently been dropped inadvertently. The golden ornament is a small cone-shaped container with a face hammered in relief in the side (fig. 11). Objects like this served as plume holders for plumes worn in the headdress of men.

Funerary urns were the traditional mode of burial of adults at Ica during most or all of the history of independent Ica in the Late Intermediate Period. In the burials of commoners the body of the dead was placed from the beginning in its urn. In the tombs of nobles, however, urn burial took place only after the flesh was largely gone, perhaps a year or more after the original interment. It appears that at that time a special rite took place in which the bones of all the dead in the tomb were painted red. Then the bones of the principal dead were placed in the urns, while those of other individuals in the tomb were returned to their original resting place. With the nobles in the urns were placed their most personal possessions of gold or silver, including the dishes from which they ate and drank, their personal ornaments, and a special face mask for the dead. This part of the customary burial ritual had not yet taken place when tomb Td-8 was closed, since the principal dead were still in their mummy bales and the urns empty.

Not only were the principal dead of tomb Td-8 still outside of the urns, but the gold dishes, personal ornaments, and the masks of the dead were all missing. Only the golden plume holder, apparently dropped inadvertently, is a remnant of the kinds of objects that should ordinarily have been found in the funerary urns. The absence of these valuables from the urns is unique for an undisturbed tomb of an Ica noble. A possible explanation is that the most personal valuables of the principal dead were removed from the tomb at the time of its premature closure, perhaps because the burial rite was incomplete, or for some other reason.

On the ground beside the empty funerary urns were the remains of the bodies of nine or more youths, whose precise age and sex have not been determined. Unlike the principal dead, these youths had not been wrapped in bales. We may suppose that they had been members of the retinue of the noble's household who had been buried with their lord, and who had been placed close to what should have been the lord's final resting place. One of these youths, who was lying pressed against the urns, had worn golden ear plugs, a kind of ornament probably used only by men at Ica. The use of gold for the ear plugs probably merely signified that he had been a member of the lord's household, although it is also conceivable that he could have been a relation. This youth also had a thin

flake of gold in his mouth, another indication of distinction. Thin flakes of metal were commonly placed in the mouths of the dead of this time, but the flakes were usually of copper.

The youth with the gold objects had by his side a copper bell and a pottery ocarina (fig. 12A). The ocarina or ''sweet potato'' is a simple musical instrument similar in function to a simple flute. Pottery ocarinas and copper bells are typical musical instruments of the Inca occupation period of Ica, together with other instruments such as vertical flutes made of pottery or cane, pottery whistles, and barrel-shaped drums with painted skin heads. The pottery flutes have been described as having a very loud, pleasing sound.[34] They all have five stops which produce sounds on a five-note scale unlike our own (fig. 13). Very pleasing, arresting music on a five-note scale is still being played on flutes and other wind instruments by native peoples of the highlands of Peru. As we have seen earlier, the nobles of the coast were regularly accompanied by their musicians, along with other members of their retinue, and music played an important part in their feasts. Mournful music was also played at the great wakes for the dead, which lasted four to ten days, depending on the rank of the noble. Presumably the youth with the ocarina had performed as a musician in the lord's household, although this was not necessarily his only occupation.

The same youth also had about his person the remnants of a large, circular silver pendant, parts of necklaces of *Spondylus* shell pendants, and half-spool-shaped bone beads. Entire *Spondylus* shell halves were also lying by his side. *Spondylus* shell was a valuable commodity in ancient Peru from at least as early as 1,000 B.C. These shells had to be imported a long distance, from the warm waters near the equator. Like the gold and silver, *Spondylus* shell signified prestige, though the prestige of these shells was evidently different in kind from that of gold and silver. *Spondylus* shells played an important part in religious ritual.

Two other kinds of objects accompanied this distinguished youth. One has been described as a double-pointed bone implement with incised circle and dot decoration. This piece is missing. Objects corresponding to this description have been said to be weaving tools, but the evidence for such use is not conclusive at present.

The last category of objects accompanying the youth with the golden ear plugs is singular. It consists of a set of five pairs of peculiar sticks which may have been used in a game of some kind, perhaps one similar to rolling dice (fig. 14). Each of four pairs of the sticks has a different length, while the fifth pair constitutes an additional set of the shortest length. The graded lengths are approximately 5¾ inches (14.6 cm.), 5½ inches (14 cm.), 5¼ inches (13.4 cm.) and 4½ inches (11.4 cm.), respectively. As we see, the first three length intervals between pairs are regular at a quarter of an inch each, while the shortest set of two pairs is three quarters of an inch shorter than the next longest pair. The sticks have rounded ends and vary from three quarters of an inch to a little under one inch in diameter. The surface of the wood is smoothly finished and rounded, except for one facet, which is flat. For each of four graduated pairs, one stick is plain and the other has an ornament carved into the rounded surface. Two categories of ornaments are used. The ornaments on the two larger decorated pieces are variants of each other, as are the designs on the two smaller decorated pieces.

Both pieces of one of the two shortest pairs are undecorated. Both of the shortest pairs are further distinguished in having each stick pierced lengthwise by a central hole, unlike the other sticks. Like the musical instruments accompanying the youth, the sticks may have been objects he required in the role of entertainer.

Uhle lists other objects from the floor of the tomb chamber without specifying their location. They probably accompanied the bodies of some of the other youths lying beside the funerary urns, since several of the objects are the same kind as those found with the youth with the golden ear plugs. Among these objects are three additional fragmentary double-pointed bone implements like those found with the youth with the gold ear plugs.[35] Also found in this group was a spindle for spinning, a sewing needle with an eye, made of a long cactus thorn, and an incurving gourd bowl with burnt black decoration, of a kind frequently used to hold yarn for weaving. The presence of spinning and sewing tools on the floor of the chamber suggests that spinning and sewing were among the tasks performed by the youths beside the urns.

Other personal ornaments like those found with the youth with the golden ear plugs are recorded by Uhle from the floor of the tomb chamber, and may have accompanied some of the other youths. Among them were the wedge-shaped *Spondylus* shell pendants that had once formed necklaces, as well as complete halves of *Spondylus* shells, which were also sometimes used as pendants.[36]

Remnants of two or three additional large round silver disk pendants were also present. The disks are about 3½ inches (9 cm.) in diameter, and have small holes drilled in the bottom section of the periphery of the pendant. Complete examples of such pendants show that the holes served as points of attachment for smaller, oval metal pendants which dangled from the larger disk. Some of the other tombs excavated by Uhle contained the smaller oval disks.[37]

Uhle lists one other object in the assemblage found on the floor of the chamber, a very large half of a mussel shell *(Mytilus chorus),* which shows no markings indicating its use. Uhle believed it could have been used as a spoon.

Bones of one or more llamas sacrificed at the time of burial were found on the floor of the tomb chamber. In an earlier tomb of the same kind remains of sacrificial llamas were more completely preserved and showed that one of the animals had worn a silver forehead ornament, an indication of the highly ceremonial nature of its interment.[38] The sacrifice of llamas formed an important part of religious ritual in the time of the Inca Empire and before.

In the upper layers of the tomb chamber, about halfway between the floor and the roof, 15 bodiless human skulls of men, women and a child had been buried. The adult skulls ranged in age from about 21 to 35 years, and the child was approximately 8 to 10 years old. The skulls had been painted red, and had been taken from a burial place elsewhere and reburied here. They had no personal connection with the principal dead and their retinue on the floor of the tomb chamber. Bodiless skulls of this kind were present in all the Ica tombs found by Uhle, as well as in the burials of commoners at this cemetery. Their presence indicates an extraordinary part of the burial customs of Ica, one that has not been recorded in historical accounts. The bodiless skulls must have come from other tombs of nobles, for only in such tombs were the dead subjected to a secondary burial ritual that included painting the bones red. Perhaps these skulls were reburied in the newer burials for good luck, or so that the old dead might help the new dead in the other world. These are only speculations, however.

The wooden seat which we discussed earlier was buried just below the lattice roof of the burial chamber, above the three principal dead. Its position there is peculiar and suggests that its purpose was symbolic, to pronounce the rank of the principal noble and his family. The importance of the stool is emphasized by the presence at its side of sacrificial llama bones, a wooden dish, and a pair of pottery dishes. These objects must have been placed there in a special ceremony at the time the tomb was concealed.

Somewhere above the burial chamber of tomb Td-8 Uhle found two small, simple burials of three adults. These were probably sacrificial burials accompanying the noble and his retinue in the deeper tomb (burials Td-1 and Td-2). Their close connection with the deep tomb is indicated by the style of the pottery vessels found in one of them (Td-1). Their probable sacrificial nature is suggested further by additional peculiarities in their position and manner of interment, as we shall see.

The two burials were found about 6 feet below the surface, at or slightly below the level of the concealed grave posts, a position indicating that these burials must have been made at or before the time of closure of the tomb. Uhle does not tell us their exact alignment with reference to the tomb chamber of Td-8. However, they may have been found near the entrance to the tomb, for that was the position of another burial of this kind above another large tomb of an Ica noble of the same period.[39]

Like the retainers beside the urns on the floor of the tomb chamber Td-8 the dead in the more superficial burials had not been placed in funerary urns. However, they had been wrapped in mummy bales, like the adult dead in the chamber. The manner of burial in grave Td-1 was unique. Two bales of adult dead were placed side by side in the sand and covered with a single striped cloth. No other double burial of adults has been recorded at Ica for burials of commoners, nor is there a record of a double burial anywhere where two individuals were covered with the same shroud. Only one of the two mummy bales in burial Td-1 has been preserved, and neither has been identified by sex. However, at least one of them may have been a woman, as suggested by an item of apparel.

The other burial, Td-2, was evidently found near Td-1, and was almost certainly that of a man. An X-ray photograph of the mummy bale shows the individual wearing ear plugs, an ornament not recorded for women's apparel at Ica. This burial was accompanied by a sling, a man's weapon, in further support that this was the burial of a man.

Both burials Td-1 and Td-2 contained weaving and sewing equipment. The presence of such equipment in burial Td-2 constitutes evidence that men as well as women could be buried with such tools at Ica during this time. This probably means that both men and women could engage in weaving and sewing, though such activity may have been done for different purposes or in different contexts.

The weaving kits in burials Td-1 and Td-2 consist of similar inventories. In each burial there was a twilled work basket containing the smaller weaving and sewing tools. These included cactus thorn needles with eyes, various sizes and thicknesses of thorn and wood spindles, different kinds of pottery spindle whorls (weights for spindles), weaving swords used for beating down

weft (horizontal) threads in the weaving process, and yarns of cotton and alpaca wool. Needles were kept in hollow cane tubes with stoppers, or were wrapped in small reed mats. Some of the yarn was wrapped around spindles or various other kinds of sticks, and some of it was wound into balls. The work basket in burial Td-1 also contained a small, ornamented bone beam of a balance for weighing small, light materials, in this case perhaps yarn. Larger weaving swords and yarn sticks were found in burial Td-1 outside of the work basket, some of them tied to at least one of the mummy bales.

Burial Td-2 was accompanied by a supply of coca leaves wrapped in a finely woven cotton cloth, two feet square. The leaf of the coca shrub acts as an anaesthetic when it is held in one cheek together with burnt lime, and has been so used in the Andean area for several thousand years (see also chapter 6). It keeps people from feeling hunger, cold and fatigue, and is, of course, a most effective anaesthetic against all kinds of pain. In other areas, coca was more commonly carried in cloth bags, in some areas with shoulder straps.

Uhle recorded no coca leaves from burial Td-1. However, he did record a cloth of exactly the same size and proportions as the one that had contained the coca in burial Td-2. Cloths of this size and shape apparently were used during this time at Ica in place of bag containers for coca and other objects, at least in some contexts. The burials that contained the cloths did not contain bags.

Most of the textiles that had enveloped the mummies had rotted as a result of their contact with the naturally decaying body parts of the dead, and Uhle did not preserve the remnants. Only the shroud that had covered both bales in burial Td-1 was recovered and described by Uhle. Unfortunately it was subsequently lost. However, the few textiles that had been placed beside the dead are remarkably well preserved. In addition to the yarns contained in the work basket and wound around the larger weaving sticks, these textiles include the two square cotton cloths and sling, mentioned above, and a woman's belt from burial Td-1.

Uhle describes the shroud only as a "striped cloth." It may have resembled the container cloth from burial Td-2, which is made of finely spun and woven cotton decorated with a pattern of warp stripes. This means that blocks of the vertical (warp) threads in the loom were arranged in the striping pattern and densely spaced, while the horizontal (weft) threads were more widely spaced, and were thus concealed by the tightly bunched warp threads. Many colors were used in the warp stripes of the container cloth, including red and several shades of blues, greens, browns and tan to cream.

The second cloth of this kind is ornamented with alternating stripes in cream-colored cotton and brocade of alpaca wool.[40] The sling and belt are made entirely of alpaca wool. In the alpaca ornamentation red and gold colors predominate, as they do in the yarns found with the weaving equipment. As noted earlier, red and gold was the most common color combination in the time of the Inca Empire, at least for the area of the central and south coast. In Ica and neighboring valleys to the south it was commonly used for belts, coca containers and many slings.

To illustrate the predominance of the red and gold patterning, the presumable container cloth from burial Td-1 is a good example (fig. 15). It is a highly ornamental textile in which stripes of light cream cotton done in a pattern of gauze weave alternate with plain cotton weave entirely covered by brocade decoration in alpaca wool in six colors. The wool stripes are arranged in a particularly intricate pattern of ornamentation.[41]

When we consider that this fascinatingly complex ornamentation was used in the decoration of what was probably only a container or "purse" cloth belonging to a retainer in the service of a minor noble, we can begin to appreciate the intricacy of the textile art of ancient Peru. Complexity in design arrangement and patterning is also typical of south coast textiles from other valleys.

Burial Td-1 also contained a belt or sash in a good state of preservation (fig. 16). Similar belts were sometimes found tied around the outer wrappings of mummy bales. In life they were used by women as sashes tied around the waist. The evidence for the latter use was recorded in written chronicles. Uhle found archaeological evidence for it in his excavations at Pachacamac.[42] He found sashes like the one from burial Td-1 as items of apparel of women who had been sacrificed in Inca times and buried on a platform of the great Inca Temple of the Sun at Pachacamac. This kind of sash was called *mamachumpi* or "principal belt" in the Inca language.[43] In most parts of the Inca Empire women wore a wrap-around dress made of a large rectangular cloth which covered them from neck to feet, and which was tied tightly around the waist by a sash of this kind. The sash was thick and wide, and was often decorated with heraldic designs (*t'oqapu*), like those found on men's tunics.[44] The sash from burial Td-1 has such designs.

Uhle found 29 sashes of varying lengths and in four different styles in the burials of sacrificed women at Pachacamac. One of the sashes he found is like the sash from the Ica burial Td-1 in details of construction and color pattern, which is also predominantly red and gold.[45] The sash from burial Td-1 is about ¼ inch thick. To achieve this thickness thick wool cords were used as

a base around which fine wool yarn was wrapped in some sections, and embroidered onto them in others.

The sash is about 26½ inches (69 cm.) long, including a set of four tapering cords at each end of the solid band. A tie cord about ¼ inch (6 mm.) in diameter and 4 feet ¾ inches (1.45 meters) long terminates the sash at each end. The sash is a little over 4 inches (10.5 cm.) wide at its center, and about 2¼ inches (5.75 cm.) wide at each solid end. Uhle recorded the manner in which this kind of sash was worn at Pachacamac. The widest part of the sash, with the heraldic ornament on it, was worn at the front of the waist, so that the sash had to be tied at the back.

The yarns used in the decoration of the sash from burial Td-1 appear to be some of the same ones as those used in the container cloth. Red and gold predominate, while very light cream and dark brown are used to enhance the two large diamond figures (the heraldic designs) which adorn the front of the sash. Both in construction and decoration the sash from burial Td-1 is particularly characteristic of objects showing close association with provincial Inca styles and Inca government in the provinces.

As noted, burial Td-1 was also accompanied by two pottery vessels, a jar and a bowl. The bowl was filled with peanuts. The jar had presumably once contained liquid. The style of these two pottery vessels is very distinctive, and is discussed with relation to the vessels in the tomb chamber Td-8.

It is typical of the art of pottery, textiles and other kinds of remains of the time of the Inca Empire that a variety of different art and dress styles, both local and of foreign origin, were used in the same area. This is a situation likely to occur when different nations live under a single centralized government. Detailed studies of association patterns reveal that these different styles were not solely means of artistic expression, but that they also symbolized different kinds of political affiliations, occupations, and social rank, both in terms of the imperial Inca hierarchy and in terms of local society.

Four major style categories of pottery were represented in tomb Td-8. Examples of each of these categories were also found in other tombs of gold nobles, but most of the vessels are in styles not found in other kinds of burials.

The largest number of vessels from tomb Td-8 (22 pieces) consists of Ica imitations of pottery shapes of the Cuzco Inca style. They differ consistently from the Cuzco Inca vessels in details of shape and decoration. Several groupings of provincial Inca styles have been found at Ica sites in different patterns of associations.

The associations indicate that these styles were used by different segments of Ica society. The provincial Inca vessels from tomb Td-8 belong to the categories called Provincial Inca A and Imitation Provincial Inca A.

Eighteen Provincial Inca A vessels were found in tomb Td-8. These vessels are decorated with imitations of Cuzco Inca designs. The designs differ in some or many details from Cuzco Inca designs, and incorporate features of native Ica decoration. Such designs are therefore distinguished by the term *Ica-Inca*.

Inca shapes that are most commonly imitated in the Provincial Inca A style of Ica are jars with necks and a pointed bottom (figs. 17A, B), a shallow plate with a handle (fig. 18), and a cooking pot with a foot and sometimes a lid (fig. 19). The cooking pots show no evidence of ever having been used for cooking, and represent, rather, the prestige that was associated with the pottery of the Incas.

Provincial Inca A pottery was found only in the burials of gold nobles, and in a burial of a distinguished commoner who belonged to a separate, segregated community with special affiliations with the Inca administration (Ica, grave Tk; see also chapter 2). The Provincial Inca A style evidently symbolized prestige connected with the Inca administration of Ica, an occupation which engaged both the gold nobles and the members of the segregated community.

Provincial Inca pottery is not found in burials or settlements of Ica commoners who lived in separate rural communities away from the capital. In contrast, one of the retainer burials accompanying tomb Td-8 did contain a provincial Inca vessel that reflects the association of this burial with the noble's tomb (fig. 20). The vessel is a small version of the large, wide-mouthed Inca jar shown in figure 2.

A set of four identical provincial Inca plates from tomb Td-8 has decoration entirely in the local tradition, and may represent a slightly less valued category (fig. 21). Such local decoration usually occurs on native Ica vessel shapes. Native shapes with native decoration are found mainly in the refuse and burials of rural Ica communities away from the capital, where they appear to the virtual exclusion of other styles. The people from the rural communities were relatively poor, without social distinction.

The bowl in figure 22 is from a sacrificial infant burial, which accompanied the tomb of another noble. Both shape and design are in the local Ica style. Such local vessels are found as a minority category in the tombs of nobles at Old Ica. They may have belonged to the retainers of the nobles rather than to the nobles themselves.

Ica-Inca designs also appear on vessels that are not imitations of Cuzco Inca shapes, although the shapes incorporate Inca loan features. Although these vessels show a stylistic affiliation with Inca art, they are too different in shape as well as design to be called "provincial Inca," and are therefore called *Ica-Inca*. Ica-Inca shapes with Ica-Inca decoration belong to the Ica-Inca A group. Ica-Inca A vessels are found in tombs of gold nobles, but not in burials of lesser nobles or commoners. They symbolize prestige of the native Ica nobility under the Incas.

Two bottle forms are the principal Ica-Inca A shapes. One of them resembles an Old World oil lamp, and is therefore called "Lamp Bottle" (fig. 23). Eight Lamp Bottles were found in tomb Td-8. The other bottle shape is an imitation of the cylindrical drums of Ica. This shape is therefore called "Drum Bottle" (fig. 24). An identical pair of Drum Bottles and a third bottle of this kind formed part of the pottery inventory of tomb Td-8.

The two pottery vessels, an identical pair of dishes that were found buried with the sacrificial llama bones beside the wooden stool below the roof of tomb Td-8, belong to another style category (fig. 25A). The shapes are in the native style of Ica, but they are made of smoked blackware instead of oxidized redware. Instead of regular painted decoration applied before firing, these vessels are decorated with special Ica-tradition designs incised into the soft clay. After the pottery was fired, the design areas were painted in brightly colored red and gold resin paint.[46]

Incised blackware is an innovation of the Inca occupation period. The vessels found next to the stool in tomb Td-8 accompanied bones of a sacrificed llama, evidently as a special offering. A bowl of the same kind of incised and resin-painted blackware was found in the sacrificial retainer burial Td-1 (fig. 25B). It appears that one function of vessels of incised blackware may have been sacrificial.

Most pottery ocarinas and flutes were made of smoked, incised and resin-painted blackware (figs. 12B, 13). The ocarina found with the distinguished youth lying against the burial urns in tomb Td-8 is unique in not having been smoke blackened, even though it was incised and resin painted like the vessels and musical instruments of smoked blackware (fig. 12A).

In all recorded tombs of nobles except the prematurely closed tomb Td-8, the final funerary rite described earlier had taken place. After this final rite the contents of the urn and the skeletal remains from the rest of the tomb were removed from some of the tombs in pre-European times, probably by stealth. As we have seen, the skulls taken in this way were evidently subsequently reburied in other burials. Presumably the families of the nobles in these tombs did not care for this kind of looting, because the tombs were eventually hidden and the grave posts cut down in pre-Spanish times as well. Some of these tombs were closed in time to prevent removal of the remains of the dead and their most personal belongings, while others were closed only after some looting had taken place.

Uhle found only one tomb of a gold noble which remained intact after the secondary interment rite. This tomb was exceptional in that it was a fresh tomb built expressly for the secondary interment, and was evidently closed immediately after the last rite (tomb Tc). Thanks to this circumstance we have a fairly good record of a secondary urn interment of a gold noble under the Incas, a noble of about the same rank as the personage in tomb Td-8.

The grave chamber of the secondary tomb Tc was just big enough for a single funerary urn and the few remains directly by its side. The urn contained the complete skeletal remains of one adult. Uhle does not give the necessary data that make it possible to identify this individual's sex. Two tweezers accompanying the remains were tools used for plucking out men's facial hair. A golden mask covered the face of the skull (fig. 26). Two golden beakers with faces modeled in the sides were found below this head on one side, "as if . . . the head would have been inclined upon them," according to Uhle (fig. 27). Like the skeletal remains, the beakers and death mask had been painted red. A golden dish containing the golden tweezers was found below the body, "more or less in such a position as if the body had been inclined over it," as Uhle describes it (fig. 28). Several additional bodiless skulls covered with red paint, all secondary interments, were also found in the urn.

Immediately above the principal in the urn were the remains of a child's body, probably one that had been sacrificed for this interment. A golden head band was found mixed with the bones of this child. The band must have been the head ornament of the dead principal rather than part of the accompaniments of the child, for it is of regular adult size. Headbands of this kind made of gold or silver have been found with other important dead. The remains of another child were found on the floor on one side of the urn, and the remains of an adult on the other side. The adult had a pair of silver ear plugs, evidently as befitted the retainer of a gold noble.

The only other objects from this special secondary interment of a gold noble were one undistinguished pottery vessel in the native style of Ica, and two undistinguished wooden carvings. It is clear that in the secon-

dary rite, accompaniments other than personal valuables were almost perfunctory, of no special significance. It is also possible that these simple accompaniments belonged to the sacrificed children or the adult retainer beside the urn and had no connection with the dead noble in the urn.

Uhle did not give nearly as detailed information concerning the remains of the tomb of a pre-Inca noble of Late Intermediate Period Epoch 6, which he also uncovered (tomb Th-1). Some of the differences in customs from those of the Inca occupation period are nevertheless evident. First, the pre-Inca tomb was not associated with human sacrificial burials. Human sacrifices may have been introduced to Ica only with the Inca conquest. Second, both gold and silver objects were found with the dead in the funerary urn. In independent Ica gold and silver evidently did not have the strict symbolism related to different degrees of rank which they did under the Inca system.

Like the secondary burial of the gold noble of the Inca period in tomb Tc, the skeletal remains of the personage in the pre-Inca tomb were accompanied by his most personal possessions of gold, including the death mask (fig. 29), forehead band, a beaker (fig. 30), and another kind of drinking cup (fig. 31A). There also were many ovoid pendants of gold of the kind sometimes attached to circular disks. Here they may have been used as sequins sewn on garments, as indicated by some textile fragments still adhering to the reverse side of similar ornaments of silver. The same kind of ornaments were also found among the remnants of some of the other tombs of gold nobles of the Inca period which Uhle uncovered. A gold flake was found in the mouth of the dead.

While the inventory of gold objects with the remains of the noble was thus much like that of the gold nobles of the Inca occupation period, the Ica 6 ornaments differ from those of the Inca occupation period in stylistic detail, as can be seen by the illustrations provided here. Furthermore, the gold of the pre-Inca period is quite different in appearance, thicker, of a darker hue, with pronounced reddish streaks. By contrast, the gold of the Inca occupation period is made of thin sheets which are for the most part a light yellow color, with only occasional traces of reddish streaks.

The noble in the pre-Inca tomb had with him a pair of gold armlets, a kind of ornament not recovered from tombs of the Inca occupation period. Such armlets are also found with distinguished dead in earlier tombs of the Late Intermediate Period, both at Ica and elsewhere. They date back to the time of the Huari Empire. Together with the drinking cups and other associated features, the armlets point to the descent of the Ica nobility from a distinguished elite class of the Huari Empire, some 700 years before the Inca conquest of Ica.

In addition to the gold objects, a great many drinking cups and food dishes in the funerary urn of the noble in tomb Th-1 were of silver (fig. 31B). A pair of ear plugs of an alloy of gold and silver was also found, as well as personal ornaments of silver, including finger rings and sequins for a garment.

The noble in tomb Th-1 was a much wealthier personage than any of the Inca occupation period found by Uhle. Not only was there greater wealth in objects of precious metals in the tomb, but also in pottery. About 250 pottery vessels were present on the floor of the tomb chamber. Like the objects of precious metals in the urns, the pottery is stylistically distinct from that of the Inca occupation period, while at the same time showing its stylistic relationship to the later forms. It includes remains of 25 bottles which are the equivalent of the Ica-Inca Lamp Bottles in the tombs of Late Horizon gold nobles (figs. 32A, B). In contrast to the Lamp Bottles, the earlier native Ica bottles are distinguished by a very long, gracefully shaped neck, a rounded body, and a strap handle which connects the neck with the body. The decoration is entirely in the Ica tradition, and is of the same kind as that found on other Ica pottery of this time.

All the rest of the pottery in the pre-Inca noble's tomb is stylistically ancestral to the poor man's pottery of the Inca occupation period, both in shape and decoration (fig. 33). In contrast to the later pottery, however, it is of nearly uniform high quality in artistry and workmanship. Pottery of the same high quality of artistry and workmanship is found in great abundance throughout the valley, and was used by rich and poor alike. It is one of the indications that in these pre-Inca times the quality of life of nobles and commoners throughout the valley was in some respects on the same high level. Only under Inca rule does one see marked contrasts in life styles between ordinary commoners and different ranks of nobles and non-nobles.

The Uhle collection contains a remarkable portrayal of what was evidently the family in a household of independent Ica living in Late Intermediate Period Epoch 6 (fig. 34). The portrayal consisted of a group of ten figurines, nine of which are still preserved in the collection. These figurines, together with a few other objects, were left behind by looters after the Spanish conquest, who had robbed a tomb like the Ica 6 tomb Th-1 just described.

The figurines are modeled in unbaked clay. The unbaked clay is very fine-grained, and therefore disintegrates easily, so that most of the figurines are considerably damaged. It is nevertheless possible to recognize differences in age, sex and occupation because of the remarkably skillful depictive modeling. The facial expression of all the figurines is one of serious dignity.

The group now includes six adults and three children of different ages. A small infant in arms was also present originally but has been lost. The children can easily be identified by their relatively small size, as well as other details. In addition to differences in size, differences in head form, headdress and posture also indicate differences in age and condition of life.

The adults include a young man and woman, the woman being the one who was found originally with an infant in arms. There also is a middle-aged man of dignified mien, and two middle-aged, kneeling women. The women are holding a vessel in the crook of the arm, as in the act of offering refreshment. The sixth adult represents an old man playing a panpipe.[47]

4

The North Coast of Ancient Peru,
Tumbez to Pachacamac

A. Geography and Late Pre-Spanish Archaeology

The archaeology of most provinces of the Inca Empire is not as precisely recorded as that of Ica. The most important province, in many ways, and probably the greatest challenge to the Incas in their course of conquest, was the great Kingdom of Chimor. The territory of this kingdom extended along the entire northern part of the coast of ancient Peru, from Tumbez, near the present Ecuadorean border, south to the town of Caraballo on the north side of the Chillón Valley. The Chillón Valley forms the northern periphery of the cultivated plain of Lima on the central coast of modern Peru. The extent of the kingdom, north to south, was 620 air miles.

Important studies of ruins, occupation refuse, and burial remains have been made in the former territory of the Kingdom of Chimor, particularly in its northern part. However, there is not as yet the kind of detailed information on the nature of art styles which would make possible a sufficiently closely dated sequence of historical events, or serve to explain the nature of social relationships at any given point in time. Some studies in this direction, based on architectural remains, are currently in progress. Uhle made some collections in the territory of Chimor which also help shed light on these aspects of the history of this territory, especially for the time under Inca domination. Furthermore, in his excavations south of the territory of Chimor Uhle found burials, remains of looted burials, and refuse of the time of the Inca Empire in which a few objects in the style of Chimor were found together with objects of other styles. These associations help to fix particular features of the styles of Chimor in time. Historical data on the Kingdom of Chimor have been collected and summarized by John H. Rowe.[48]

The territory of the Kingdom of Chimor included the largest and most densely peopled river valleys of the coast of ancient Peru. At the time of the Inca conquest of Chimor, groups of valleys that were close to each other had been converted into irrigation complexes, in which canal systems were built in such a way that more or less continuous cultivation was possible between adjacent

rivers in each system. The largest of these river systems, the Lambayeque complex, is located in the northern part of the territory. These systems went out of use soon after the arrival of the Spaniards between 1528 and 1532, as a result of depopulation and political chaos. A bare 10 to 20 years later the chronicler Cieza de León crossed arid deserts where there had once been cultivated fields.[49] Even today irrigation is less extensive in most areas than it was before the arrival of the Europeans.

The geography of the northernmost area of the Kingdom of Chimor differs from the rest in that there is a much broader expanse of coastal lowland between Tumbez and the Lambayeque Valley than from Lambayeque south, where the large irrigation systems lie. What rivers exist have to cross a much wider desert than farther south. Because of these geographical peculiarities the main coastal route of the Inca highway proceeded inland from Tumbez to the Lambayeque system, along or near the natural waterways. From the northern border of the Lambayeque area south it veered toward the coast, ending at the capital of the Kingdom of Chimor at the mouth of the Moche River. South of there the main coast road remained near or at the shore, until it reached another widening of the coastal plain northwest of Ica. The main trunk road of the Inca highway thus followed a natural route of communication, one that was also used in earlier times. The desert north of Lambayeque also differs from the rest of the coastal deserts in that hardwood trees *(Prosopis chilensis)* and cacti grow over large stretches between valleys. South of this area most of the desert between valleys is without visible plant life.

Tumbez, the northernmost valley of the Kingdom of Chimor, borders on a region of moister, semi-arid climate of modern coastal Ecuador. The Tumbez River also differs from the coastal rivers to the south in that it flows north through its entire lower course, ending in the Gulf of Guayaquil. The Gulf of Guayaquil is a great indentation in the coast, and its waters are much warmer than the open waters of the coast to the south, where the effects of a cooling ocean current make themselves felt. Perhaps partly because of these geographic peculiarities, which orient the Tumbez Valley toward the hotter, more humid north, the history of the people of Tumbez before the time of Chimor seems to have differed considerably from that of the people to the south.

South of Tumbez, the large Chira and smaller Piura Rivers follow the more or less standard pattern of coastal rivers in flowing in a westerly direction from the Andes into the cooler waters of the Pacific Ocean south of the Gulf of Guayaquil. The Chira and Piura Rivers cross a broad desert, and come within close proximity to one another only for a short distance in their middle reaches. No inter-valley canal system was possible between them. Communication between them was relatively easy only across the short stretch of desert in their middle sections. Along the coast their mouths are widely separated by desert, with an even wider expanse, the great Sechura Desert, separating the mouth of the Piura River from the Lambayeque to the south. A nearly as large, hilly desert separates the lower Chira from the Tumbez Valley to the north and east. These geographical features probably account for some degree of cultural isolation of the people of the Chira-Piura area. The upper courses of the main branches of these two rivers are also widely divergent, separated by mountain ranges. Only the upper course of the Piura furnishes a fair possibility of communication with the coast to the south.

At the time of the Spanish conquest, the people of the Chira and Piura Valleys spoke the same language, called Sec, which was unrelated to the languages spoken in the Kingdom of Chimor from Lambayeque south.[50] However, the style of some pottery objects recorded from the Piura region shows that the people of this area were in touch with the heartland of the Chimor tradition at least as early as the Early Intermediate Period.

South of the Sechura Desert begins a coastal section about 275 air miles long, where human communication is easier due to the closer proximity of river valleys to each other, and the possibility of inter-valley irrigation. This area was the homeland of the culture of Chimor. It extends from the Lambayeque Valley system in the north to the Casma Valley in the south. South of the Casma there are some 85 miles of mountainous, arid coast with only two small, isolated rivers, until the next large river system is reached. Apparently this latter section also constituted a slight bar to easy, informal communication, though it did not prevent communication when special circumstances created a desire for it.

As noted, the most extensive ancient irrigation system was the Lambayeque complex, south of the Sechura Desert, which was joined to the neighboring Pacasmayo (Jequetepeque) system. The ancient irrigation system of the "Lambayeque" Valley was centered around the large Chancay River, which is divided into several major canals in its middle and lower reaches. The name of the central canal, the Lambayeque, is used most commonly to designate the entire valley. The Lambayeque irrigation complex also included the smaller Leche and much smaller Motupe Rivers to the north, and the north side of the smaller Zaña River to the south. The south side of the Zaña, in turn, was connected by extensive canals to the large Pacasmayo River to the south. The area of continuous ancient irrigation from the Motupe to the Pacasmayo covers a distance of about 77 air miles (140 kilometers).[51]

The Lambayeque and Pacasmayo plains contain remnants of some of the largest cities in ancient Peru. Most of these cities were occupied at different periods throughout a long history, however, and the archaeology done so far does not tell us how much of each settlement was occupied at any given time. The styles of remains at these settlements indicate that the most extensive canals probably had their origins in the time of the Huari Empire and later in the Middle Horizon. However, fairly extensive canals must have been constructed earlier, in the Early Intermediate Period, and some must have been built in the Early Horizon. At least some of the large Middle Horizon canals may have come into some degree of disuse during the middle of the Late Intermediate Period, undergoing renewal and some extension and changes in the times of the Kingdom of Chimor and the Inca Empire. Architectural remains indicate that under the Kingdom of Chimor, as well as under the Incas, further additions were built at sites located near strategic irrigation outlets and at highway communication points. Some were built at new sites, others in areas where old settlements had existed.

The styles of the archaeological remains from the Lambayeque-Pacasmayo region suggest that in late pre-Chimor times this area was not as influential a culture center as earlier. The greatest flowering of culture centers in that region apparently took place between the time of the Huari Empire and the first half of the Late Intermediate Period. In further support of this observation, Cieza de León, in describing his travels in the 1540s, singles out only the Chira Valley (site of Poechos), the Motupe Valley (site of ancient Jayanca or Xayanca), and the Pacasmayo Valley (site of Farfán) as seats of especially impressive centers at the time of the Inca conquest. Cieza does not refer to sites of particular importance in the central Lambayeque area, merely remarking that the valleys were prosperous and populous, and that he saw great ruined structures giving silent testimony to past greatness.[52] Cieza's observations are supported by an archaeological study which indicates that while there are ruins of large cities with late pre-Spanish occupation remains in the Lambayeque Valley, these sites lack great ceremonial structures or palaces that might indicate that these had been special prestige centers at that time.[53]

Only about 17 air miles (28 kilometers) south of the Pacasmayo River lies another river complex which includes the large Chicama River on the north and the smaller Moche on the south. The point of origin and capital of the Kingdom of Chimor were located in the smaller Moche Valley. The area of the capital of Chimor near the northern mouth of the Moche River was irrigated through two principal canal systems, one from higher up in the Moche Valley, the other from Chicama Valley.[54] This latter inter-valley canal must have been built under the rule of Chimor, but a forerunner of it could have existed some time in the Middle Horizon.[55]

South of Moche there are only two relatively large river complexes, separated by long stretches of arid coast. South of the Moche River there follow at relatively short distances the small Virú and very small Chao Rivers. Some 65 air miles (about 110 kilometers) south of the Moche flows the peculiar Santa River. Although rich in water and with a long course through the high mountain ranges, the Santa has only a small irrigable coastal plain enclosed by Andean foothills. South of the Santa there is another long stretch of coast with rivers comparatively poor in water, including the nearby Nepeña and Casma, and the more distant Culebra and Huarmey. The Culebra and Huarmey are very poor in water, the Culebra being particularly small. As noted earlier, for about 85 miles south of Casma the coast, which is hilly and rough, is almost devoid of water, the Culebra and Huarmey being the only water-carrying courses.

At the southern end of this long, barren stretch of coast there is another larger isolated river complex, in which the small Fortaleza, large Pativilca and small Supe Rivers had an interconnected irrigation plain.[56] Miguel de Estete, who traveled with the first Spanish expedition to this area in 1533, notes that under the Incas, Supe was subject to Pativilca (i.e. Guamamayo).[57] We shall see later that this does not appear to have been the case in the Middle Horizon, when the principal occupation in this river system evidently was in the Supe Valley.

South of Supe there are two independent, moderately large rivers, the nearby Huaura and the more distant Chancay (not to be confused with the Chancay River in the Lambayeque system). About 30 miles south of the Chancay is the northern boundary of the heart of the central coast, where two rivers, the smaller Chillón and larger Rimac (Lima), share a continuous irrigation plain. In pre-Spanish times the area of continuous irrigation of Lima probably extended south to include the lower Lurín

Valley and religious center of Pachacamac. Estete reports that the first Spanish expedition to Pachacamac crossed an extensive area of continuous cultivation before reaching Pachacamac from the north.[58]

No comparable river complex exists south of Pachacamac, though there are single valleys with abundant water and large irrigated plains. The largest of these are the Cañete (ancient Huarco or Lunahuaná) and Chincha, about 90 and 133 miles south of Lima, respectively.

At the time of the Kingdom of Chimor, the people of Moche shared their language, Quingnam, with the people of the two small valleys to the south, the Virú (Guañape) and Chao, who also used it as a native language. A closely related language to Quingnam, Muchic, was spoken in the entire area of the large river systems north of Moche, from the Chicama Valley to Motupe.[59] The language of the kings of Chimor, Quingnam, was spoken all the way to the southern boundary of the kingdom at the town of Carabayllo.[60] However, as Rowe points out, the historians do not say whether Quingnam was the native language of all the people in the southern area, or whether it was used here as an official language for administrative purposes only under the Kingdom of Chimor.

The language boundaries of late times reflect a long, complicated and sometimes agitated history of changing community patterns in the area, a history that can be inferred from the archaeological record. The language boundaries do not necessarily coincide with political or other cultural boundaries at any given time.

The capital of the Kingdom of Chimor, once called Chimor and now known as Chanchan, was a great city which is now in ruins. It lies northwest of the modern city of Trujillo, on a desert plain on the north side of the Moche River, overlooking the sea. The ruins of the formal core of the city have been reported to cover 3.7 square miles (6 square kilometers), and are still one of the great landmarks for visitors. The larger metropolitan area of Chanchan has been reported to extend over 6, 9 or 15.2 square miles (10, 14.5 or 24.5 square kilometers), respectively, in some of the most recent publications.[61] It was one of the largest, perhaps the largest, city of ancient Peru.

Chanchan was not an ordinary city (fig. 35). Its central area was occupied by nine or ten great rectangular compounds of varying sizes, from about 656 to 2,158 feet (200 to 650 meters) on a side, enclosed by great walls.[62] Less elaborate planned living areas are present near the great compounds.[63] The enclosing walls of the elaborate compounds had a height estimated in some of the latest publications at 25 or 30 feet (7.50 or 9 meters).[64] Each of six of the large compounds is divided into three sections, with a single, elaborate entry from the north. The northern two sections are further subdivided into courts, corridors, colonnades, formal reception halls, living quarters and storage areas. They also include kitchens and walk-in water wells. The central section in each compound was the most elaborate. Either the central or rear section of nine of the compounds contained a burial platform prepared for the most distinguished dead.[65] These burial platforms have been largely destroyed by looters. The rear sections of the compounds are thought to have been used by service personnel and contained one or more walk-in water wells.[66]

Most parts of the walls of the formal structures of Chanchan are said to be built of rectangular bricks of dried clay (adobes), while some parts are said to be made of clay poured into frames that formed longer wall sections (a building technique called "tapia" construction). Some walls were made at least in part of river cobbles set in clay. The surfaces of the large walls taper from a 4 meter (about 13 foot) thick base to a 1.5 meter (about 5 foot) thick top, a technique that lends greater firmness to the structure. Walls with an inward slant of the exterior surface are described as having a "batter." The technique was an old one in this area, used in the construction of pyramids as early as the Early Intermediate Period. A batter was also used in the construction of large walls built by the Incas, who may have borrowed this technique from Chimor, since they did not make use of it before their conquests.

The great compounds of Chanchan were not ordinary dwellings, but enormous, elaborate residences, storage centers and reception halls. The walls of these reception halls and burial mounds are famous for their ornate decorations in modeled clay relief. At each end of the city there are large, depressed areas said to have been gardens.[67] At one time the storage rooms, colonnades and perhaps some living quarters were roofed with cane, matting and mud plaster, providing cooling shade and protection from wind and dust. The city was famed for the extraordinary wealth and pomp of its inhabitants, and the luxury of its palaces. Three large truncated pyramids which must have served ceremonial purposes stand outside the compound area, and one stands within this area.[68] On the outskirts of the formal building area were informal, densely crowded quarters where ordinary people lived, and a large network of irrigation canals and outlying rectangular buildings apparently used for administrative functions.

Each of the nine largest, most elaborate compounds of Chanchan which contained a burial platform may have

been the residence of one of the kings who are reported to have ruled the Kingdom of Chimor until the Inca conquest. Although ten kings are recorded, the first was probably mythical. The people living in each compound probably included the king's family, retainers and government aides. Large parts of the compounds appear to have been used only for conducting government business.

After the death and burial of a king and his retinue, his compound may have been abandoned or, alternatively, it could have served as the residence for his family and descendants, except for the heir to the throne.[69] Under the Incas, joint residence and other group distinctions marked the families and descendants of the kings and emperors who ruled at Cuzco. These groups formed separate social units (royal "ayllus"), each with its own identity and special loyalties. The Incas borrowed many of their techniques of social structure, government and administration from the Kingdom of Chimor, and the grouping of the families and descendants of each ruler as a separate social unit may have been one of these borrowed ideas. A large archaeological expedition has explored Chanchan in recent years.[70]

Although large ruined cities with some features similar to those of Chanchan also occur in the area of the Pacasmayo and Lambayeque River systems to the north, the size, elaboration and number of the great compounds of Chanchan are unique. Perhaps the largest of all the late cities, Pátapo (ancient Cinto) on the Taymi canal in the Lambayeque Valley, had no palace at all, nor did ancient Collique, a second large city of late date on the Reque (Lémape) canal in the same valley.[71] Other impressive settlements in the Lambayeque system are most notable for the great number and large size of pyramids with long ramps of access, built around open areas. At one such great city, Pacatnamú, at the mouth of the Pacasmayo River, 57 pyramids are associated with rectangular compounds of some sort.[72] By contrast, pyramidal structures at Chanchan are much fewer in number, and they are smaller than many of the pyramids in the Lambayeque system.

Most of the northern settlements with numerous pyramids evidently had their origins in the Middle Horizon; a few had pyramids probably datable to the Early Intermediate Period. The style of the Middle Horizon and later pyramids represents the continuation of a much older north coast tradition appearing as early as about 2000 B.C., near the end of the Preceramic Period or the beginning of the Initial Period. These observations reinforce the presumption that the city map of Chanchan as it existed at the time of the Inca conquest was in major part a product of late construction under the kings of Chimor, with innovations in architecture and city planning combined with older architectural features.

No cities of comparable size existed in the Kingdom of Chimor south of the Moche Valley. However, smaller settlements with compounds similar in plan and construction techniques to the smaller, less elaborate compounds of Chanchan have been recorded for the Virú Valley.[73] These sites presumably originated under the rule of Chimor. Structures of the same building tradition, but probably of earlier date, have been recorded as far south as the Casma Valley.[74]

The great superiority in luxury, wealth, size and number of the palaces and associated remains at Chanchan compared with all other settlements, large or small, under the Kingdom of Chimor, reflects the great concentration of power and prestige at the capital. These features are one of the indications of the high degree of control exercised by the rulers at Chanchan over the world they had conquered.

A further light is shed on the existence or nonexistence of great prestige centers under the Kingdom of Chimor by the absence or presence of structures built in a different style by the Incas after their conquest of Chimor. Published accounts fail to record Inca-style constructions at Chanchan. Only a few Inca constructions have been recorded at other sites with palaces in the style of Chimor. The greatest number of buildings in a provincial Inca style are found in Chimor settlements without palaces in the Lambayeque Valley.[75]

The archaeology of other areas of the Inca Empire indicates that for strategic reasons the Incas built complete new administrative centers in areas where there were no great capitals at the time of their conquests. If important capitals were present, the Incas usually allowed them to continue as such under their local rulers, who, however, had to acknowledge Inca overlordship. The formal and ceremonial buildings already present at these centers continued in use under the Incas, the Inca rulers only adding some building sections if they saw a need for them.[76] The presence of numerous constructions built entirely in an Inca style thus usually means that at the time of the Inca conquest the region was lacking in political importance of a secular nature and had no prestigious capitals. This observation does not apply to important religious centers found by the Incas at the time of their conquests, where they made a point of erecting conspicuous new temples and associated buildings in their own style. Like the Europeans, the Incas made religious mission an excuse for conquest.

Written accounts, like the records of other remains, show the Kingdom of Chimor to have been of relatively recent origin. Four kings governed Chimor under Inca rule, from between 1462 and 1470 to the time of the arrival of the Spaniards between 1528 and 1532. If we estimate the average length of rule for the kings of Chimor on the basis of the known dates for the four last pre-Spanish rulers, the first king of Chimor would have begun his rule about 1300, that is, in Late Intermediate Period Epoch 6.

The archaeological record shows, however, that the occupation of the area of Chanchan and the tradition of Chimor culture formed an uninterrupted sequence from the Middle Horizon on. The area of Chanchan was occupied by Middle Horizon Epoch 2 or 3, 600 to 800 A.D. The evidence for this contention is based in part on the relative dating of style features of pottery vessels found in a large cemetery adjoining the city.[77] In part it is based on the stylistic differences in clay reliefs on walls. At least one of the pyramid mounds on the outskirts of Chanchan, the so-called Huaca Cientopies or El Dragón, has relief decoration probably datable to the Middle Horizon.[78]

We see, then, that the establishment of the late dynasty of the Chimor kings at Chanchan did not initially represent any major cultural innovation, but only a local political event. As in most of the accounts of the beginnings of the 15th century kingdoms, the first king of Chimor is said to have come to the valley from somewhere else. It was a legendary and politically useful convention for describing vaguely recorded beginnings of dynasties before they engaged in political and military expansion.

So local was the beginning of the Chimor dynasty, that the first two reported kings did no more than gain control over neighboring local chieftains within the small Moche Valley. The first major expansion was not undertaken until the time of the grandson of the first reported ruler, under whom the upper reaches of the Moche Valley were brought under state control, as well as neighboring valleys north to the northern border of the Pacasmayo canal system at the Zaña Valley, and south to the Santa Valley. It is important to observe that these boundaries lie within the boundaries of an ancient cultural community on the north coast, known as the Moche culture, datable to the second half of the Early Intermediate Period (see also chapter 6). This expansion movement of Chimor probably took place some time around 1350 or perhaps a little later, still in Epoch 6 of the Late Intermediate Period.[79]

According to historical accounts, no further expansion of the Kingdom of Chimor took place until the time of the last independent ruler, Minchançaman, who still ruled when the Incas conquered Chimor. Rowe suggests convincingly that this late expansion movement by

Chimor may have been undertaken by the King of Chimor in response to news of the military expansion of the Incas in the south after 1438, that is, in Late Intermediate Period Epoch 8.[80] No detailed account exists of the stages by which this late conquest by Chimor was achieved. However, Rowe points to evidence that suggests that the Lambayeque area north of Zaña must have been taken over early in Minchançaman's reign or possibly slightly earlier, and that there may have been significant frontier points in the course of the southern conquest. One of these southern frontier points may have been at Huarmey, and the other at Paramonga on the north side of the Fortaleza River near its mouth, that is, in the northern part of the isolated river complex that included the Pativilca and Supe Valleys.

The most difficult part of the conquests of Chimor probably took place south of the Fortaleza-Pativilca-Supe river system. From at least as early as Middle Horizon Epoch 1B there existed a cultural division between the Supe Valley and the next valley to the south, the Huaura, a division that separated peoples with different pottery traditions and, presumably, differences in other customs and points of view. From the Middle Horizon on the Huaura Valley evidently formed the northern periphery of a culture area that had its focus in the Chancay Valley, the next valley to the south. This culture area included the coast to the south as far as the Chillón Valley.[81] In Middle Horizon Epochs 1B, 2A and 2B this entire area was incorporated into the Huari Empire. After the fall of Huari, Chancay became the influential center of development of a distinctive style of art and culture in this area. The artistic influence of the Chancay culture extended in modified form even beyond these boundaries.[82] Unfortunately, very little archaeological information exists on this period for the valleys directly neighboring this area to the north and south.

A trustworthy historical account sheds some light on the possible broader alliances of the peoples of this region. One of the first acts of the Spaniards after kidnapping and imprisoning the Inca Emperor 'Ataw Wallpa was to send an expedition to Pachacamac, the great religious center south of Lima. The first action of the Spaniards there was to destroy the shrine and its powerful priesthood. When the news was spread that the Spaniards had destroyed the authority of the shrine of Pachacamac and taken its place, the lords of a certain number of neighboring valleys promptly came to pay homage to the conquerors. Evidently these lords had stood in a special relationship of homage to Pachacamac, and were now transferring their allegiance to the new

authority. These lords came from as far north as Huaura (Guarva) and as far south as Chincha.[83]

Thus, when we read that at the time of the conquests of Chimor, Lima had a very powerful ruler who controlled the area south to Pachacamac, and that he succeeded in defeating the forces of Chimor after three major Chimor assaults from the north, the combination of archaeological and historical information becomes suggestive.[84] It is possible that in the face of the military threat from Chimor, the lords from the area with special ties to the shrine of Pachacamac acted as allies against the forces of Chimor. Chimor evidently succeeded in taking over the territory of the Chancay culture area, but was finally stopped at the border of the territory of the Lord of Lima at Carabayllo.

We see, then, that at the time of the Inca conquest of the Kingdom of Chimor the area between the Santa and Lima Valleys, on the one hand, and from Lambayeque north on the other, had probably undergone profound but quite recent upheavals, resulting in the bare beginnings of changes in former cultural boundaries. Although some common traditions existed in this entire area, Chimor culture came as a more foreign element and probably a greater shock to the peoples south of Casma than it did to the peoples to the north. The conquests of Chimor must have been completed only some 12 to 15 years before the Inca conquest. It would be difficult to find archaeological evidence that might isolate so brief an occupation period under the Kingdom of Chimor before the Inca conquest.

The Inca conquest was superimposed on this complicated recent history of abrupt changes and upheavals, and added further complexities. Having conquered Chimor, the Incas proceeded to show their respect for its institutions and products by borrowing a great many of them. As a result, institutions, art styles, and technologies of the culture of Chimor were spread much more widely under the Incas than before. The Incas adapted many techniques of government from the system of government of Chimor. Rowe points out that the political organization of the Inca Empire was worked out in the main by the Emperor Thupa 'Inka after the conquest of Chimor, some time between 1471 and 1493.

In addition to the system of government through a hereditary nobility, mentioned earlier, the Incas probably learned the use of a special class of civil servants for government services, the rectangular town plan, mass production methods in pottery, textiles, adobes and perhaps other technologies, metal working techniques, and perhaps refinements in tapestry weaving and feather cloth making from the people of Chimor. North coast workmen were much respected and worked directly for the Inca government at Cuzco, as well as elsewhere.[85] The Incas were ingenious inventors as well as borrowers, however, and also contributed new features of administration, art and technology, which in turn were superimposed on the coastal cultures.

The Incas were astute politicians whose concern was to impose their authority, when possible, in such a way that it would result in the loyalty of their new subjects to the Inca cause. Initially they bestowed great distinction on the kings of Chimor, and the capital at Chanchan continued to be a great administrative center. Although Minchançaman himself was taken to Cuzco as an honored hostage, to ensure the loyalty of his subjects, his son and grandson both continued to rule over the entire territory of the former kingdom. However, some time during the reign of the grandson, the Inca administration underwent major changes, all oriented toward more absolute control of the provinces. The unity of the Kingdom of Chimor and the extraordinary power of its kings were destroyed. Each valley or valley system of the territory of Chimor was put under the control of an independent governor, either a descendant of the former kings of Chimor, or of the governors installed by them, each now under the direct supervision of the government of Cuzco.

Evidence from Ica and Chincha recorded by Uhle shows that great changes took place in the archaeological record at an estimated date of about 1485-1490.[86] These archaeological changes indicate greater and more standardized Inca influence. They suggest that a major change took place in the administration of the Inca Empire at this time, leading to greater state control of the conquered provinces. The historically recorded administrative reorganization of the former Kingdom of Chimor must date to about the same time. This event would have taken place late in the reign of the Emperor Thupa 'Inka.

While the succession of major historical events in the territory of Chimor between about 1440 and 1550 cannot fail to have left its mark on the archaeological record, it would take careful observations of details of many associations of objects on and in the ground, and of the differences in the styles of the remains, to discover this mark. Observations of this kind have not yet been made in sufficient detail, although there are many excavation and survey records.

We may expect that in the original expansion area of Chimor between the Zaña and Santa Valleys we would find Chimor ("Chimu")—tradition remains without major style changes from the time of the later expansion movement of Chimor (about 1440, in Late

Intermediate Period Epoch 8) to about 1485, 20 years or more after the Inca conquest of Chimor.[87] With finer control of associations and style analysis, it may be possible to discover some less striking innovations in the archaeological remains for the period between about 1462 and 1485. Beyond the boundaries of the early expansion area of the Kingdom of Chimor, we may expect local and regional styles, different from those of Chimor, to occur from the time of the independence of these areas through the occupation of Chimor and the subsequent early years of the Inca occupation until about 1485. After about 1485 there were considerable changes in the archaeological record everywhere, as noted in chapter 1. There probably were no major changes in the archaeological record of most areas from the later Inca occupation to the early Spanish occupation.

In assessing the archaeological record, we must also keep in mind that at the time of the Inca conquest the most hierarchical class structure in the Andean area was found in Chimor where the nobility and common people were believed to have been descended from different stars.[88] The pomp and riches with which the kings of Chimor surrounded themselves exceeded those of all other areas, including Ica. We have seen that at Ica these social differences found clear expression in the archaeological record, and therefore we should expect to find them even better represented in the archaeology of Chimor. The Chanchan Project expedition is said to have discovered remnants of the looted tomb of a noble, but the work is still in progress.[89]

The peoples of Chimor were great metallurgists. Like the Ica and Inca nobles, the kings and nobles of Chimor used gold and silver ornaments and dinner ware as symbols of distinction. It is reported that much of the great Inca art in gold and silver, robbed and melted down into ingots by the Spanish conquerors, had been refashioned by the Incas from remarkable art objects and other valuables that had once belonged to the kings and nobles of Chimor.[90] What was left in Chimor by the Incas was subsequently looted by the Spaniards and their successors. Most surviving archaeological remains of the property of Chimor nobles are torn out of context, and therefore cannot be easily identified as such or compared with the remains of commoners.

There is no good record of the pattern of associations of objects in the burials of commoners of Chimor either, since the looting fever has been directed even to the remains of the poor. Even though Uhle and a few other archaeologists have found burials of commoners, they either failed to record the associations, or simply gave an inventory of a few of the objects that came from a particular burial, omitting a complete description of their finds.[91] Our example of Uhle's burial records from Ica shows that without such records a reconstruction of the most interesting part of culture history is not possible. For these reasons we can do no more than guess at the historical and social significance of some of the finds, using Uhle's data from Ica, Chincha and Pachacamac for comparison.

Uhle made collections of pottery vessels reflecting the late period under discussion at three sites in the territory of the Kingdom of Chimor. All of these vessels lack a record of burial associations, and the dating of the collections must be done on stylistic grounds alone. The sites where Uhle made the collections are the capital at Chanchan, the nearby site of Moche, and a site called Olivar or Oliva, near Chuquillo, in the Pativilca Valley of the isolated southern river system.

Uhle collected only a few simple pottery vessels at Chanchan. Although he does not specify the location where they were found, their simplicity suggests that they probably came from a cemetery belonging to commoners.

Uhle made a fairly large and more important collection at Moche, at a small cemetery about 208 yards (190 meters) south of the great Early Intermediate Period pyramid Huaca del Sol (see chapter 4C). In his publication Uhle gave the site the letter designation d, but Kroeber cataloged it as Site B in the University of California Museum collection.[92] Uhle observed that the pottery vessels from these burials matched some of the refuse fragments of pottery he collected from the surface of a settlement on the plain between the two pyramids at this site. The latest occupation of the site dates to the Inca occupation period, as Uhle observes, with a style of remains which probably stayed unchanged through the early years after the arrival of the Spaniards.

The late settlement at the site of Moche was small and undistinguished in appearance. It lacked public buildings of adobe or stone construction or residences of persons of distinction. Uhle describes the surface of the site as being densely covered with doughnut-shaped stones of a kind used as clod breakers in plowing, as well as other kinds or ordinary refuse associated with everyday life. However, the site did have one special distinction. It was located on the route of the main coastal trunk road of the Inca highway.[93] The early chroniclers customarily made no reference to minor highway stops, and they made none to this site. Nevertheless, at least some of the residents must have performed services on behalf of the government, as was customary at sites along the highway.

The Site B cemetery belonged to the occupants of the settlement between the two ancient pyramids, which had long since fallen into disuse. Most of the pottery Uhle collected from the Site B burials is attributable, on stylistic grounds, to the latest occupation period, probably the period after 1485. However, some of the burial pottery is attributable, also on stylistic grounds, to a much earlier time, probably datable to the first two or three epochs of the Late Intermediate Period.

Uhle makes no description of the site of Olivar in the Pativilca Valley, except to say that it was found near the site of Paramonga. Paramonga is just north of the Fortaleza River, near the sea.[94] It was one of the main junction points where an Inca road connected the coastal and highland trunk roads.[95] The site of Olivar was evidently a cemetery where Uhle excavated a few small burials. Although he kept no notes on burial associations, most of the objects he found are attributable to the Inca occupation period after 1485, and some belong to the early part of the Spanish occupation before 1570. The dating is again based on observations of art style of the pottery, and on the presence of Spanish glass beads datable to the early Colonial Period.

In summary, the objects collected by Uhle from the three sites within the territory of Chimor mentioned above must have belonged to commoners living in the later part of the Inca occupation period. At least some of these commoners were probably engaged in government service. Most of the people whose possessions Uhle collected probably had no particular social distinction, but they were not destitute either. One of the striking observations is the great similarity, in part identity, of some of the pottery vessels from all three sites.

Many features distinguish the stylistic tradition of the fancy categories of pottery of Chimor. These features include distinctive vessel shapes, the large-scale use of a smoke-blackened, polished finish, and the use of molds for making shapes and designs ("press-molding"). The pottery of the Inca occupation period of Chimor also has incised decoration (designs made by grooves, i.e. incisions, in the soft clay before the vessel was fired), and designs made by putting a glossy polish on some areas and leaving others matte ("pattern-burnished" decoration). It is possible that these last two design techniques were confined to pottery of the Inca occupation period. Another decorative technique consists of checkerboard design patches created by pressing a paddle with such a design grooved into its surface into the moist surface of the vessel body before it is fired. This technique results in a reversed decorative pattern of raised lines ("paddle-marked" decoration). The use of a paddle to make designs is a time and labor-saving device, used in this region most commonly on vessels without special artistic distinction and with a relatively careless surface finish.

Although smoke blackened fancy ware is far more common than other kinds, grayish orange colored fancy ware, some with painted decoration, also occurs. Some fancy vessels are made of a soft, light, cream colored ware.

Cooking vessels of the Chimu tradition are also distinctive. Most of them are small to medium-sized ollas with round bodies, a short raised rim with an outward slant from tip to rim base (a beveled rim), sometimes two short lugs attached to the rim and upper body, and a dark grayish surface. Many are encrusted with soot from use in cooking. Some are plain, some have press-molded designs. Some of the utility ollas show no sooting, are a dull orange red, and have either simple painted decoration of a few white stripes, or molded bumps that cover the surface. All have a matte, unpolished surface. Large jars were also collected by Uhle at Moche, some of similar workmanship to the utility wares.

Some of the pottery collected by Uhle reflects imitations of the Inca style in shape or design features. Part of the dating of the pottery from the site of Moche to the late Inca occupation period is based on the associations of pieces with the same style features in correspondingly late graves from Chincha and Ica, and on style features of vessels excavated at a cemetery of the late Inca occupation period at Pachacamac.[96]

The most striking examples of imitations of the Inca style of Cuzco are provincial versions of Inca jars with pointed bottoms. The shape, size and decorative characteristics of these jars distinguish the style of provincial Inca jars from the territory of Chimor from those of other provinces of the Inca Empire. Uhle found three such jars, two at the site at Moche (figs. 36A, B), and one with unspecified location (fig. 37). All three are small. Two are of smoked blackware, and one is made of dull orange ware with painted decoration. One blackware jar is plain, while the other has press-molded decoration. All three jars have very rounded, nearly pot-bellied body contours, unlike Cuzco Inca jars, and unlike most provincial Inca jars from the coast to the south. They are also smaller than most Cuzco Inca jars.

The painted jar and the plain blackware jar are from the highway site at Moche (figs. 36A, B). Neither is mold made, unlike most Chimu-style pottery but like Inca-style pottery. They are of careless manufacture, with an uneven, irregular surface, uneven surface color reflecting careless firing, and a poor polish. Both have a few style features that tie them more closely to the Cuzco Inca style than other such jars from the territory of Chimor. Thus, both have a characteristic Inca-style lug on the upper front of the body, in addition to the standard pair of side handles at the lower body. The blackware jar, with a partly missing neck rim, retains one of a pair of standard small pierced lugs on the lower surface of the rim, a typical Inca-style jar feature. Although the rim is missing from the painted jar, this piece shows equally close affiliation with the Cuzco Inca style in its decoration, which is an imperfect imitation of a standard Cuzco Inca design for such jars.

The style features of both jars from the Moche site thus reflect especially close ties to the Cuzco Inca style. They suggest, by inference, that their owners may have had a special tie to the Inca government, closer than that of other kinds of citizens under the Inca Empire. These persons may have belonged to the special class of civil servants who were under more direct supervision of the Inca government than other people, and who were used for various government services. The relatively poor manufacture of the vessels suggests that they carried no particular distinction or value.

The jar collected by Uhle from an unspecified location has fewer Inca features and more Chimu-style features (fig. 37). Unlike the other jars, it is mold made, and it has Chimu-style press-molded decoration on the upper body. It lacks the Inca lug on the upper front body and the pierced lugs on the lower rim of the neck. It has Chimu-style pattern-burnished stripe decoration on the neck and on the pointed bottom of the body. Its standard of manufacture is higher than that of the jars from the Moche site, showing more careful shaping, surface finish and firing. The contrast in style features and manufacturing techniques suggests that the press-molded jar may reflect a different kind of social affiliation of the owner than the jars from the Moche road stop.

The press-molded design of the jar without provenience has style features that are important aids in dating aspects of the Chimu style. The body of the vessel is divided vertically into quarters by means of glossy dark molding ridges, and also has a circular ridge at the top below the neck. Each quarter of the vessel is a matte, sunken, medium gray area decorated with small projecting, glossy dark bumps, that is, "stipples." In the center of each quarter section is the raised depiction of a bird. Two birds are very stylized, and two are more naturalistic representations of sea birds (cormorants) shown eating fish. In the Chimu style of the Inca occupation period, as in the Ica style, this is a very popular design motif. The presence of this Chimu design pattern on an imitation Inca shape helps to tell us which features of the Chimu style were in use during the Inca occupation period.

Uhle collected five blackware bottles at Moche and one at Olivar in the Pativilca Valley. These bottles can be assigned to a "Chimu-Inca" style category (figs. 38A, B). They differ from the provincial Inca jars in being local shapes that do not occur in the Cuzco Inca style, but have some style features borrowed from Inca shapes. Most of the bottles are very similar in shape, size and decoration. They have a medium-high neck and a strap handle from neck to body. The body is slightly angular at the point of maximum diameter, and has a flat bottom. The point of maximum diameter varies from middle height to the lower third of the height of the body. The combination of this kind of angularity and its position on the body, together with the proportions of the flat bottom, are modified Inca loan features which also occur in other coastal styles of the late Inca occupation period after about 1485. Some of these Chimu-Inca bottles have the additional Inca loan feature of a short, everted neck rim. This rim is sometimes flat at the top.

These Chimu-Inca bottles also have many non-Inca Chimu-style features. Some have a bulge in the top of the neck on which modeled features depict the eyes and beak of a bird. On some bottles the strap handle is in the form of a monkey, with a modeled head and arms at the top, with or without modeled legs and a tail at the bottom. On one bottle, the monkey tail is in its customary place, but the head and arms of the monkey are placed on the upper body of the bottle in front of the neck, instead of at the top of the handle (fig. 38A). Some bottles have pattern-burnished stripes on the bottom or neck, like the provincial Inca jar described above.

Almost all the bottles have press-molded decoration on the upper body, arranged in principle like the design on the provincial Inca jar. One of its important distinguishing features is that the bulging seams of raised clay which mark the area where the two halves of the mold had been joined are parallel to the handle in a front-to-back position. This feature is especially popular in the late Inca occupation period. In the preceding epochs, the seams of the mold are most commonly, or perhaps always, side-to-side rather than front-to-back on bottles.

These Chimu-Inca bottles show only indifferent care in manufacture. Their appearance and their apparently common occurrence suggest that they were not considered objects of particular distinction.

There is another category of Chimu-Inca ware, one that probably denotes distinction of some kind. Uhle

found an example at the site of Moche (fig. 39). It is a double-chambered vessel in which two bottles with long, narrow necks are joined by a hollow tube through the lower bodies and by a flat, solid bridge below the rim of each neck. These bottles are most commonly made of plain, finely finished smoked blackware. The fragmentary piece found by Uhle at Moche is of a rarer kind made of a soft, cream colored ware, also with a fine, glossy finish. The stains now visible on the surface are the result of damage sustained after burial. Like the provincial Inca jars from this site, this vessel is not mold made. Like the other vessels described above, this bottle category appears to be confined to the Inca occupation period, probably after 1485. The only feature that may be the indirect result of Inca inspiration appearing on these bottles is a flat or slightly curved, horizontally projecting rim on each neck. Only one of these necks is open. The other is closed, and contains a whistle on the inside.

If these double-chambered whistling bottles are partly filled with liquid and then tilted back and forth, the whistle makes a small, agreeable sound. It would have been a pleasant and gracious way to serve a drink. The top of each whistling neck is always ornamented with a beautifully modeled little figure. The one found by Uhle at the site of Moche has the modeled figure of a monkey, greedily eating corn from a large cob held in its hands. Unfortunately, the rim of the other neck of this vessel is missing.

A pair of very finely made blackware bottles of the same kind as the one found by Uhle at Moche was found by him in an Ica burial of the Inca occupation period after 1485 (burial Tk). The manufacture and style of these vessels indicates that they were probably not made at Ica, but imported. The glossy, very smooth, very black surface finish suggests that they may have been made at Pachacamac, where this finish is typical. Like other vessels of the Late Horizon at Pachacamac, they are not mold made. The modeled figures on the top of one spout of these bottles are fine, life-like representations characteristic of the style of Chimor. One represents a female dog with two suckling pups, the other a fisherman carrying two enormous fish (fig. 40). That men actually carried fish larger than themselves can be inferred from a recent photograph taken in eastern Peru, where a man carried such a fish (fig. 41). Presumably equally large fish could be taken from the sea.

The Ica burial from which these vessels came belonged to a person of distinction, but not a member of the nobility (cf. chapters 2, 3). Persons buried in such graves at Ica had property characteristic of a special style assemblage associated with a segregated community, probably of civil servants, dating to the time after the administrative reorganization of the empire. Fragments of fancy vessels like these double-chambered whistling bottles are rare or do not occur in household refuse. They were probably government gifts for meritorious service. They appear to have been valued objects of the more distinguished members of this community. Burials of Ica nobles contained similar vessels, but with important stylistic differences: they were locally made imitations, not imports.

In the light of the evidence from Ica, it is possible that the fancy Chimu-Inca whistling bottle found by Uhle at the site of Moche also may have belonged to a non-noble of distinction engaged in government service. It is equally possible, however, that the association pattern of this vessel category in the area of Chimor was different from that of Ica.

Uhle also collected vessels at the site of Moche which are entirely in the Chimu style. Most of them date to the later Inca occupation period, on stylistic grounds. They include a more traditional category of double-chambered whistling bottles (fig. 42), a bottle with an animal-head spout (fig. 43), and the famous "stirrup-spout" bottles which are the trademark of the north coast tradition from the Early Horizon on (figs. 44A, B). An animal-head bottle virtually identical to the one found by Uhle at Moche was found by him in a burial from the Chincha Valley, datable to the early years after the arrival of the Spaniards, probably before 1541.[97]

There is a possibility that one or two of the bottles Uhle collected at Moche Site B may predate the later part of the Inca occupation period by a short span of time, for they have some more traditional Chimu-style features.[98] These pieces may date to the early part of the Inca occupation period before 1485, or possibly as early as independent Chimor of Late Intermediate Period Epoch 8.

B. The Ruins of Chimu Capac

The river complex of the Fortaleza-Pativilca-Supe Valleys played a strategic role in the Huari Empire, especially in Middle Horizon Epoch 2. For a period of about 150 years after the fall of Huari, during Middle Horizon Epochs 3 and 4, and perhaps longer, the people living in this river system came under the extensive sphere of influence of a powerful culture center of the north coast. The prestige of north coast culture appears to have declined sometime after the early part of the Late Inter-

mediate Period, and the peoples in different localities apparently reverted to greater cultural isolation. The archaeology of the Pativilca River system reflects these changing conditions.

During the Middle Horizon the principal occupation of the Pativilca River complex was in the Supe Valley. Although the Pativilca River is the source of the largest amount of water, its valley is enclosed by mountains which leave room for only a relatively narrow valley plain. While the Supe River does not carry water in its lower reaches during the dry season in the mountains, it has the widest valley plain. The lower reaches of the Supe Valley could not have had an important occupation without canals that brought water from the Pativilca. Such ancient canals exist.[99]

One of Uhle's most valuable archaeological studies was undertaken at a unique outpost of the Huari Empire in the lower Supe Valley. In much later times, long after the site was in ruins, it became known as *Chimu Capac*, an Inca term. The ruins of Chimu Capac are located about 2.5 miles (4 kilometers) north of the Supe River and 2 miles (3.2 kilometers) from the sea, immediately north of the main houses of the sugar hacienda San Nicolás, on and at the foot of a group of isolated hills in the valley plain.[100]

Uhle describes the site as consisting of two parts. One part was composed of two heavily fortified hills about 500 feet (152 meters) high. Several heavy fortification walls of stone enclosed the hills. The forts at the top of the hills consisted of various kinds of stone buildings, including what may have been storage structures. Uhle describes the latter as "cell-like constructions." The forts occupied an area of about ¼ mile by nearly ⅓ of a mile (500 by 400 meters).

The second part of Chimu Capac was a formal settlement at the western, seaward foot of the fortified hills. The settlement was built on a rectangular plan, about 620 by 440 meters (about 2,033 by 1,443 feet) in area. It was enclosed by "several straight thick walls, which form several more or less rectangular squares." When Uhle saw them, the walls were much weathered. They had been built partly of stone and partly of lump-shaped adobes. The mixture of building materials and the shape of the adobes suggested to Uhle that the adobes were re-used remnants of earlier structures at the site, which had been destroyed in the course of construction of the settlement of Chimu Capac. The principal building was a rectangular pyramid directly at the foot of the hills. This pyramid was composed of several terraces. The higher terraces enclosed a sunken court on three sides. This was no ordinary dwelling, and must have served a public, and probably ceremonial purpose.

Although Uhle gives no further description of the site, the impression conveyed is that of a planned settlement with important ceremonial functions, heavily protected against possible military attack.

Uhle notes that on "the whole coast of middle Peru" there exist only two sites where the Huari presence is strongly represented, namely Chimu Capac and Pachacamac. Pachacamac was a competing center of Huari religion and power in the Huari Empire during Middle Horizon Epoch 2. Uhle points out that whereas Pachacamac continued as a religious center for centuries until the time of the Spanish conquest, Chimu Capac did not survive the Middle Horizon.

The platforms of the terraces of the pyramid at Chimu Capac were used as cemeteries, like the terraces of the Huaca del Sol in the Moche Valley, and like the forecourt of the Huari temple of Pachacamac. Uhle supposed reasonably that the burials at the temple of Pachacamac must have been those of people who had some business connected with the shrine and its oracle. So too, the burials on the platforms of the pyramid of Chimu Capac very likely had some connection with the ceremonial purpose of this structure.

The cemeteries on the platforms of the pyramid were densely crowded with burials. The style of the pottery, textiles and other remains Uhle recovered from his excavations indicates that almost all the burials date to the Middle Horizon, including specimens datable to Epochs 1B, 2A, 2B, 3 and 4. The only exception consists of remnants of what was apparently a single small burial datable to the early half of the Late Intermediate Period, probably Epoch 3. The Late Intermediate Period burial must have been placed there at a time when Chimu Capac was largely abandoned.

Although Uhle's archaeological record for Chimu Capac is poor, the data he does furnish can be used to great advantage because of the limited period of occupation of the site and the unusually good preservation of the perishable remains. Uhle did make a list of some of the contents of six burials, but he gives no further description of the burials and makes no reference to the human remains.

Uhle gives a general description of the kinds of burials found at Chimu Capac. Some burials were placed in square underground chambers of stone masonry which contained one or two dead. Other burials were placed simply in the ground without any structure or housing. Some of the dead were placed near a stone wall (presumably a terrace wall). All adult dead appear to have been wrapped in mummy bales with false heads and other accompaniments also characteristic of Middle Horizon burials at Ancón, Pachacamac, Ica, Nasca and presumably elsewhere.

The mummy bales from Chimu Capac presumably resembled those from elsewhere on the coast in composition and general appearance. None has been preserved as a bale, though Uhle's collection contains many parts of bales, including false heads. Unlike most false heads of Middle Horizon mummy bales from farther south, the heads from Chimu Capac were made of wood (fig. 45). Such carved wooden heads are a northern trait. A false wooden mummy head in the same style has been recorded from the Santa Valley.[101] These heads resemble the heads of wooden carvings used as a part of sacrificial offerings in shrines in the Moche Valley on the north coast of (cf. chapter 4C). The faces of the wooden mummy bale heads are usually painted with red resin paint from chin to eyebrows, the whites of the eyes and teeth are painted white, and the round pupils in the center of the eyes are black, made of a thick, tar-like substance. The false mummy heads were inserted into the bale by means of a stick protruding from their base.

The forehead section of the false heads was unpainted and covered with a headdress. The headdress consisted in part of a crown of reed or lace-like basketry. Some of the false heads were ornamented with a feather plume above the crown. In at least one example, a wig with many small, very long braids covered the head under whatever headdress was used. A wig like it was found on a Middle Horizon 2A mummy bale head from Ancón.[102]

The false mummy heads with their adornments were covered with a cloth, like the false mummy bale heads elsewhere. Uhle collected a neck wrapping for one of the bales, which resembles the ends of long forehead bands of Middle Horizon mummy bales at Ancón, which were also tied around the neck of the bale (4-7779).

Around the girths of some of the bales, either outside or within the outermost wrapping, long sausage-shaped cloth pouches with small, rectangular pendent pouches were attached. Either the long master pouch or the pendent pouches or both were filled either with coca leaves, or with raw cotton which included fiber, seeds and fragmentary leaves and sticks.

For the importance of coca, see chapters 3 and 6. Textiles also had a great and ancient value in the lives of the peoples of the Andes from as early as the use of coca. Cotton fiber was the main raw material grown on the coast for the production of textile art, just as llama and alpaca wool were the raw products contributed by the peoples of the highlands.

Some of the hollow mummy belts and their pendent pouches were made of plain cotton weave and painted with abbreviations of religious designs that also appear on cloth paintings of exclusive religious function. The inclusion of coca leaves and raw cotton in the pouch belts, to the apparent exclusion of other kinds of contents, reflects the extraordinary value that must have been attached to these products.

The mummy bales of Chimu Capac were accompanied by many other grave goods, and some were dressed in very fine clothing. The bodies inside the bales were also clothed and adorned with personal ornaments. Unfortunately, perishable remains placed close to the body of the deceased were not generally preserved. Inner garments of the deceased, and garments enclosing the outer wrappings, may have differed slightly in some details.

Pottery vessels accompanying the dead of Chimu Capac are numerous and furnish the greatest amount of information concerning the dating of the site. The pottery is also particularly informative on the cultural affiliations of Chimu Capac. The collection contains 253 vessels.

Only three vessels are datable to Epoch 1B of the Middle Horizon, that is, the early time of the Huari Empire.[103] The painted decoration on two of these vessels is a simple pattern in common use on Epoch 1B pottery of the Huari capital. These vessels are modeled jars representing important lay personages. One of the personages is seen wearing a four-cornered hat, the head covering of men of distinction under the Huari Empire.

One fragmentary pottery vessel is datable to Epoch 2A, and about 30 vessels are datable to Epoch 2B, the later time of the Huari Empire. Of the Epoch 2B vessels, ten were found in one burial (grave 6), and twelve in another (grave 5). The Middle Horizon 2B pottery of Chimu Capac is stylistically unique compared with the pottery of other important provinces of the empire. Most of the ornamented forms are provincial variants of highland Huari forms that otherwise are found only at the capital and its greater highland environs. These highland shapes and designs belong to the more common, ordinary pottery of the capital. They do not include a few highland Huari prestige forms which are found at important sites in all parts of the empire.

Of equal importance is the scarcity of vessels in the provincial Huari style of Pachacamac, particularly those shapes and designs most commonly associated with the Pachacamac Griffin (a mythical being with a feline body and eagle head). The Pachacamac Griffin is the supernatural being that distinguishes the Pachacamac branch of Huari religion under the Huari Empire in Middle Horizon Epoch 2 (see also chapters 4C, 4D and 5). In Epoch 2 the Griffin was not represented in religious art centered in other parts of the Huari Empire, though it

was an important mythical figure in the art of Tiahuanaco (cf. chapter1).

The sparsity of Pachacamac-style remains at Chimu Capac is the more remarkable since remains in the Pachacamac style are common on the coast south of Supe. In contrast, Pachacamac influence was no stronger north of Supe than at Chimu Capac. The moderate influence of Pachacamac religion from Supe north was counterbalanced by a moderate amount of influence of north coast religion at Pachacamac under the Huari Empire in Epoch 2.

Taken together, these observations suggest that Chimu Capac probably functioned as a strategic outpost of the Huari government, designed to curb the growing power of two serious coastal rivals to Huari power, Pachacamac and an important center of religion and worldly power on the north coast. The danger from these rivals may have been particularly acute in Middle Horizon Epoch 2B because they showed signs of merging into a cultural, and therefore potentially political, alliance. The Pativilca River system was the ideal geographical choice for establishing a Huari control center to block such an alliance. It lay directly north of a regional cultural community centered around the Chancay Valley which, though forming no particular threat to Huari, had close ties to Pachacamac. It may have been politically difficult to isolate any part of this community from the influence of Pachacamac, so that a Huari control center would have to be placed outside its northern border.

Let us now see what features of the pottery art suggest these inferences. Two categories of tumblers and a cup shape, together with their decoration, are the clearest Middle Horizon 2B examples of the highland Huari style at Chimu Capac. Plain tumblers are shown in figs. 46A-C, 47; tumblers with a modeled face in the side in figs. 48A, B; and a fragmentary cup in fig. 49. While tumbler and cup shapes are also typical of other provincial Huari styles, the Chimu Capac forms differ in contours, proportions, and modeled features, resembling instead the corresponding shape categories at the capital.

Huari-style pottery decoration in all provinces, including Supe, is distinguished from most other styles by being painted in up to six standard colors. These colors include red, white, a cream to light orange hue, purple, gray and black. Red is used as a background color, and black for outlining designs and for small design details.

Highland Huari decorative elements which distinguish the Chimu Capac style from other provincial Huari styles include both an over-all checked design (fig. 46C), and a kind of stepped, checkered design (fig. 48B, rim design), both so-called ''feather motives.'' The position and arrangement of secondary filler elements are also peculiar to the highland Huari style. The bodiless deity heads with rayed headdress represent a religious motif that occurs with greatest frequency in the pottery art of the Huari capital, and much more rarely in Huari provinces other than Supe (figs. 47, 49, 50). The Pachacamac Griffin, in the form of an abbreviated bodiless head, appears on only three of the vessels from Chimu Capac, two of them tumbler shapes in the highland Huari-style variant (figs. 46B, 48A, 54). The presence of these heads on vessels basically in the highland style indicates that the blocking of the rival religion of Pachacamac took the form of severe curtailment in a context of official sanction, rather than total prohibition. It suggests that at this time some care may have been taken by the Huari government not to let matters come to open conflict.

While Chimu Capac versions of highland Huari-style vessels are most common among the Epoch 2B pottery, imitations of north coast pottery are also present. The flat top of the body in double-spouted bottles is a north coast feature (figs. 50, 51), as are the modeled representations of felines shown alone or devouring prey, of a mother and child (fig. 53), of a monkey eating an ear of corn, or of a seal. A single double-spout bottle entirely in the Pachacamac style, and with a Pachacamac Griffin head depicted on it, was found at Chimu Capac, and is illustrated in figure 54 for comparison with the bottles with north coast features.

The use of molds for making shapes and designs is another north coast technique in the Middle Horizon 2B pottery art of Chimu Capac. Vessels with north coast shape features were shaped in molds. Two of these vessels are decorated with press-molded designs in low relief (figs. 51, 55). One of these, a double-spout bottle, also has the remnants of mold-made figures adorning the strap ("bridge") that connects the two spouts (fig. 51). For more complete modeled remnants of such bridges from the site of Moche, see figure 52. Press-molded vessels are not painted with the Huari colors. Much of the surface is commonly left unpainted. Small areas are painted with very simple designs in one, two or three north coast colors, namely red, off-white and black. One of the press-molded vessels is made of smoked blackware, which precludes painting before the clay is fired.

Middle Horizon 2 press-molded designs at Chimu Capac and Ancón differ from Middle Horizon 3 examples in that the relief is very low. When fired as smoked blackware the relief appears on a well-polished surface. On the oxidation-fired example the design surface is largely unpolished. The contrast between raised and recessed areas in these designs is so slight that it is not easily visible. Some design outlines and the mold-made grooves marking design details were retraced manually with a pointed tool after the mold had been removed and before the vessel was fired, presumably to make the designs more easily visible.

Religious ideas of the north coast are present in the press-molded ornamentation of only two Middle Horizon 2B vessels from Chimu Capac (figs. 51, 55). It appears that under the empire representations of religious ideas entirely of Huari origin were by far the more common. This means that the Huari government was able to exert the control necessary to keep its official religion dominant at Chimu Capac, a situation that changed abruptly after the fall of Huari.

The largest amount of pottery from Chimu Capac is attributable on stylistic grounds to Middle Horizon Epochs 3 and 4. Most prominently during Epoch 3, and still strongly in Epoch 4, the culture of Supe, together with the culture of the entire coastal area to the north, continued to flourish, developing regional expressions of a mixture of Huari and north coast religion. This happened after the fall of the empire, at a time when the one-time Huari capital had dwindled to the status of a powerless village or town, and the power and influence of Pachacamac were sharply curtailed. South of Supe north coast influence continued to be less prominent, though its presence there was also significant.

During Middle Horizon Epoch 3 religious expression in the coastal cultures from Supe north played, if anything, a more dominant role than before. The great quantity of religious depictions among the remains of Chimu Capac leaves no doubt that religion here was of over-riding importance. Many burial accompaniments were entirely religious in character. Many other objects basically non-religious in function, such as fine garments, bags, pottery vessels, gourd containers and other kinds of objects were decorated with religious scenes. In this religion the north coast tradition played a much stronger part than before, and derivatives of Huari religious motifs without north coast elements are rare.

In pottery, the religious scenes are represented almost entirely through the north coast technique of press-molding, rather than the Huari technique of painting. Most press-molded designs of Epoch 3 differ from those of Epoch 2 in technical detail (figs. 60, 61, 64, 65, 68). The molds were more effective in creating clear design depictions. Designs appear in greater relief, and the mold-made grooves marking design detail are deeper. Design grooves were only rarely retraced after the mold had been removed. Most press-molded designs of Epoch 3, smoked blackware as well as the oxidized pieces, have a dull, unslipped, unpolished surface. The only exceptions are examples of one religious scene (a copulating deity couple) in which the surface has a polish (fig. 64). At least some of the press-molded designs on vessels made of smoked blackware were once painted with red and perhaps gold resin paints after they had been fired. The visual effect must have been very handsome. Only traces of the paints remain.

In Epoch 4, press-molded designs apparently declined in quality as well as quantity. On one vessel from a burial probably attributable to Epoch 4 (grave 1) the press-molded scene has very blurred outlines and low relief, even though the design is entirely unpolished. The grooves that are supposed to mark the design detail are very shallow, hardly visible, but, like the Middle Horizon 3 examples, lack manual retouching.

The Middle Horizon 3 religious scenes of Chimu Capac have distinctive features which are depicted not only in pottery but also in other art forms. The most complete representations appear as paintings on plain cotton cloths, the cloths merely serving as canvases for the designs. Religious expression is the only function of these cloths. The cloth paintings help us to understand the more abbreviated religious scenes depicted in other art forms (figs. 56-59).

The painted cloths from Chimu Capac are rectangular, usually between 55 and 90 cm. (about 1¾ and 3 feet) on the short side and between 104 and 125 cm. (about 3½ and 4 feet) on the long side. The larger cloths are made of two webs (separately woven pieces) sewn together. Most paintings are designed to be viewed with the larger dimension in horizontal position. The designs are painted in one, two or three colors on the off-white cotton base. A dark pigment (black or brown) is most commonly the principal design color and is sometimes used alone. As a rule, red or gold or both are added as supplementary colors. The pigments are sometimes faded, but many are preserved as new.

Although the designs seem to be simple at first glance, closer examination shows them to have intricate compositions. Despite the many design conventions that make the style of these paintings easily identifiable, no two are exactly alike, and each piece shows particular originality in composition. The achievement of balance without adherence to monotonous symmetry in these compositions is intriguing.

As Carrión Cachot has pointed out, all or most Middle Horizon 3 religious scenes found on the coast from Supe north are relatable to fertility and represent appeals for abundance in agriculture and fishing.[104]

The most important religious scene is a sky scene with a central Sky God in front-face posture (figs. 56-60; for a color photo, see Rowe, 1974, pl. LII). The Sky God is male. An arc over his head represents the sky (figs. 57, 59). The arc usually ends in a serpent head at each end and has a serrated top border. The rest of the sky scene is filled with depictions of stars, animals and, rarely, "angel" figures (see below). In painted cloths this scene is shown almost to the exclusion of others. All other religious depictions at Chimu Capac are relatable to the Sky God scene in a subordinate or secondary role.

The arc of the Sky Serpent is part of the religious tradition of the north coast. To this day, the serpent is thought to unite the sun and the ocean in north coast religion and is seen in general as a mediator of opposing forces.[105] In scenes showing the Sky God, the sky arc is frequently modified into two separate arcs which come out of the top of the god's head (fig. 56). The loin cloth tie cords shown on some of the Sky God representations also end in serpent head appendages, as they do on mythical beings of the old north coast religion (cf. chapter 6). Nevertheless, the Sky God is basically of the Huari tradition, as indicated by his front-face posture, fully human body, and arms extended at the sides. Some depictions show the Sky God with a headdress of ray appendages enclosing the entire head, as on Huari gods (fig. 58). Others are shown with a crescent-shaped headdress on an upright support, an ornament of the north coast tradition (figs. 57, 59).

In some examples the Sky God is depicted holding a club in one hand and a hafted axe or north coast knife (tumi) in the other (fig. 56). In one example, a round shield replaces the axe or knife (fig. 56), and in another there is a small object resembling a double-ended canoe paddle (fig. 57). In Inca religion, which was derived from that of Huari, the second-ranking god after the Sun was the "Thunder, God of Weather, to whom prayers for rain were addressed. He was pictured as a man in the sky and identified with a constellation. He held a war club in one hand and a sling in the other, and wore shining garments."[106] The historic description of the Inca God of Thunder is close enough to the Sky God image of Chimu Capac to suggest that the latter also may have represented the God of Thunder, a Huari deity. As bringer of water, such a god must have had importance in a religion centered around fertility. For an example of the corresponding deity in Huari religion, see figure 62.

A variety of circular, rectangular and star-shaped figures in the sky scene patently represent different kinds of stars. Similar star-like, light-colored circles form parts of the rayed headdress of the Huari deity (fig. 62). Some of the stars on the painted cloths from Chimu Capac have small faces and are framed by rays. Below and between the stars there are depictions of birds, serpents, fish and fish-like figures, felines, and sometimes monkeys. Like the Sky God, these figures represent a union (syncretism) between religious ideas of the north coast and Huari. In highland Huari religion of Middle Horizon Epoch 1A, mythical felines and griffins appear in religious art (fig. 63). Star-like, light-colored circles adorn their tail feather tips and headdress. In Inca religion some stars and constellations were represented by animal spirits, that is, "Star Animals."[107] The animals in the sky scenes at Chimu Capac may also represent Star Animals of this kind.

A special religious syncretism is apparent in many of the representations of animals resembling felines in the sky scenes in press-molded pottery designs (fig. 61). Like most Huari and Tiahuanaco feline spirit animals, they have a long tail that commonly arches over the body. In addition, some of the north coast spirit animals have a back-curved line projecting from the top of the snout, different from the ray appendages that project from the mouths of some angels and spirit animals in Huari religion (fig. 66; for comparison, see sleeve and tunic border designs, fig. 76B). The curled snout projection is the marking of an ancient sky spirit of the religious tradition of northern Peru, which has its origins early in the Early Intermediate Period and is known as the Moon Animal. It is sometimes shown seated within the narrow sickle of the young crescent moon, and is also represented alone under the arc of the Sky Serpent (see chapter 6).

In some Middle Horizon 3 examples the long tail of the Moon Animal is converted into a sky arc curving over the body.[108] Apparently the feline Star Animal of Huari religion and the Moon Animal of north coast religion were similar enough in concept to become identified as the same spirit in the north coast religion under the Huari Empire and after.

Only one example of a sky scene from Chimu Capac is datable to the time under the Huari Empire. This scene is press-molded and incised into the side of a small jar (fig. 55). In it a single Moon Animal is the only central figure, seated under the sky arc. A long curved line projects backward from the top of the head. This line is a distinctive head marking of the ancient Moon Animal, a marking that has not been recorded in Middle Horizon 3 examples (cf. chapter 6). Huari features in this depiction are suggested in the contours of the head and snout, and in the spirit animal's having a human hand and foot. However, these features all differ in stylistic detail from those of the Huari style proper. Features with clear Huari execution appear only in the details of the appendage heads at each end of the sky arc, and in additional appendage heads that emerge from the mouths of the sky arc heads. These heads resemble feline appendage heads of Huari religious design.

The religious syncretism manifested in the Middle Horizon 2 sky scene is minor compared with the syncretism in the Middle Horizon 3 scenes. It is part of the evidence leading to the inference that the main thrust of syncretism between north coast and Huari religion did not appear at Chimu Capac until Middle Horizon Epoch 3, after the fall of the Huari Empire, during a time of greatly increased north coast power.

Monkeys appear only occasionally in sky scenes, but regularly in more explicit fertility scenes seen only in pottery design. They have no connection with the Huari tradition. Most commonly the monkeys are seen in scenes showing a copulating deity couple.[109] In published illustrations of vessels of unknown provenience in this style, algarrobo trees (Prosopis chilensis) with an abundance of pods are commonly shown below the couple, with the monkeys seated in the branches, some of the monkeys collecting the seeds. In these depictions, seeded branches of such trees sometimes entwine the male god and project toward the female. It appears that monkeys symbolized fertility primarily in the context of sexual activity. In one remarkable example from Chimu Capac, the copulating deity couple is pictured within a modeled, gable-roofed house, with monkey and human figures press-molded in spaces at the sides (fig. 64).

In another scene subordinate to the sky scene, the central figures are two mythical humans in profile, facing one another (fig. 65). Similar profile figures appear in Huari religion as attendants or messengers to the gods (i.e. "angels"—figs. 66,67). At Chimu Capac the angels appear most commonly as press-molded designs on pottery and only rarely as principal figures in cloth paintings. In the only example of such a cloth painting in Uhle's collection, each angel is holding a club in one hand (4-7165). In pottery designs the angels usually hold a north coast knife, analogous to the knife held in one hand of the Huari Angel figures. The north coast angels have long hair strands that proceed from the top of the head in two great arcs ending in serpent heads. These arcs are distinguishable from similar head ornaments of the Sky God only by their lack of a serrated top border. Symbolic serpent head appendages emerge from the mouths of the angels and form the ends of the loin cloth tie cords. In one angel scene mythical birds and felines are depicted below the angels as secondary spirits, adding to the resemblance to the Sky God scenes (fig. 65). However, unlike the Sky God, the angels rarely appear beneath the sky arc.

Another scene relatable to the sky scene, which appears only in pottery design, shows a god resembling the Sky God holding corn (maize) plants in each hand. Carrion Cachot illustrates the close relationship between this fertility god and the Sky God.[110] This close relationship is also seen in a north coast bottle shape from Chimu Capac, in which a Sky Serpent emerging from a modeled deity head arches over four modeled tubers.

Many jars from Chimu Capac are converted into deity representations. The lower part of the neck is modeled into a deity head, and there are appropriate press-molded designs in low relief on the upper part of the jar body. Long press-molded hair strands at the back of the head and upper body, and in front of each ear, end in serpent head appendages, like the hair strands of the Sky God and the angels (fig. 68). Often an S-shaped, double-headed serpent in low relief curves over each shoulder of the jar body, a symbolic figure that appears elsewhere most commonly in the more explicit fertility scenes and occasionally in the Sky God scenes.

In pottery art the most complete mythical scenes logically appear on the largest available surfaces, on jar bodies, in two opposing panels (figs. 60, 61, 65). More abbreviated scenes appear regularly in the decoration of the smaller drinking cups (tumblers). Tumblers are an important emblem of the gods in Huari religion, and also appear as secular prestige vessels in Huari culture (figs. 46-48).

There are two other common vessel categories in Middle Horizon Epochs 3 and 4: flaring-sided food bowls and cooking ollas. Many of these vessels are ornamented only with bands of geometric designs which are press-molded into the lower outer sides of the food bowls and the upper surface of the cooking ollas. However, religious elements are also commonly used in such design bands. These elements consist of rows of depictions of secondary spirit animals from the sky scene, including birds, felines and serpents or fishes. The use of these designs in the decoration of much-used, sooted cooking ollas is an indication of the degree to which religious thought ruled daily activities in the lives of the people of Chimu Capac.

Secondary sky animals also appear in the form of painted wooden carvings. Carvings of serpents are most common (figs. 69A, B). The carved serpents ordinarily have a cord attached to a hole in the tail. In some of the cloth paintings, serpents are also depicted trailing a cord-like appendage (fig. 56). The carvings also include figures of birds, monkeys and small heads of a kind appearing as stars in the sky scenes.

A common carving is a small object resembling a double-ended canoe paddle. The Sky God in one of the cloth paintings from Chimu Capac is shown holding such an object in one hand (fig. 57).

Some of the smaller cloth paintings are merely decorated with bands of geometric designs of a kind used as secondary ornamentation in the sky scenes, or with bands of sky animals. Simple wooden boards, presumably serving a religious purpose similar to that served by the smaller cloth paintings, are also painted with such geometric or sky animal designs.

The story of Chimu Capac is revealed in a great many other objects excavated by Uhle. We can do no more than illustrate a few especially interesting ones here.

Incurving gourds were used as containers, primarily for yarn that formed part of the weaving equipment accompanying some of the dead. A few of these gourd containers are ornamented by a process of etching or burning the design into the surface ("pyro-engraving"). Two of these are decorated with religious designs. One probably dates to Middle Horizon Epoch 2A, or possibly to Epoch 1B, on the basis of the design style (fig. 70). The other dates to Epoch 4, on the basis of its burial associations (fig. 71).

On the Epoch 4 gourd the design is relatable to the religious scenes on the cloth paintings and press-molded pottery of Epochs 3 and 4 (fig. 71). Each of two design panels contains the depiction of a bodiless deity head, presumably of the Sky God, as suggested by two great arcs emerging from the top of the head. However, this head differs in other stylistic details from the heads on cloth paintings and in pottery designs.

The design on the Middle Horizon 2A gourd is different in style (fig. 70). A band containing four mythical fishes, each in a panel, circles the sides. The features of these fish figures are in a very conservative Huari style. The top of the container is only partly preserved, showing the remnants of two long serpentine appendages ending in fish tails. The design details of these figures designate great sanctity in Huari designs in all parts of the empire. However, in the highland Huari style, designs with such explicit fish features have not been recorded as principal decoration. Apparently as early as Epoch 2A the fish motive had greater importance in religious depictions on this part of the coast than in the highlands.

Uhle recovered many objects which appear to be ceremonial clubs. Perhaps these were symbols of distinction, presumably belonging to men. Tools of warfare such as clubs and spears, with accompanying shields, also were part of ancient religious rituals of the north coast, a tradition that persists to the present day.[111]

The clubs from Chimu Capac are of painted wood (figs. 72, 73). Below the club head is a carved human face, and on some a circular or rectangular carved shield is attached to the handle below the head. Most of these ceremonial clubs are probably attributable to Epochs 3 and 4, but the one in figure 72 was found in an Epoch 2B grave. The painting and carving style of this piece is distinctive and more painstaking than on most of the other clubs. Furthermore, this piece, as well as another that may be contemporary with it, are "Janus-headed;" that is, they have two faces, one front and one back. Presumably Janus-headed figures had a special symbolism in Middle Horizon Epoch 2B. They were also found at Pachacamac.[112]

One remarkable object without special evidence of religious symbolism in Uhle's collection is a wooden tube with a carved figure of an important human personage near one end, and a small lug for a cord attachment at the back (fig. 74). Tubes of this kind were probably used as lime containers, as part of the socially correct equipment employed in coca chewing (see chapters 5 and 6). White stones inlaid in a tar-like substance represent fancy ear ornaments of the carved figure, and traces of red resin paint remain on the face. The rest of the tube was also ornamented with stone inlays. In its original condition it must have been a very handsome piece.

Perhaps the most exceptional part of Uhle's collection from Chimu Capac is the large number of textiles. Many are in an unusually fine state of preservation, though almost all have sustained some damage through decay.

Some of the textiles are in the same style as textiles found by Uhle at Pachacamac in the lowest burial stratum in front of the old temple. Most of the contents of this stratum are attributable to Middle Horizon Epoch 2B, and a few to Epoch 3. A fragmentary textile in the same style as those from the lowest stratum at Pachacamac was recorded by Uhle among the contents of Middle Horizon 2B grave 5 from Chimu Capac. Other textiles from Middle Horizon 4 grave 1 and Middle Horizon 3 grave 2 serve as further guides to an understanding of the stylistic changes in textiles from Chimu Capac between Middle Horizon Epochs 2B and 4.

Men's tunics are among the finest textiles recovered by Uhle. Tunics in the Huari style proper are sleeveless and knee-length or longer. The example in figure 75 is entirely of alpaca wool, ornamented with religious motives of the Huari style, probably datable to late Epoch 2B. Uhle also recovered a smaller rectangular cloth in the same style. Its size and proportions suggest that this cloth may have been a woman's shoulder mantle.

More men's tunics from Chimu Capac are in a different, coastal style. They have sleeves and are broader than the Huari-style tunics. Many are also shorter, some short enough to have revealed elaborately ornamented hip cloths or aprons attached to the front of some loin cloths. In the Middle Horizon this kind of

tunic has been recorded on the coast from Pachacamac north. Sleeveless tunics with the same short, broad proportions are also found at Chimu Capac, as well as on the south coast, and probably elsewhere (cf. chapter 5).

Religious ornamentation is as common in elaborately woven textile design as it is in pottery design. One of the best preserved textiles, a very fine, large, sleeved man's tunic, furnishes a good example (fig. 76). This piece probably dates to Middle Horizon Epoch 2B, late in the Huari Empire. While the designs are in the main within the religious tradition of Huari, some stylistic details and religious features of the north coast tradition distinguish this ornamentation from that on garments in the Huari style proper. The tunic is 92 cm. (about 3 feet) long, 130 cm. (about 4¼ feet) wide, with sleeves 24 cm. (about 9½ inches) long, and 15 to 18 cm. (6 to 7 inches) wide.

The sleeves and shoulder section of this tunic are of undecorated, undyed cotton weave. The rest of it is ornamented in an intricate arrangement of three kinds of bands in different weaves composed of alpaca wool and cotton. The most elaborate religious designs appear in two widths of bands of tapestry weave. The narrower bands, 8 to 10 cm. (3 to 4 inches) wide, are separate webs sewn on as borders of the sleeves and the bottom of the tunic. The broader band, 20 cm. (about 7¾ inches) wide, crosses the breast and back below the plain cotton shoulder section, as part of the same web. Between the top and bottom webs of the tunic there is another web, 48 cm. (about 19 inches) wide, made in a different weaving technique ("interlocking warp and weft"), with simpler religious ornamentation. This composition of different weaves, webs and band designs is standard for sleeved tunics of this time.

The tapestry designs are of fine alpaca wool in at least 12 contrasting colors: dark red, light red, lavender, gold, white, black, dark brown, light brown, dark blue, light blue, gray and green. The principal religious design appears on the tapestry band that crosses the breast and back of the tunic. Depictions of the winged Huari Feline-headed Angel, each bearing a Huari staff, appear in adjoining rectangles (fig. 76A). Design details, especially in the vertically compressed proportions of the angel heads and the narrow proportions of the toes, fingers, wing feathers and some other design details, are typical of the north coast strain of Huari textile designs. For the earliest form of the Huari Feline-headed Angel, see figure 67.

The narrow tapestry band borders are composed of separate rectangles with alternating ornamentation. The principal designs are mythical animals with a combination of attributes of the Huari Feline Star Animal and the north coast Moon Animal, one of the early examples of religious syncretism at Chimu Capac (fig. 76B). The principal Moon Animal feature is the angular, back-turned snout top. Alternating rectangles are made of a checkered, lace-like tapestry web without depictions. The bands are bordered by "Step Fret" designs.

The largest body section of the tunic is ornamented with simpler representations of the Feline Star Animal in alternating rectangles. Two natural shades of undyed cotton were added to eight colors of dyed wool to make the ornamental pattern.

The sleeve of another tunic of this kind is shown in figure 77. The arrangement of bands and weaves is almost the same as in the tunic shown in figure 76, but the principal designs of the tapestry border differ, and are in the style most characteristic of tapestries of this period from Pachacamac. Each principal design figure is S-shaped, with fret ends and stepped outlines. Each bulged portion of the S figure is converted into a fish-like head. Each fret end of the figure terminates in an eagle head.

C. The Ruins of Moche and Cerro Blanco

One of Uhle's most important excavation series was undertaken at the great site of Moche in the valley by that name. The site was either the capital or one of the most important centers of north coast ("Moche") culture in the Early Intermediate Period, but lost its position as a major power center under the Huari Empire. Despite this fact one of its great pyramids continued as a shrine throughout the Huari Empire and the subsequent independent flourishing of north coast culture in Middle Horizon Epoch 3. After Epoch 3 the site appears to have lost special significance as a shrine, though it continued to be inhabited until the time of the Spanish conquest.

This is the summary of the information furnished by Uhle's excavations and site descriptions. The site of Moche lies on a small plain between the Moche River on the west and a prominent hill 1100 feet high, the Cerro Blanco ("White Hill"), on the east (fig. 78). The top of the Cerro Blanco was used as a shrine for offerings in the Middle Horizon and, to a minor extent, in much later times, as Uhle's collections and site data indicate. At the foot of the Cerro Blanco stood the smaller of two pyramids, the "Pyramid of the Moon" ("Huaca de la Luna"). This pyramid was built and used by the people of the Moche culture from nearly its beginning (about 100 A.D.), undergoing much remodeling and expansion through time.[113]

Even while the Huaca de la Luna was in use, a much bigger pyramid, the "Huaca del Sol" ("Pyramid of the Sun") was being constructed on the opposite side of the plain, by the river (figs. 78, 79). By the time of the Huari Empire the Huaca del Sol had come to replace the Huaca de la Luna as the principal shrine and ceremonial center of Moche.[114]

The plain between the two pyramids was occupied over a period of perhaps as much as 2000 years (about 500 B.C. to 1550-1570 A.D.). Upon excavating into the plain, Uhle found that the occupation remains formed a deposition nearly 6 meters (20 feet) deep. Below the refuse Uhle found remnants of walls of more ancient structures. Some of these ancient walls were made of small, tack-shaped adobes, a form that probably dates to very early in the Early Intermediate Period or possibly to the end of the Early Horizon. In some sections of the plain Uhle found burials datable to different epochs of the period after the Huari Empire.[115] The thickest part of the refuse deposit of the plain dated to the time before the Huari Empire, however. Uhle found burials of the Moche culture of the later half of the Early Intermediate Period on the lower slopes of the Cerro Blanco and in the front terrace of the old Huaca de la Luna (see chapter 6).

One of Uhle's most important excavations was made on the southern platform of the great Pyramid of the Sun (Kroeber's Site A). The importance of this excavation rests in the fact that the remains on the platform span the late period before the Huari Empire (Early Intermediate Period Epoch 8 and perhaps also Epoch 7), the time of the Huari Empire, and a brief period of the great aftermath in Middle Horizon Epoch 3, when the north coast, though not the site of Moche itself, had once again become a brilliant cultural center of great power and influence. The Site A remains thus reflect a succession of revolutionary events which led to great changes in north coast culture history over a period of about 400 years.

From late in the Early Intermediate Period (Moche Phase IV) on, the southern platform of the Huaca del Sol was evidently used as a site for religious offerings. In Middle Horizon Epoch 3, and to a lesser extent probably also in Epoch 2B, the platform was used also as a cemetery.

The Pyramid of the Sun is a spectacular landmark on the desert plain, visible from at least as far as the sea, about 5.75 kilometers (3.5 miles) away (fig. 79). Its highest point is 41 meters (135 feet) above the plain. The entire pyramid was some 493 meters (1,615 feet) long, including a 90 meter (295 foot) long and 6 meter (19.5 foot) wide ramp of access from the north. This ramp led to a rectangular platform 18 meters (59 feet) high, about

175 meters (574 feet) long. This platform evidently was also used as a Middle Horizon 3 cemetery, but Uhle made no collections there, confining himself to a brief description of the remains. Behind this platform, to the south, lies the main and highest part of the pyramid, resting on the 18 meter high base of another, larger, southern platform.

The southern platform is also rectangular, but with a westward displacement relative to the axis of the ramp and northern platform. It is 228 by 136 meters (748 by 446 feet) in ground plan, enclosed by five 3 meter (10 foot) high terraces that led to its top. The higher pyramid, smaller in ground plan, rises from the top of the southern platform in seven steep terraces to the 41 meter high summit, 23 meters above the base platform. The height and prominence of this pyramid proclaim its focal importance. It is one of the most spectacular structures of ancient Peru.

A 29 meter (95 foot) wide terrace separates the base of the high pyramid from the southern wall of the foundation platform. This terrace is Site A. Its position at the foot of the high pyramid is a gauge of its ceremonial importance—no comparable terrace appears to have bordered the high pyramid on its other sides. The Site A terrace and its uses are analogous to the terraces of the pyramid of Chimu Capac and their uses in the Supe Valley.

On the Site A terrace Uhle found loose soil to a depth of 80 cm. (2.6 feet), filled with scattered remains of human and animal bones, a great many fragments of pottery, and some fragmentary textiles and bits of cane.[116] Uhle interpreted these as the remnants of burials. However, some of the debris he describes in no way resembles a looted cemetery, nor, as Uhle also concluded, occupation refuse. The only two intact deposits recorded by Uhle were small caches, evidently offerings. The style of many fragments in the loose soil proclaims their sacred character. Furthermore, parts of complete vessels and musical instruments were found scattered over areas of up to 20 meters (65.6 feet) across. These objects were broken at the site, probably deliberately, and scattered by later disturbances. Such a deposition pattern is found elsewhere in the Huari domain at partially disturbed sites of sacred offering deposits of Middle Horizon Epochs 1 and 2. The bones could have been the remnants of sacrificial offerings, which also have been found elsewhere.[117]

The burials that Uhle found on the Site A terrace contained unbroken or only slightly broken pottery in some, but not all of the styles represented by the fragmentary pieces in the loose soil. Mainly, the burials did not contain painted depictions of Huari-style religious themes. The burials were excavated into the walls of the pyramid, or were built against the walls and enclosed by new walls.[118] The mortar of one of these burial walls contained the fragment of one of the Middle Horizon 2 tumblers of which other pieces were scattered in the loose soil.[119] This proves that the burial was made after the tumbler had been broken, probably at a time when no special significance was attached to it.

From brief remarks and a few illustrations furnished by Uhle, one gathers that the burial pottery included for the most part press-molded smoked blackware. Some of this pottery resembles Middle Horizon 2 pottery from Chimu Capac, and some resembles the corresponding Epoch 3 pottery. A few vessels in a modified form of the Huari style with non-religious decoration, probably of Epoch 3, also were present in the burials.

The earliest style of remains in the loose soil is Phase IV of the Moche tradition, datable to the time before the Huari Empire. However, Uhle found only very few remains in this style. One pottery fragment is of special interest, for it represents a precursor of the deity figure that came to dominate north coast religion from the Middle Horizon on (fig. 80). The piece was part of a modeled figure from the top of a Moche-style bottle. The protruding fangs of the head are the marks of a Moche Lord from before the time of the Huari Empire (cf. chapter 6). Under the Huari Empire and later, the successor of the Moche Lord lost his fangs. In Middle Horizon 2 and later pottery vessels, deity figures appear most commonly as smoked blackware, with a number of other innovations in stylistic detail (figs. 81A, B). By this later time the focus of north coast power and influence had shifted to great sites in the Lambayeque-Pacasmayo River system, where the pieces in figure 81 originated.

The most numerous offerings from the southern platform of the Pyramid of the Sun are fragments of trumpets and whistles of orange-tan pottery made by the technique of press-molding. Uhle notes that these fragments were scattered by the thousands through the loose soil. Press-molded into their surfaces are depictions of a deity. Like other particularly sacred offerings in Huari religion, the trumpets appear to have been deliberately smashed. Their presence supports other, abundant evidence that musical instruments played an important role in the rituals of Huari religion, as well as in earlier religions.

Most or all of the fragmentary musical instruments from the offering area probably date to the time of the Huari Empire, like most of the other fragmentary remains in the loose deposit. Their depictions form an interesting link between religious figures of the Moche tradition of the Early Intermediate Period and the Middle

Horizon 3 Sky God of Chimu Capac. Like the design themes, the press-molding technique employed to make the designs on the musical instruments has its origins in the pre-Huari Moche culture (cf. chapter 6).

Most of the depictions on the musical instruments are of a man with mythical attributes, who is holding a club in one hand and an unidentified object in the other (fig. 82). He wears an elaborate headdress, which usually has at its center the crescent-shaped plume of the north coast tradition (figs. 83-85). This plume is either enclosed by rayed appendages in the style of Huari religion (figs. 83, 84), or it is covered by a Sky Serpent arc of the north coast tradition (fig. 85). These are all features also shared by the Sky God of Chimu Capac. On many figures the entire body is enclosed by toothless serpent-head appendages, and on many a big pendant below the neck ends in a serpent-head appendage at each side. All the figures are shown with large ear plugs of the kind worn by personages of distinction in the time of the Huari Empire.

Like the Sky God, most of these deity figures do not have fangs, but Uhle found one fragment on which the old Moche Lord fangs are retained (4-2580c). This example appears to represent the latest occurrence of fangs of this kind of deity head (cf. chapter 6).

One of the whistle fragments from the loose deposit on the platform of the Pyramid of the Sun is a head in the same style as the other Middle Horizon deity heads, but with a headdress like that of a mythical being represented on a whistle from a Moche IV grave (fig. 86; cf. chapter 6). This is a particularly interesting example of traditionalism in the religious offerings of the platform, for it provides a further link between the religious depictions of the Middle Horizon deities and their Moche predecessors. Like the Moche IV whistle, the Middle Horizon example was covered with paint, in this instance red ocher, after it was fired. None of the other Middle Horizon fragments shows traces of such paint.

Whistles, trumpets and small containers of form similar to those from the offering platform on the Pyramid of the Sun at Moche have been recorded also from sites in the Santa Valley.[120] Some were found in burials, others in what may have been an offering deposit.[121] The press-molded representations on these objects are like the Sky God figures, except that they have no mythical attributes. This contrast with the fragments from Moche serves to bring out the great emphasis on religious sanctity of the offerings on the platform of the Pyramid of the Sun.

Other offerings with religious depictions from the loose soil of the platform apparently were for the most part within the expression of Huari religion. However,

Uhle also found fragmentary pieces of press-molded blackware with both Moche and Huari features, including some that represent the north coast deity figure whose main center of development was, to all appearances, north of the Moche Valley in the Lambayeque and Pacasmayo Valleys.[122] Some of the fragmentary remains in the loose soil were nonreligious in appearance, including both north coast and Cajamarca-style pottery of Middle Horizon Epochs 2 and 3. The latter style belonged to the highland center neighboring the Moche Valley, later an important ally of the Kingdom of Chimor.[123] Secular pottery, including that of the Cajamarca style, has also been recorded as part of a sacred offering deposit of Huari religion near the Huari capital, datable to Middle Horizon Epoch 2A.[124]

Uhle found one offering cache in the Moche style of the Early Intermediate Period below the accumulated debris of the platform, embedded between the adobes of the floor. The cache consisted of pieces of very fine jewelry of gold and blue stone. Among the finest pieces is a hollow, trapezoidal ornament described by Uhle as the clasp of a necklace. It is made of gold, ornamented with a lizard in relief inlaid with blue stones (fig. 87). The cache also included three gold figurines and the head of a fourth; and according to Uhle it also included parts of a necklace, all with blue stone inlays (fig. 88).[125] The rest of this cache consisted of many round, hollow beads, half of gold and half of blue stone, and a large disk of blue stone. Perhaps the cache was part of a dedicatory offering made at the time of the completion of the pyramid, or perhaps it was an offering made on some other occasion. Its contents reflect the beauty of the jewelry used by the distinguished elite of Moche, and the great technical skills that went into its creation.

Another, simpler cache was found by Uhle "standing between adobes in a wall in front." This cache is datable on stylistic grounds to Middle Horizon Epoch 1B, the early period of the Huari Empire. It included two simple pottery vessels, one a small, simple Huari-style ("Chakipampa B") jar, and the other a small cooking olla. It also included a pair of pottery figurines in the Moche style, both depictions of females, one shown suckling an infant (4-2544-2547).

Uhle apparently found quite a few fine textiles among the loose debris of the offering soil.[126] Some of the textiles he illustrates in his publication have close resemblances to some of the textiles found on the burial platforms of the pyramid of Chimu Capac. Only one of the pieces illustrated by Uhle is in the collection deposited at the Lowie Museum. This piece is a unique remnant of Huari textiles with religious designs. It is a fine tapestry band of many colors, datable on stylistic grounds to the early days of the empire in Epoch 1B (fig. 89). It is one of only two recorded textiles with Huari religious depictions of this epoch.[127] The piece shows two Feline-headed Angels of Huari religion. In Middle Horizon Epochs 1A and 1B such depictions have been recorded only in the context of sacred offerings; there is no record that they ever appeared in secular burials (cf. fig. 67).

Among other sacred offering remains of the debris of the southern platform is the fragment of a wooden tumbler, a section of its entire side from rim to bottom. The tumbler had a religious design carved in relief as a central ornamental band around the side (fig. 90). This piece is probably also datable to Epoch 1B, although it could be as late as Epoch 2A. The depiction is a part of a "Floating Angel" of highland Huari religion (fig. 91). Floating Angels are winged figures in horizontal position, as if in flight, each carrying a staff which parallels the bottom border of the design band. As noted earlier, tumblers of this kind were an important emblem in the hands of the gods of Huari and Tiahuanaco.

Large pottery tumblers with Huari religious designs also formed part of the offerings in the debris of the south platform. Fragments of three large tumblers are attributable to Middle Horizon Epoch 2 on stylistic grounds (fig. 92). They are all painted with Huari deity heads. On one fragment the deity head is modeled in relief in the side, a very conservative trait confined in other known contexts to sacred offerings (fig. 93). This piece may date to Epoch 2A. A plainer fragment of such a tumbler, also with a modeled deity head in the side, probably represents a variant of the ceremonial Epoch 1B style of Huari (the "Robles Moqo" style), which is reserved for sacred offerings.

Of the variety of remains of the Huari Empire from Moche Site A, only one fragment of a tumbler, datable to Epoch 2B, shows part of a depiction of the Pachacamac Griffin.[128] All the other fragments with religious designs have highland Huari traits. Pachacamac religious influence apparently was not very strong at Moche. But even if the Pachacamac Griffin representations were relatively scarce, this figure was not excluded from Moche, anymore than it was from Chimu Capac.

The two blackware vessels illustrated in figures 94, 95 are presumably from the burials and not from the offering deposit. Unlike the offering remains, the vessels that Uhle indicates as having come from burials do not show evidence of having been deliberately smashed at the site, and some are preserved in unbroken condition. All the blackware vessels are press-molded, with molded ornamentation. The jar illustrated in figure 94 shows the depiction of a Huari deity. The tiered bottle in figure 95 is a north coast version of a Huari-style bottle shape, and is attributable to Middle Horizon Epoch 2 on stylistic grounds.

Another shrine was built on the top of Cerro Blanco (Kroeber's Site H). Much of this shrine and its offerings had been partly destroyed through human activity, and partly washed away by the periodic rains that fall on this part of the coast. However, Uhle still found "large and extended walls surrounding the summit." Uhle collected enough remnants of the shrine to show that it must have been virtually identical in ornamentation to the "Huaca El Dragón" at Chanchan.[129]

The Huaca El Dragón is a small pyramid built perhaps in the later part of the Middle Horizon, to judge by the style of painted ornaments in clay relief which cover many of its walls.[130] At the shrine of Cerro Blanco, Uhle found fragmentary remains of red and white painted clay wall reliefs, their style and depictions like those of the Huaca El Dragón. Even though by Epoch 2 the capital of the Moche Valley probably had been transferred from the site of Moche to Chanchan, we have seen that the Pyramid of the Sun did not lose its use until after Middle Horizon Epoch 3. The shrine on the Cerro Blanco may have been built as a rival shrine representing the new order in the Moche Valley. Placed in a more prominent position near the old temple, it would have served as a politically useful device to counteract the old order.

In the Huaca El Dragón of Chanchan the murals are repetitious depictions of a sky scene, in which a voracious Sky Serpent arches over pairs of Moon Animals. The heads of the Sky Serpent are seen eating human figures beneath them. This depiction sets the theme of human sacrifice for the shrine. Smaller mythical animal figures appear in spaces and panels between the Sky Serpent scenes. The friezes are enclosed by bands of figures probably derived from the Moon Spirit Man in Moche religion (cf. chapter 6). With the possible exception of a staff carried in one hand of each figure, as by Huari angels, there is no hint of Huari religious tradition in these designs. It is evident that the sky deity cult in its native north coast expression dominated the shrines of the Huaca El Dragón and Cerro Blanco.

The Huaca El Dragón is of very different construction and much smaller than the Pyramid of the Sun at Moche. It is a rectangular building enclosed by a large, high wall with a batter, an architectural pattern more like that of the structures of the Kingdom of Chimor. Within the walled enclosure was the pyramidal shrine, built on several levels. A ramp of access from the base to the top of the structure is in the tradition of the Pyramid of the

Sun. The central shrine is enclosed by fourteen small, cell-like rooms without doors or windows. These rooms were the repositories for offerings. The offerings included the dismembered bones of human adolescents, a great many shells and worked shell fragments, and carved wooden figures. The shells were the exotic *Spondylus princeps,* imported from the warm waters of the north, which figured greatly in religious ritual before, during, and after the Huari Empire. The idols represented various kinds of figures, both male and female, among whom were litter bearers.[131] In the north coast tradition, litters were used to transport distinguished personages. By extension, Moche Lords are also shown conveyed in litters (cf. chapter 6).

Uhle found remains like those of the Huaca El Dragón among the ruins of the shrine on the Cerro Blanco, "imbedded between the tiles of adobe of the wall-like constructions" which he found in collapsed condition. Carved wooden figures of litter bearers and bearers of great covered jars (presumably liquid containers) are among those he collected. The litter bearer shown in figure 96 is identified as such by the concavity of the shoulder, where the litter bar rested, next to the raised arm. Part of a wooden litter was also recovered by Uhle.

The litter bearer is depicted as a person of distinction in his own right, as shown by his hat and forehead ornament, both in a style of the Huari tradition signifying distinction. He has large ear spools in his ears, also an emblem of social importance. The figure is ornamented over the entire body with the remnants of shell inlays representing birds in flight. Eyes, fingers, toes and loin cloth ornaments were also once shown as shell inlays, though most of the shells have disappeared and only the inlay grooves remain. The figure is made of hard desert wood *(Prosopis chilensis).* This carving is in most details identical to one of the litter bearer figures from the Huaca El Dragón.[132] The hooked nose and red-painted face resemble the corresponding features of the false mummy heads of Chimu Capac and the Santa Valley (fig. 45).

With each of five carved figures Uhle found a human skull, painted red. These were evidently the remains of sacrifices, as at the Huaca El Dragón. As at El Dragón, most were children or adolescents between the ages of 6 and 14 years; one was an adult woman.[133] Uhle also found wooden staves with figures carved at the top, like carvings from the Huaca El Dragón. Above all, there was, as at the Huaca El Dragón, a great quantity of exotic shells imported from the Gulf of Guayaquil. Two kinds of shells were present at the shrine of Cerro Blanco, *Spondylus princeps* and *Conus fergusoni.* As at El Dragón, the shells occurred both in their natural state,

and in different stages of workmanship toward the creation of ornaments, presumably shell inlays, and perhaps other kinds as well. Shells of this kind, whole, fragmentary, and even in the form of dust, were used as highly valued sacred offerings in religious rites down to the time of the Inca Empire.

D. The Necropolis of Ancón

One of Uhle's most important excavation projects was undertaken at the famous "Necropolis of Ancón." The name "Necropolis" is the Greek term for cemetery, that is, "City of the Dead." This site is located in an isolated bay about 35 kilometers (22 miles) north of the city of Lima on the central coast of modern Peru, about halfway between the valleys of the Chillón and Chancay Rivers. In modern times the bay has been used as a beach resort, for which it is ideal.

The Ancón Necropolis has the distinction of being the first site of ancient Peru where a systematic archaeological excavation project was undertaken on a large scale, in the later half of the 19th century.[134] This excavation soon made Peruvian archaeology famous, though it did not at that time add greatly to an understanding of the Andean past. The excavators were Germans, and one, Alphons Stübel, befriended Uhle, and inspired him to engage in field work in the Andean area.[135] Not unnaturally, the Necropolis of Ancón was one of the sites Uhle chose for excavation when his opportunity came in 1904.

Many other excavators, including some archaeologists and many treasure seekers, were attracted to this famous site. In 1942 the archaeologist Gordon R. Willey, in collaboration with the physical anthropologist Marshall T. Newman, excavated twenty tombs in the southeastern part of the cemetery, in a follow-up to Uhle's excavations.[136] Excavations were virtually continuous from 1945 to 1954 or perhaps later. This episode of work was initiated by Julio C. Tello, the Director of the Museo Nacional de Antropología y Arqueología of Lima. It began with excavations in the northwestern section of the Necropolis under Toribio Mejía Xesspe, a project that was continued in 1947 by his colleague Cirilo Huapaya Manco.[137] Another important scientific excavation was conducted at this extraordinary site in the 1950s by the Peruvian archaeologist Marino Gonzales Moreno. A section drawing of Gonzales' work was made by E. Chumpitaz C.[138]

The only extensive publication ever made on the Necropolis of Ancón was by Reiss and Stübel. It was not customary at that time to present association data, and their publication is chiefly useful for its beautiful illustrations. However, Uhle published an invaluable summary of his excavations, which does contain references to associations and stratigraphy.[139] It is clear from both this article and Uhle's article on the ruins of Moche, which appeared in the same year, that many data of this kind were recorded by him but were not entered in his field catalog and letters, the only documents that accompanied the collections deposited at the Lowie Museum. Maps, plans, sketches, and many other kinds of field data must have been contained in a separate record which Uhle kept in his possession. A few of these additional data were incorporated in Uhle's published articles. Therefore, when Uhle's published data are used in conjunction with the collections and catalog at the Lowie Museum, they yield much more information than can be learned either from the publications or the collections alone.

William Duncan Strong used Uhle's publication on Ancón, in conjunction with the field catalog and collections at the University of California, to make a preliminary study of the pottery from Uhle's excavations.[140] Subsequent research has made it possible to see a great deal of additional significance in the data collected by Uhle, and the ways they shed light on the Andean past.

The Bay of Ancón is approximately horseshoe-shaped, formed by a shallow, 3 kilometer (1.8 mile) long north-south indentation of the coast.[141] This stretch is a beach with a gently rising desert plain behind it. On the south this coastal indentation is protected by a similar, but hilly, east-west indentation that ends in a rocky promontory toward the northwest, about 2 kilometers seaward. The southern part of the bay and the promontory are fruitful sources of shellfish, and were exploited for these animals by small communities of fishermen from well before 2,000 B.C. until about 800 B.C., and again in much later times. The early fisherfolk lived along the southern, hilly section of the bay, nearest the source of shellfish supply. Fish and other forms of sea life were also important food resources for these people. In Uhle's time a small fishing community existed near the same area, on the plain.

Slightly brackish but drinkable water is available near the beach at a depth of 2 meters (6.5 feet). Uhle noted that when he was there numerous wells provided drinking water for the modern fishing community, as they must have done for the ancient communities.

The refuse of fishing communities that consume their catch locally is easily distinguishable, because it consists of dense layers of discarded shells and some blackish earth, in addition to general occupation refuse. It also has a strong ammonia-like stench when exposed.

The Necropolis of Ancón lies in a different area. It extends along the plain behind the beach along the southern end of the north-south indentation of the bay (fig. 97). On the south it borders the area of the ancient and modern fishing communities, extending 1100 meters (1,203 yards) north from there and 800 meters (875 yards) inland. The name "Necropolis" is somewhat misleading, because the site was not only a cemetery. The burials were merely the natural accompaniments of a settlement which was established on this plain at the beginning of the Huari Empire, in Middle Horizon Epoch 1B.

It is of particular interest that the occupation refuse of the Middle Horizon settlement has an entirely different character from the refuse of the ancient and later fishing communities. Shell and fish remains are scarce, and the earth is a compact, brown to tan deposit. These features suggest that even though the main activities of this community could have been fishing and shellfish collecting, only a small part of such products was consumed locally, since their remains are not there. Uhle found house wall foundations of stone, house posts, and remnants of cane walls with mud plaster, in the eastern, inland part of the site, leading him to believe that the disintegration of these house remains must have contributed to the appearance of the brown deposit.

Uhle also found foundation walls of old courtyards, the yards containing llama dung, in the inland section of the site. Llamas normally live and graze in cool highland plains, but they can also graze on fog-shrouded coastal hills during the winter season. They are able to live on the coast if provided with food. In ancient times, as today, llamas were used as burden animals for transporting goods between the coast and highlands, and perhaps between different parts of the coast as well. Their presence at Ancón suggests traffic in goods between Ancón and other areas, probably including the highlands, at the time of the occupation that created the brown earth depositions.

The contrast in occupation refuse is the more striking because at a later time the site was again used by simpler fishing communities that built up shell mounds much like the ancient ones, indicating mainly local consumption of sea products. This later refuse was deposited partly over the remains of the Middle Horizon settlement and cemeteries. Uhle's studies show that the occupation of the Ancón Necropolis was continuous from Middle Horizon 1B to the time of the Inca Empire. Uhle's summary observations on the relationships of deposition layers indicate that the change in the nature of the settlement must have taken place after the early part of the Late Intermediate Period, about Late Intermediate

Period Epoch 4. This is about the time when the great north coast culture centers appear to have undergone a decline, and when the entire coastal area entered into a time of greater regional isolation.

Some time before this change in the nature of the settlement at Ancón, a wall was built around the ancient town. The north and east sections of this wall were still preserved in Uhle's time. The date of the construction of the wall is made evident by the fact that a part of a large Middle Horizon 4 cemetery extended under the north-eastern section of the wall into the plain beyond, and must therefore have been made before the wall was built. However, the Middle Horizon 4 graves are sparser below and outside the wall than inside it, and later graves are not found below or beyond the wall. It means that the wall must have been built in Middle Horizon Epoch 4.

The ancient town was also protected by a hill fort on the highest hill, which borders the bay some 300 meters (328 yards) south of the southeastern, inland part of the Necropolis. The hill was enclosed by three concentric fortification walls. Uhle noted that these walls were analogous to the wall of the ancient town, and that the fort was therefore probably built at the same time.

Uhle's observations and collections thus indicate that at the beginning of the Huari Empire a settlement was established on the plain of Ancón unlike any that came before, which had a function related to activities over a larger area. Perhaps this settlement was designed to provide neighboring areas, including the highlands, with sea products, which were particularly bountiful at this site. After the fall of the empire the settlement continued to fulfill the same kind of function until the early part of the Late Intermediate Period. Some time before it ceased this larger function, there must have developed a general condition of strife that gave rise to fear of attack, causing the site to be heavily fortified in Middle Horizon Epoch 4. The wall must have been built at about the same time that the stronghold of Chimu Capac at Supe was abandoned.

The earliest settlement under the Huari Empire was established on the southwestern part of the plain near the more ancient fishing communities, the modern fishing community, and the sea, that is, the part of the plain nearest the area of shellfish supply (Uhle's section P). Here Uhle found the early refuse deposit very sparse in marine products. This deposit reached a height of 1.22 to 2 meters (4 to 6.5 feet) above the unoccupied desert floor. Graves of Middle Horizon Epochs 1B, 2 and 3 had been dug into the sterile ground before any refuse had accumulated. A few of the late Middle Horizon 2B and Middle Horizon 3 graves had been made in some sections where a 10 to 30 centimeter (4 inch to 1 foot) layer

of brown earth refuse had accumulated. On the seaward end of section P of the site (area Z) Uhle excavated a few graves datable to Middle Horizon Epoch 4 and Late Intermediate Period Epoch 3, respectively, which could not have been made before about half of the brown earth deposition had accumulated at this point. Thus, this oldest part of the settlement apparently continued to be occupied until the event befell the site which led to its return to local isolation.

Presumably the llama corrals found by Uhle on the inland border of the site, or others like these, were established at the time of the first Middle Horizon settlement.

After Ancón returned to its regional isolation, mounds rich in shell layers and fish remains accumulated to considerable heights all over the site. Uhle estimated that there must have been about 100 such mounds. Perhaps some of these mounds cover additional Middle Horizon occupation refuse.

Agricultural produce was consumed throughout the occupation of the Necropolis from the Middle Horizon to the Late Horizon, even when sea products formed the main part of the refuse. They included corn (maize), lúcuma (a native fruit), avocados, beans, and probably other foods. Therefore, even though there was a change in local use of sea products in the Late Intermediate Period, other foods continued to be imported at least to some extent, since there was insufficient water available for cultivation at Ancón itself.

Uhle recorded no buildings of more durable materials than cane and mud at Ancón. Huapaya Manco reports remains of walls of field stones and adobes in the black shell refuse layers of the later occupation.[142] However, except for the fort and town wall there were evidently no major public constructions at Ancón. Their absence is an indication that the purpose of the Ancón settlement was not to serve as an administrative or ceremonial center. This observation supports the impression that this settlement was probably established to exploit the resources of the sea, and had no other special significance.

Despite the absence of public buildings or elaborate mansions, however, people of good social standing, perhaps government administrators, lived at the Necropolis under the Huari Empire. Uhle recorded six early and late Middle Horizon 2B tombs in which the principal dead, all mature individuals, were accompanied by objects of gold and silver. There were not many such objects, an indication that these were not people of extraordinary social standing, but what there was designates some distinction. These tombs were all found in the oldest part of the town, in section P.

Men of distinction wore gold and silver in their

headdress. A man's headdress consisted of a basketry crown, adorned with a frontlet enclosing it and a plume standing upright in front. In one Middle Horizon 2B tomb, the plume and perhaps the frontlet were of silver, while thin gold sheets probably represented the eyes of the false head (P-14). In another tomb of the same epoch a frontlet of tapestry accompanied a silver plume (P-12). Other contents here and elsewhere show that tapestry was a highly valued cloth. Another man in a very late Middle Horizon 2B tomb, perhaps an individual of somewhat lower rank, had a frontlet of silver, though he lacked a silver plume; he also wore silver ear plugs (P-18). Apparently less important personages had plumes of feathers and head bands of plainer cloth than tapestry, to judge by Reiss and Stübel's excavations (fig. 98). Unfortunately the contents of the tombs excavated by Uhle were in a much poorer state of preservation than Reiss and Stübel's, and most perishables, like feathers, were not preserved or only very poorly preserved. Uhle also mentions an unidentified gold fragment from another Middle Horizon 2B tomb from this area (P-21).

One woman's burial of Epoch 2B was accompanied by a gold spindle whorl (P-25). Another tomb with some contents suggesting the property of a woman contained gold beads (P-17).[143] Other Middle Horizon 1 and 2 burials contained neither gold nor silver, and were perhaps the remains of people of lesser distinction.

In Epochs 3 and 4 of the Middle Horizon, both gold and silver continued in use, but were apparently scarcer than in the time of the empire. In Uhle's collection neither of these metals occurred as a headdress ornament. Uhle recorded only one Middle Horizon 3 tomb with objects of precious metals, which included two pins (tupu) of silver, of the kind used to fasten women's garments at the shoulder, and six long tubular gold beads (P-24). He also recorded an armlet of gold with a Middle Horizon 4 burial of a man (T-13), and two hollow gold balls with a man's mummy bale in another tomb of this epoch (T-14).

Uhle uncovered one burial datable approximately to Late Intermediate Period Epoch 3, in which one of the four principal dead had an embossed silver frontlet on the false mummy head (C-102). This burial is the latest example of mummy bales with false heads, and also the latest burial in which he found objects of precious metals. This burial dates to near or about the time when the change in settlement probably took place at Ancón.

False mummy bale heads were in general use for adult dead from Epoch 2 on throughout the Middle Horizon. The record does not indicate how common the use of false mummy bale heads was in the early part of the Late Intermediate Period. In Middle Horizon Epoch 1B some dead were wrapped in bales with false heads, but apparently most were not.[144]

At Ancón the shape of the burial chambers, as well as the style of the contents, changed almost with every phase, so that burial structures are good indicators of the date of the burial. Most burials of Epoch 1B are long and shallow, with the dead buried in extended positions. This pattern reflects the burial custom of the people of this area before the time of the Huari Empire. With the empire came a new burial custom in which the dead were buried seated, with their knees drawn up. Some graves of Epoch 1B contained more than one dead, and sometimes one of these was seated while the other was extended on his (her) back. These graves reflect the fact that the cultural impact of the Huari Empire was not as all-embracing in its beginning stage as it became after its reorganization in Epoch 2. Uhle uncovered only one grave datable to Epoch 1B, in which a single adult lay in extended position (P-7).

Thereafter all dead were seated with knees drawn up, enveloped in mummy bales with false heads. The small sample suggests that in Epoch 2A the burial chambers were deeper and narrower than in Epoch 1B, either rectangular or slightly trapezoidal, and contained one to three mummy bales.[145] At least some of the bales of this epoch were proportionately broader than the later ones.[146]

The Ancón graves of Epochs 2B and 3 of the Middle Horizon were spectacular, and are almost unique in the Middle Horizon record. The only other place where such tombs have been recorded is the site of "El Teatino" in the Chancay Valley. This is the site that gave its name to the most common pottery style of Chancay and Ancón in Middle Horizon Epochs 1B, 2 and 3 (see below).[147] The tombs consisted of some 2 to 3 meter (about 6.5 to 10 foot) deep, tapering shafts, round in horizontal section, with one to three side chambers at the narrow bottom. Each side chamber was the resting place of one adult dead wrapped in a mummy bale.[148] The shaft tombs datable to the earlier part of Epoch 2B also had separate entry chambers at the top, into which were placed lesser (possibly sacrificial) dead and their accompaniments.[149] Some of the very late Middle Horizon 2B shaft tombs and those of Epoch 3 lacked separate chambers at the top, to judge by Uhle's and Huapaya's sketches, though they also had burials or at least burial goods in the upper part of the shaft.[150]

Middle Horizon 4 graves were shallower and straight rectangular in vertical and horizontal section, without a taper, and without side chambers at the bottom. The only remnant of such chambers was an occasional shallow recess in the wall at the bottom.[151] As in the earlier tombs, one to three principal dead were normally placed at the bottom, while some secondary interments were occasionally placed in the upper part of the tomb. One exceptional Middle Horizon 4 tomb contained four adult dead, two men, and two that were probably women, one of the latter with a child (T-14). This burial is a forerunner of burials of the early Late Intermediate Period, which contained larger numbers of mummy bales.

From Middle Horizon Epoch 3 to about Late Intermediate Period Epoch 3 a tumbler with a hole in its bottom was commonly placed in the upper part of the grave chamber (fig. 99). Sometimes the tumbler was stuck upside down on a stick. As noted in chapter 4B, tumblers had ceremonial importance in the Middle Horizon and later, and their position above the burials evidently had some special symbolic significance.

Late Intermediate Period burial chambers were simpler and more varied in structure and contents. The elaborate shaft graves of Middle Horizon Epochs 2 and 3 represent a great effort and investment in labor. Their presence would tell us, if nothing else would, that the burial rites for these dead must have been invested with pomp and ceremony. The subsequent increasing simplification of burial structures, down to simple unstructured interments in the late shell refuse, reflects the decline of pomp and hierarchy at the site, especially after Late Intermediate Period Epoch 3.

The mummy bales of Ancón were very much like those from Chimu Capac, with one exception. The false heads were not carved of wood. They were made of cloth cushions stuffed with leaves.[152] Like the wooden mummy heads of the north, the cushion mummy heads of Ancón were most commonly painted red on the face. Eyes were usually represented by pieces of shell cut into a diamond shape, and provided with black, round pupils of tar. The nose was beak shaped, carved of wood, and the mouth was indicated by sewn threads. A wig covered the head, and large ear spools of simple manufacture, sometimes only a wad of reed, were attached to the side of the cushion face. The various forms of headdress were attached over the wig, and the entire head was covered with a cloth. Only a few of the examples illustrated in the work of Reiss and Stübel show variations in the face features. Thus, the face of one false head is covered with a silver mask of the dead, and another has silver sheets for eyes. As noted, one of Uhle's Middle Horizon 2B mummy bales probably had gold sheets for eyes (P-14). Such variations appear to have been rare.

The false mummy bale heads with silver adornments illustrated by Reiss and Stübel have not been dated. Uhle's association data suggest that they probably do not post-date Late Intermediate Period Epoch 3.

As elsewhere, the styles of the pottery vessels in the graves at Ancón tell us a great deal about the cultural affiliations of the people who lived there. Pottery vessels were relatively numerous, particularly in the more elaborate graves.

From Middle Horizon Epoch 1B to Epoch 3 most of the vessels were in the distinctive regional style called "Teatino." The main center for the manufacture of this style was probably in the Chancay Valley, about 20 kilometers (12.5 miles) north of Ancón. However, Teatino-style pottery was also found in the Chillón Valley, 18 kilometers (about 11 miles) to the south, and the Huaura Valley north of the Chancay. The distribution of the Teatino style is one of the indications of the existence of a separate cultural community in this area.[153] The tradition of Teatino-style pottery persisted into the early part of the Late Intermediate Period, but with diminishing importance as well as with changes in stylistic detail. After Middle Horizon Epoch 3 the Teatino style was gradually replaced by another stylistic tradition developed in the Chancay Valley, which had its beginning in Middle Horizon Epoch 3.

The large quantity of Teatino-style pottery in Middle Horizon graves at Ancón suggests that the people who settled there under the Huari Empire were originally inhabitants of the neighboring valleys, probably mainly the Chancay. These people may have been recruited under a government draft system.

Pottery in the Teatino style is a simple, brown-colored ware. The most common ornamental vessel forms are canteen-like jars and flat-bottomed bowls, and there are also some tambourine-shaped jars and occasional other forms (figs. 100-102). These forms resemble shapes associated with Huari-related pottery styles of the coast to the north, notably Supe. Like the paste and firing, the decoration of these vessels is distinctive. It consists of small areas of simple, non-representational line designs grooved into the soft clay before it was fired. The grooves are relatively broad and smooth. At least some, and perhaps all of these grooves were filled with a white pigment after the vessel was fired, but traces of this pigment are preserved in only a few examples. Before the vessels were fired, they were apparently dipped in an unpigmented or red-pigmented clay suspension in water to give a smoother appearance to the surface. In the process, some areas sometimes remained accidentally or deliberately undipped, resulting in attractive ornamental lenses of slightly different coloring on odd sections of the surfaces (fig. 101). A few Teatino-style vessels were fired as smoked blackware.

More elaborately decorated pottery in different

styles was present in much smaller amounts, and was reserved for the most distinguished burials. In the time of the Huari Empire, in Middle Horizon Epochs 1B and 2, most of this pottery is of styles belonging to the valleys of the Rimac (Lima) and Lurín, the latter being the valley where Pachacamac is located. At the time of the expansion of the Huari Empire, the Rimac and Lurín Valleys were closely joined in a cultural community, as reflected in the pottery art and architectural remains. During the first stage of the Huari Empire in Middle Horizon Epoch 1B, the seat of power and prestige was in the Rimac Valley, where great pyramidal structures indicate the seat of an important ceremonial center. This center was probably at least in part religious in nature, and perhaps came to be allied with the official religious movement of the Huari Empire. Long afterwards, in the time of the Inca Empire, a prestigious oracle still existed in the Rimac Valley.

Up the valley from the present city of Lima are the remains of an old city, parts of which date to Middle Horizon Epochs 1B and 2 under the Huari Empire. The ruins of this city are called Cajamarquilla. Near it, on a dry alluvial fan on the valley border, is an ancient cemetery whose graves also date to Epochs 1B and 2 of the Middle Horizon, with some burials datable to the time just before the time of the Huari Empire. This cemetery probably belonged to the ancient city of Cajamarquilla. It is called "Nievería," after the name of the landed estate to which it belongs. Uhle conducted excavations at the cemetery of Nievería, but he made only a few records of associations and gave no descriptions of the graves. Fortunately, later archaeological studies, notably by Jacinto Jijón y Caamaño, Alfred L. Kroeber, Louis M. Stumer, and P.C. Sestieri in the valley of the Rimac, and by Marino Gonzales Moreno at the Necropolis of Ancón, have added further clarifications to the significance of Uhle's excavations.

The results of the work by Uhle and the others shows that in Middle Horizon Epoch 1B Ancón was under the direct influence of the great centers of the Rimac Valley, and that the most distinguished personages at Ancón must have been closely tied to the society of the Rimac. Uhle excavated only one grave at Ancón datable to this epoch (P-7). This grave was relatively poor. It contained four pottery vessels, including a cooking olla and two Teatino-style vessels. The fourth vessel is an example of a relatively coarse, relatively conservative Nievería-style vessel (fig. 103). However, some of the vessels Uhle collected at the cemetery of Nievería serve as examples for the finer kind of ornamented orange-ware pottery of Epoch 1B that can also be found at Ancón (figs. 104, 105).

After the reorganization of the Huari Empire in Epoch 2 the principal religious seat was shifted from the Rimac to the site of Pachacamac in the Lurín Valley. Although a distinctive Huari style associated with the new order was introduced at Pachacamac at this time, and soon became a symbol of religious and worldly friction within the empire, pottery in the tradition of the Nievería style also formed an important part of the pottery assemblage of Pachacamac. Its presence at Pachacamac suggests that the Rimac and Lurín Valleys may have been under a single administration at that time. Perhaps the two valleys formed a continuous irrigation plain, as they evidently did later under the Inca Empire.

The presence of both Nievería tradition and new Pachacamac-Huari pottery in some of the most distinguished tombs of Ancón indicates that at this time Ancón continued to be closely tied to the power center south of it, now at Pachacamac. Two jars from one of the Middle Horizon 2B shaft tombs at Ancón, shown here, are in the ceremonial Pachacamac-Huari style. The face-neck jar in figure 106 is painted with representations of the Pachacamac Griffin on the jar body. The modeled face on the neck evidently represents a deity figure, because in Huari religion vertical markings below the eyes are associated with mythical beings. As such, this jar is analogous to face-neck jars from Chimu Capac and the north coast.

The vessel in figure 107 is more unusual. It represents a man with a lip plug and nose plugs, seated cross-legged, holding one hand to a cheek and the other around a long-necked container. He is probably engaged in chewing coca. Long-necked gourd containers or various kinds of tubes were used to carry the lime solvent for the drug in the coca leaf. The white stripe around the man's forehead represents a forehead band, with the tie shown in the back. The man also wears an intricately strung bead necklace, of the kind recovered from burials. A mustache and chin whiskers are indicated with black paint, a very distinctive Huari trait.

The bottle in figure 108 is in the Derived Nievería style of Middle Horizon Epoch 2B. The modeled face neck on the spout is of Huari inspiration.

One relatively small Middle Horizon 2 burial excavated by Uhle at Ancón contained fine ornamental vessels relatable to the coastal styles of the north rather than Pachacamac (P-20). This burial contained pottery in the style of the early part of Epoch 2B. Two out of the four vessels in it are made of press-molded blackware in the northern style, one showing particularly clearly the distinctive Epoch 2 technique of press-molded decoration discussed in the description of the pottery of Chimu Capac (fig. 109A). This vessel is a jar with a face modeled in the neck, like the deity heads of similar jars at Chimu Capac. The body of the vessel represents a *Spondylus* shell which, as we have seen, was associated with religious ritual in the Middle Horizon. An actual shell of this kind is shown for comparison (fig. 109B). This shell is from the offerings of the shrine on the Cerro Blanco at the site of Moche, discussed in chapter 4C.

One other, slightly damaged vessel from the same grave, a flask-shaped form with its neck missing, has elaborate painted decoration in the several colors typical of Huari painted designs (fig. 110). It shows no sign of having been made in a mold. This kind of vessel is a prestige form that could be found anywhere in the Huari Empire. The fourth vessel from grave P-20 is utilitarian, with unclear stylistic affiliations.

Grave P-20 shows that north coast culture was not entirely absent from Ancón in Middle Horizon Epoch 2, anymore than it was absent from Pachacamac. However, it was present to a much smaller degree than at Supe. We are probably observing a reflection of the effects of the blocking action of the Huari outpost at Chimu Capac, which succeeded in keeping the rival power centers of Pachacamac and the north coast from forming too close an alliance. Under the Huari Empire the isolated bay town of Ancón appears to have been safely within the power sphere of Pachacamac.

With the end of Epoch 2B, the influence of the Pachacamac and Rimac Valley culture virtually disappeared from the record of pottery styles of Ancón. Only one fragmentary tumbler from above a Middle Horizon 4 grave is painted with a modified form of a Pachacamac Griffin head. The large-scale disappearance of the Pachacamac-Huari tradition reflects the collapse of power of Pachacamac with the end of the Huari Empire. Occasional derivatives of Huari forms occur at Ancón, but resemble some of the derivatives of Huari-style vessels from Chimu Capac, rather than those of the Pachacamac-Huari tradition. Press-molded pottery in the style of the north coast is slightly more common than under the Huari Empire, though it is not nearly as common as at Chimu Capac. It appears that as the power of Pachacamac vanished, the influence of a new order at Chimu Capac and north increased at Ancón. However, Ancón was never an important center for major public events, and much of the strife of this period is not reflected in its archaeological record.

Only one jar in Uhle's collection is a Middle Horizon 3 example of a north coast sky scene, in which the Sky Serpent arches over a feline spirit animal (fig. 111). Reiss and Stübel illustrate only three vessels relatable to the great north coast religion of this time.

Most of the Middle Horizon 3 pottery vessels from Ancón are in the Teatino style, as before, with only minor stylistic innovations. However, an occasional vessel is covered with a chalky white slip, which represents the beginnings of the stylistic development of the later Chancay tradition that came to dominate this area.

Press-molded pottery of the north-coast tradition is slightly more common in the Middle Horizon 4 burials. Much of it consists of face-neck jars with derivatives of *Spondylus* shell bodies, which are also common at Chimu Capac (fig. 112). In addition to other modifications in stylistic detail, these vessels are covered with the new chalky white slip of Chancay. This and other Chancay innovations are not present on the corresponding vessels from Chimu Capac.

Pottery in the Teatino tradition is much scarcer in Middle Horizon 4 burials than before, and is largely confined to cooking ollas in modified form. Most of the ornamented pottery is in a new painted style which is very distinctive. It appears to have been partly inspired by stylistic innovations of the coast to the north. Most of the designs are simple, non-representational line patterns in two or three colors, including red, white, and black (figs. 113A, B). Uhle excavated slightly later burials in the Chancay Valley which contained very similar vessels.

The new stylistic tradition of the Chancay Valley probably continued to represent the same community of peoples as the Teatino style, that is, the people of the Chancay Valley, Ancón, and the neighboring valleys to the north and south, the Huaura and Chillón. There is no significant amount of recorded information on the archaeology of the Late Intermediate Period for the valleys of the Huaura, Chillón, and Rimac. There are only a few scattered data on remains from the Lurín Valley (Pachacamac). These data indicate that in late pre-Inca and Inca times, the people of this valley belonged to a different cultural community from that of Chancay.

Uhle uncovered graves from several sites in the Chancay Valley, which show a continuous culture sequence from Middle Horizon Epoch 4 to Late Intermediate Period Epoch 8, probably including the early years of the Inca occupation period. Uhle's archaeological record for Chancay does not include remains from the time of the Inca Empire after about 1485 or 1490, that is, after the administrative reorganization of the empire under the emperor Thupa 'Inka.

Uhle's excavations at Ancón did not yield as large a record for the Late Intermediate Period as the excavations in the Chancay Valley, but there is enough to show that the people of Ancón must have formed a part of the cultural community centered at Chancay. The same is evident from Reiss and Stübel's excavation record. Not until the time of the Inca Empire did the people of Ancón once more enter into much closer ties with the newly great center of Pachacamac.

Historical records make it clear that the great shrine and oracle of Pachacamac was left undisturbed until the end of the Inca conquest, evidently because the religious influence of this center was far more powerful than any political or military power in the Incas' path. Even then, though Pachacamac had no powerful military establishment, the Incas felt it politic to make a special treaty with the priests of Pachacamac, under which the worldly as well as the religious power of Pachacamac was greatly expanded, to something like what it was under the Huari Empire, or perhaps even more.[154] The treaty between the Inca conquerors and the priests of Pachacamac was arranged about 1476.

The archaeological record shows very clearly that under Inca rule after about 1485 Ancón was once again dominated by the center of Pachacamac, as it was under the Huari Empire in Middle Horizon Epoch 2. Much of the pottery from Ancón datable to that time shows no relationship to the stylistic tradition of Chancay. Large quantities of it are in the "Pachacamac-Inca" style, a style of very fine blackware symbolizing distinction at Pachacamac and in the area under its direct influence. Uhle uncovered remnants of this style overlying the original Middle Horizon settlement at Ancón in section P of the Necropolis (fig. 114). Provincial Inca pottery of the kind found in great quantities at Pachacamac was also uncovered by Reiss and Stübel. The presence of these styles at Ancón suggests that once more administrators under the authority of Pachacamac were set to supervise activities at Ancón.

On the northeastern border of the Necropolis, the opposite corner of the site from section P, Uhle found another kind of burial of the Inca occupation period (burial E-2). This grave contained vessels in the common, ordinary pottery style of Pachacamac, which did not designate distinction, nor appeared ordinarily at sites outside of the immediate cultural community of Pachacamac. The presence of these vessels at Ancón, even more than the presence of the prestige vessels in section P, indicates that under the Inca Empire, Ancón was incorporated into the power structure of Pachacamac, to the point where Pachacamac authorities may even have settled some of their own people from the lower social ranks at the Necropolis.

In summary, the archaeology of pottery art of Ancón shows that under the centralized Huari and Inca Empires, a town at the Necropolis was controlled directly from a center at Pachacamac or, in Middle Horizon Epoch 1B, an antecedent center in the valley of the Rimac. In the intervening time the people of Ancón had their closest ties to a small, regional culture center in the Chancay Valley. From the beginning of the Middle Horizon most of the settlers of Ancón belonged to the community of the Chancay culture, but it is possible that under the Inca Empire some people of low social rank in the cultural community of Pachacamac also settled there.

Since perishable remains were poorly preserved in the graves excavated at Ancón by Uhle, the pottery constitutes the best record for the history of the site. But however fragmentary most perishables were, such fragments were found in associations of contemporaneity with other objects, and so serve to shed light on the better preserved collection made by Reiss and Stübel, and on similar objects from Chimu Capac and Pachacamac.

We have seen that in Middle Horizon Epochs 3 and 4, Ancón culture showed some degree of relationship to the culture of the people of Supe, as represented at the site of Chimu Capac. However, the remains of Ancón contain only abbreviated reflections of the major theme of religion, which played so important a part at Chimu Capac and farther north.

Religious cloth paintings equivalent to those from Chimu Capac occur at Ancón, as well as farther south along the coast to Pachacamac.[155] However, these southern paintings are much smaller than those of Chimu Capac, and the depictions are much abbreviated versions of the Sky God scene (fig. 115). In this southern area the cloths were stretched over a cane frame attached to a stick. Reiss and Stübel report that these tablets occur "either singly or in numbers, packed and tied up in bundles, sometimes stuck in the sand by the mummies . . . , sometimes wrapped in cloths."[156] The massing of the tablets in the Ancón graves is analogous to the massing of the cloth paintings in the graves of Chimu Capac.

The combined records made by Reiss, Stübel, and Uhle suggest that the grave tablets were used primarily in Middle Horizon Epochs 3 and 4. However, an excavation profile based on excavations by Marino Gonzales Moreno indicates that the use of such tablets survived into the Late Intermediate Period.[157] The record does not show any major changes in the paintings between Epochs 3 and 4 of the Middle Horizon, either in style or in subject matter.

Religious representations in other kinds of remains are scarcer at Ancón than at Chimu Capac, as noted already in the discussion of pottery art. Except for the occasional pottery vessel, depictions relatable to elements in the Sky God scenes occur only on a few of the most personal accompaniments of the dead. Such objects were placed with the dead within the mummy bales.

One category of such personal accompaniments consists of large, carved wooden ear plugs. These are handsome ornaments, worn by both men and women, and found on the bodies within the mummy bales. A good example from a Middle Horizon 4 tomb is shown in figure 116. As in the example shown here, bird figures are commonly carved in an outer band, while the central carving depicts a variety of figures, including fish-like forms, or an abbreviated Sky God, Moon Animal or Feline Spirit.

In the Middle Horizon and later there was everywhere abundant use of small balances for weighing light material. At Ancón this material was yarn, which may have been traded locally. The balances are composed of a small beam, with small weighing bags of net suspended by cords at each end. The net bags were not usually preserved. However, Reiss and Stübel illustrate a well preserved net bag of this kind filled with several balls of fine cotton yarn.[158]

The Ancón balance beams were carved of wood. Uhle found one within the outer wrapping of a mummy bale, probably of a woman, in Middle Horizon 4 tomb T-14 (mummy bale 2, one of four in this tomb; fig. 117). The top of this beam is ornamented with carved figures of monkeys which, as we have seen, figured particularly in fertility scenes of north coast religion in Middle Horizon Epochs 3 and 4. Within the outer wrappings of the same bale were also found weaving equipment and short, rectangular wood pieces which may have been used in the manufacture of netting.

Hollow pottery figurines played an important part in the burials of Ancón from Middle Horizon Epoch 2 on. At least some of these figurines were placed within the outer wrappings of mummy bales. Only one of the many found by Uhle shows a relationship to the religious cult (fig. 118). This figurine was found on a mummy bale in a Middle Horizon 4 tomb (T-7). It represents a figure with an arching head ornament similar to head ornaments of the north-coast tradition on some mythical figures, and with lines painted below the eyes, a feature usually associated with mythical beings in the Huari tradition. The figure has large ear plugs of the kind worn by persons of importance. The chest of the figurine is painted with a much abbreviated head that resembles Sky God heads in cloth paintings. Below this head, on the lower part of the body of the figurine, bird figures are depicted in upside down positions, like many of the spirit birds in the sky scenes at Chimu Capac.

Considering the location of the Necropolis of Ancón, it is striking that not many graves contained fishing tools, though many contained the short, rectangular sticks that may have been used to make fish nets.

Some burials did contain fish hooks of copper or an alloy containing it. Uhle found such fish hooks in only one grave, the Middle Horizon 2B burial of a man (P-14). The same burial also contained a metal knife, but no weapons of the kind found in other burials of men. The man in this burial probably had high social standing, as indicated by the elaborate headdress and other mummy head ornaments of gold and silver. Here, then, was a man of distinction whose burial accompaniments proclaim his occupation as a fisherman. It means that the occupation of fishing did not signify social inferiority at Ancón, in Middle Horizon Epoch 2 at least.

Although the occupation of fishing did not signify social inferiority, it does not appear to have had any special prestige attached to it either, since fishing equipment was not recorded in the other burials found by Uhle.

Only two occupations were heavily represented in the Middle Horizon graves of Ancón. They were weaving, represented predominantly or possibly even exclusively in association with bodies of women, and weapons, associated with the bodies of men. It is evident that weaving and fighting or hunting did carry with them a special social value not accorded other occupations.

The prestige of weaving, reflected in the burials of Ancón, is in keeping with the prestige reflected for this occupation in the historical and archaeological record of the Andean area, going back to the beginnings of textile art about 3000 B.C. or earlier. The art of weaving was perhaps the most highly valued of all the arts in the eyes of the peoples of the Andes, and occupied a large part of their lives.[159] It is no accident that Andean textiles are considered in many respects the finest achievement of textile art in the history of the world.

Weapons accompanying male burials consisted of clubs, spears and slings. The spears were thrown with the aid of short sticks with a hook at one end ("spear throwers"), remnants of which were also found in the graves. Both clubs and spears were over one meter (three feet) long. Some clubs had elongated, bulbous wooden heads represented by a thickened carved section of the handle. Similar clubs are also common in the burials from Chimu Capac. However, Uhle found a club head of cast bronze in one late Middle Horizon 2B tomb (P-21, 4-6306), and similar ones of stone in two Middle Horizon 4 tombs (T-13, 4-5741, T-14, 4-5658).

The presence of the bronze club head is one of the interesting indications of the use of bronze tools in ancient Peru. The bronze was a deliberate alloy made with the addition of arsenic. Arsenic bronze has its earliest documented appearance in a Moche-style ornament of the north coast, which dates to about the middle of the Early Intermediate Period.[160] The use of arsenic bronze for tools has not yet been documented for the time before the Huari Empire; its use was spread beyond the borders of the Moche culture area through the agency of the Huari Empire. Tools of arsenic bronze also included knives, and occasionally other implements, like the fish hooks.

After the fall of Huari the use of bronze tools declined drastically or disappeared entirely from many areas, including Ancón. Not until the time of the Inca Empire did the use of bronze tools become once more widespread, this time with a different metallic composition.

5

The Coast South of Pachacamac

During the later culture history of the coast of ancient Peru the peoples of the Rimac and Lurín Valleys formed a cultural pivot, receiving influences from the coastal cultures to the north and south, as well as influencing these cultures at times. Insofar as the cultures north and south of this pivotal area influenced one another, these influences were less direct, and were at times significantly filtered or transformed in the Rimac-Lurín area, often in association with neighboring communities, before being passed on. This situation prevailed particularly in the times of the Inca and Huari Empires, and in the intervening Late Intermediate Period.

The coast south of the Lurín Valley, from the Mala to the Yauca Valley, over a distance of about 450 kilometers (280 miles), is commonly known as the "Near South Coast" or "Sur Chico," to distinguish it from a longer stretch of coast south of there to the Chilean border. The reason for distinguishing this area of the coast as a separate unit has both a geographical and a cultural basis, and held true in ancient Peru as it does today. For a brief stretch south of the Yauca Valley, where the Andean foothills reach the sea, the coast is rugged and chilly in winter, soaked by heavy fog condensation. To the south of there begins a long stretch of arid coast where no rivers reach the sea. This area was always largely uninhabited, except for small fishing communities at the shore which did not participate in the mainstream of Andean cultural life, at least not from the Early Horizon on. This area formed a barrier to direct coastal communication, more severe than the coastal desert barriers between the Piura and Lambayeque Rivers, on the one hand, and the Casma and Pativilca, on the other. The peoples from water-carrying river valleys south of this southern desert barrier were isolated from easy direct communication with their coastal neighbors of the Near South Coast, and formed a more distinctive culture area.

Archaeologists normally abbreviate the term "Near South Coast" to "south coast," because this region formed the southernmost section of the main coastal culture area of ancient Peru, the area where cultural centers of power and prestige developed and strongly affected the course of Andean culture history as a whole.

Uhle's unerring instinct made him select key centers of this "south coast" as major targets for his investigations. Some of the most important ones, in different periods, existed in the Chincha, Ica and Nasca Valleys, which Uhle investigated. He also did survey work on the stretch of coast south of Nasca, including the hilly southern border section (area of Chala). Uhle's most consistent and extensive recording of archaeological data was done in the Ica Valley.

The coastal geography south of Pachacamac is slightly different from the area to the north, in that the coast becomes progressively drier toward the south. Only the Cañete and Chincha Valleys carry large amounts of water and have large irrigation plains. South of Chincha there is another widening of the coastal plain, similar to the stretch between Tumbez and the Lambayeque River system in the north. This geographical feature results in greater heat over the land and greater evaporation of moisture. The desert is perfectly dry, and the courses of the rivers cross much larger desert stretches while carrying less water. As a result the rivers central to this area, the Ica and Nasca, do not reach the sea, and carry water only four or five months out of the year even in their upper reaches. Below the points where surface water flow stops there are only sporadic oases, where underground water seepage is near enough the surface to make some cultivation and settlements possible. During some years surface flow does not arrive even in the upper reaches of these rivers, so that periodic drought is a serious problem. Because of these geographical peculiarities the most important occupation areas are about 50 to 90 kilometers (30 to 50 miles) inland, not near the sea, in contrast to the occupation centers of the valleys on the narrower stretches of the coast. In the Ica and Nasca Valleys only settlements of fishermen existed at the shore.

The Nasca "Valley" has a unique geographical feature. In its upper reaches it is not a single valley. Nine small rivers ("ravines"), with additional minor confluents, flow from the western slopes of the Andes, converging like segments of a fan into a single outlet, the "Río Grande," about 50 kilometers (31 miles) from the sea. Shortly below this point the surface river flow stops. The principal farming areas, not very extensive ones, existed along the small tributary ravines, around an elevation of about 450 meters (1500 feet) above sea level.[161] The name of this valley complex derives from one of the upper confluents, the ravine of Nasca. The ravine of Nasca was the seat of one of two major administrative centers of the Incas in the Nasca river complex, as well as the center of the formidable and prestigious "Nasca" culture of the Early Intermediate Period.

The Nasca and Ica Valleys, together with the Acarí Valley to the south and the Pisco Valley to the north, were situated along relatively easy communication lines to the highlands, which were used throughout much of the culture history of their peoples. The archaeological record indicates particularly close contact between the south coast cultures and the peoples of Ayacucho and Huari (capital of the Huari Empire), and also with peoples of the highland areas to the south. The latter included Cuzco and the Titicaca Basin, both important centers of cultural development at various times. Cultural influences from the south coast reached the highlands as early as the later half of the Early Horizon, and there is some evidence of contacts from well before that time.

Uhle came to the coast of Peru as an archaeological pioneer, when nothing of its culture history was known. He discovered and identified the remains of the "Nasca" culture, first in the Ica Valley and then in the Nasca area, and he placed these remains correctly as predating the Huari Empire. Because he first discovered this style of remains in the Ica Valley, he called them "the new-found style of Ica." After his field work in the valleys of Nasca he called them "proto-Nazca."[162] It turned out later that the "Nasca" culture dominated most of the south coast, to Yauca in the south and Chincha in the north. At times its influences were even more extensive.

Although Uhle did not realize it, he had also discovered remains of an antecedent ot the Nasca culture, called the "Paracas" culture ("Ocucaje" Phases 8 and 9 of Early Horizon Epochs 8 and 9). These remains date to the time when religious and artistic innovations originated in the valleys of Ica and Nasca, innovations that formed the foundations of the distinctive Nasca culture that succeeded them.[163] Because of an unfortunate proximity of two separate burials in one of his excavations, Uhle recorded the remains of a burial datable to Early Horizon Epoch 9 and another datable to Early Intermediate Period Epoch 3 together as a single grave, leading him to suppose that the very different styles of Ocucaje Phase 9 (600-500 B.C.) and Nasca Phase 3 (about 300 B.C.) were contemporary.[164] However, this confusion did not have a significant effect on Uhle's chronology, since he did not attempt to define differences between phases of "the new-found style of Ica" or "proto-Nazca" style.

The principal prestige and innovation center of south coast culture became fixed in the Nasca drainage in Early Horizon Epoch 10, and remained in this area through Middle Horizon Epoch 2A, that is, from about 500 B.C. to about 700 A.D. Over a thousand years of dominance, with periodic innovative movements to reinforce its people's self-esteem and influence abroad, served to entrench the standing of this cultural center. Throughout this time the valleys of Acarí and Yauca on the south, and of Ica and Pisco on the north, formed integral but secondary parts of the Paracas-Nasca culture area. North of the Pisco Valley, the people of the Chincha Valley, and sometimes the Cañete as well, were more remote, peripheral participants in this culture system.

In Early Intermediate Period Epoch 7 Nasca culture entered into an era of much increased innovative activity and cultural exhanges with more farflung areas. One of these areas was the Ayacucho Basin and the site of Huari, where a new era of Nasca influences is reflected in the pottery art.[165] This happened about 200 to 250 years before the appearance of Huari religion in the Ayacucho area, and about 250 to 300 years before the expansion movement that created the Huari Empire. It means that for at least two centuries Nasca culture, including religious ideas, stood in a relationship of special prestige to the community destined to become the capital of the Huari Empire.

When Huari religion appeared in the Ayacucho Basin in Middle Horizon Epoch 1A, it had an overpowering effect on the peoples of this area, an effect that overshadowed the influence of Nasca culture. But even though it overshadowed it, it did not obliterate it. Just as Lords and other mythical beings of north coast religion became syncretized with Huari religion in northern Peru, so did the important mythical beings of Nasca religion become syncretized with Huari religion in the south.[166] The difference was that Nasca religious art became incorporated into the religious art of the Huari capital in a way that north coast religious art did not. A degree of cultural unity of some 200 years' standing tied the Huari capital to the Nasca center, a unity that survived all adversities of the Huari government and only died with the fall of Huari.

Thus, under the Huari Empire, the entire Nasca drainage was a large, natural stronghold of Huari rule and Huari religion. By contrast, the parallel stronghold of Huari rule at Chimu Capac in the Supe Valley was only a small, artificially created strategic outpost. After the reorganization of the Huari Empire in Middle Horizon Epoch 2 the competing Huari center of Pachacamac was able to maneuver between these two Huari strongholds with some freedom. It is a measure of the effectiveness of this maneuvering that in Epoch 2B the Pachacamac variant of Huari religion, represented by the dominant figure of the Pachacamac Griffin, replaced the Nasca-Huari religion and associated secular aspects of art and culture in the Ica Valley. The strength of Pachacamac-Huari religious art in the Ica Valley in Middle Horizon Epoch 2B was such that it may reflect the establishment of a branch oracle of the shrine of Pachacamac at Ica, in analogy with branch oracles established by Pachacamac during a renewal of power in much later times.[167]

As a result of the power expansion of Pachacamac, a strong cultural boundary came to separate the communities of the Ica and Nasca Valleys in Middle Horizon Epoch 2B, for the first time in nearly a thousand years. This boundary was not natural to the traditional community relations of the people of this area, and it began to disintegrate as soon as the Huari Empire had fallen and the power of Pachacamac had collapsed with this fall.

It would be natural that the loss of the satellite Ica and the adjoining satellite valleys to the north in Middle Horizon Epoch 2B would have had a depressing effect on the self-esteem of the people of the Nasca drainage. The effects of the collapse of the Huari Empire about 100 or 150 years later were apparently even more disastrous for the people of Nasca, probably because of their close ties with the Huari capital.

The succession of these two disasters at the beginning and end of Middle Horizon Epoch 2B, respectively, provided the antecedents for a change in the traditional cultural relationship between the people of the Ica and Nasca Valleys. The people of Ica became more innovative and independent in their art and culture, and with the end of the Middle Horizon they initiated an archaizing movement that ended by making Ica the center of cultural innovation, with Nasca and other neighboring valleys in secondary prestige positions.[168] From Middle Horizon Epoch 3 on we may begin to speak of an independent Ica culture. Except for this change in cultural relations, the traditional and natural communications between the communities of the Ica and Nasca Valleys were resumed after the fall of the Huari Empire.

The special cultural relationship between Nasca and the Huari capital in the time of the Huari Empire is reflected in both the religious and non-religious art of both areas. Huari religious pottery of the Nasca drainage is only slightly different in style and depictions from that found at Huari. No distinctive mythical being distinguishes Huari religious art of the Nasca drainage from that of the capital. The special relationship between Nasca and the Huari capital becomes particularly clear if we contrast it with the other principal coastal prestige centers under the Huari Empire, namely Pachacamac, the north coast centers, and Chimu Capac.

The center at Pachacamac may be described as a direct new transplant of Huari religion to the coast at the time of the reorganization of the empire at the beginning of Middle Horizon Epoch 2. The prestige art of Pachacamac associated with the religious cult is nearly as similar to that of the capital as the corresponding art of Nasca, except that the stress is on the depiction of the Griffin. Although the Griffin is present in the earliest manifestation of Huari religion in Middle Horizon Epoch 1A, it does not play a part in the religion of the Huari capital in Epoch 2. In contrast, it dominates the religious expression of Pachacamac. A serious religious rivalry between the capital and Pachacamac is implied in this divergence.

We have seen earlier that the north coast had as powerful a religious tradition of its own as did the Nasca culture. The difference here was that no special ties linked the north coast culture centers to the community of the Huari capital before the time of the empire. On the evidence, Huari religion and other aspects of Huari culture did not succeed in penetrating nearly so strongly the powerful, independent traditions of the north coast, so that the religious and cultural expressions of the latter were never obliterated by Huari religion. The north coast traditions asserted themselves even more strongly after the fall of Huari, and the survivals of Huari religion and culture were less obtrusive and more subtly mingled with the native traditions.

As an artificial, strategic outpost, Chimu Capac was also in a very different category from the Nasca culture seat under the Huari Empire. The part played by Chimu Capac was ephemeral compared to that of the other seats of power.

Sacred religious offerings played a powerful part in the operations of the Huari Empire. They were most impressive and most clearly separated from all other aspects of life in Middle Horizon Epoch 1A, before the imperial expansion, and in Epoch 1B, at the beginning of the expansion movement. In Epoch 2A, worldly, non-religious objects began to play a significant part in sacred offerings, and by Epoch 2B the offerings appear to have become even less impressive.[169] Up to now, sacred offerings of the kind found at or near the Huari capital in

Epochs 1B and 2A of the Middle Horizon have been recorded elsewhere from the center at Nasca and a closely related center much farther south on the coast (the Ocoña Valley).

Offerings of this kind were apparently confined to important religious centers. Since they were buried after the offering ceremonies were completed, they are ordinarily found only by accident.[170] It is not generally known that Uhle discovered a principal offering site in the Nasca drainage in 1905, well before anyone else did. Since he did not realize the significance of his find, his discovery remained unrecorded except for the listing of specimens and site provenience in his field catalog.

The offering site Uhle discovered is known as "Pacheco," after the name of the section of land ("fundo") on which it was found. The land is part of the large estate ("hacienda") of Soisongo in the lower ravine of Nasca. Uhle refers to this area only as "a cemetery near Soisongo," that is, near the main buildings of the hacienda. The exact location of his finds is unmistakeable, however, because of the nature of the objects he collected. In this region such objects occur only at this site. Uhle collected seven thick-walled fragments of very large urns and a tumbler, all sacred offerings attributable to Middle Horizon Epoch 1B. Uhle found them lying on the surface, apparently where the offerings had been disturbed by the activity of people or other creatures.

In later excavations conducted by Julio C. Tello and Ronald L. Olson at this site, thousands of fragments of offering pottery were unearthed from pits, where they had been ceremonially broken. Painstaking reconstructions showed that a limited number of vessel and design categories were produced in large numbers of duplicates. This was not done by a mass production process, except for some press-molded features. Most parts of the vessels were not done with the use of molds, and were painted individually with Huari designs in seven colors. The workmanship of these offering vessels is outstanding, and the finished products were beautiful.

Two of the fragments found by Uhle were parts of a modeled deity head, of the kind found in the side of nearly two foot (58 cm.) high, thick-walled tumblers (fig. 119). For comparison, a reconstructed example from the Museo Nacional de Antropología y Arqueología of Lima is shown in figure 120. Olson observed in his field notes that these vessels had been smashed deliberately with a blow that struck the deity head in the face. This is a form of sacrifice or "ceremonial killing," and also may have been designed to protect the sacred vessels in their undamaged state from desecration.

It will be seen that the designs around the rim of the reconstructed tumbler, above the deity head, are depictions of plants. These are all highland food plants, both grains and tubers, most of them not grown on the coast, such as quinoa, tarwi, ullucu, oca, potato and añu.[171] These plant designs not only reflect the highland origin of the religion, but also show that the religious depictions were such faithful reproductions of highland models that even the foreign plants were represented. The other fragments found by Uhle also show depictions of these highland plants (figs. 121A, B). However, the fragments are parts of another, more common offering vessel, a huge, thick-walled urn with side handles modeled to represent two intertwined mythical serpents or serpentlike figures.[172] These urns are over two feet (up to 66 cm.) high. A similar, reconstructed urn is shown in figure 122. The abundance of plant depictions in association with depictions of deities reflects the preoccupation with abundance of food in the religion of Huari, as it did in earlier religions.

While many of the urns were decorated in the main with depictions of highland plants, many others were painted with depictions of deities, "angels" and other mythical beings of Huari religion. These representations are very clear, and help to explain similar depictions in other parts of the domains of Huari and Tiahuanaco religion. The descriptions of the mythical beings of Inca religion, recorded by historians, are entirely in harmony with the religious depictions found in the sacred art of Huari and Tiahuanaco. Here we see particularly clearly the ancient basis of most of Inca religion, which persisted over a period of perhaps 1000 years.

Many Middle Horizon 1B offering urns from the ravine of Nasca are painted with pictures of a deity couple (fig. 123). Two pairs of these deities are painted over the entire side of the urns, both inside and out. On the inside they are shown standing side by side. The goddess on the right can be identified as female by her garments, a long, dark wrap-around cloth covered with a shoulder mantle tied in front. On the left and in figure 122 the god is seen wearing a man's tunic and belt. The lower part of the clothing probably represents the ornamental apron of a loin cloth, since the belt at the waist suggests a tie cord. Parts of the loin cloths with ornamental aprons were uncovered by Uhle at Pachacamac in the Middle Horizon 2B stratum.[173] If this is the right interpretation of the depiction, then it presupposes that the tunic worn by this figure must have been the short variant which is also found among the remains of garments of the Huari Empire (figs. 76, 124).

The middle Horizon 1B offerings mark the first appearance of a goddess in Huari religion. In Inca religion, which continued the Huari tradition, the principal god, next to the Creator, was the Sun, who had a wife, the Moon.[174] The divine couple on the Huari offering urns matches the accounts of the Sun God and Moon Goddess of the Incas. The rays around the heads of the Huari god and goddess may represent the rays of light that emanate from the heavenly bodies.

The divine pair does not appear in the recorded Huari religious depictions of Epoch 1A, where similar urns show only a single male deity, also with a rayed headdress (fig. 62). As we have seen in the discussion of Chimu Capac, another god of Inca religion, second only to the Sun in importance, was the Thunder, a male deity who stood alone. Perhaps the solitary deity depicted on the Middle Horizon 1A offerings represented the Thunder, just as a comparable depiction carved in stone on the lintel of a doorway of the sacred precinct of Tiahuanaco and the similar figure on the sacred painted textiles at Chimu Capac may have done.

Although the Creator was supreme in Inca religion, greater than the Sun and Thunder, the concept of this Creator was first postulated early in the time of the Inca Empire, by the first Inca emperor, Pachakuti, on theological grounds.[175] Emperor Pachakuti was a religious reformer of great brilliance, as well as an extraordinary leader, and his innovations had a profound impact on the peoples of his empire. However, except for the concept of the Creator, Pachakuti's religious reforms were in terms of reorganization rather than innovation, and were based on existing beliefs of the peoples in the former domains of Huari and Tiahuanaco.

The concept of the divine couple implies the idea of fertility, an idea that was expressed even more explicitly in the divine couple represented in press-molded pottery of Middle Horizon Epoch 3 on the north coast (fig. 64). Both the north coast and the Nasca and highland Huari manifestations of the divine couple are associated with cultivated plants. The plant appearing with the sacred Huari couple of Epoch 1B is invariably corn (maize). The god has only four corn ears tipping four of seventeen rays in his headdress. The goddess, on the other hand, has more and a greater variety of corn ears about her, some showing kernels and some corn silk. Four of thirteen rays in the headdress are tipped with corn ears, as is the end of one of her staves, and corn ears also ornament her garment. Thus the goddess, more than the god, embodies fertility in Huari religion. In contrast, in north coast art of Epoch 3, the plant depictions are branches of a tree laden with fruit, concentrated around the god, extending in the manner of sexual organs toward the female. The more specifically sexual theme appears to be a north coastal reinterpretation of the concept of abundance and fertility in Huari religion.

The single deity painted on the Huari religious offerings of Epoch 1A has no plant depictions associated, anymore than does the Sky God of Chimu Capac. It is possible that this god was an earlier concept in Huari religion, and that the Sun and Moon as a divine couple became important only slightly later. As we have seen from the painted textiles and other depictions of Chimu Capac and farther north, most mythical scenes had some relationship to fertility in the sense of abundance of food, and to sky from where fertility was plainly thought to come. Fertility and abundance were also the principal themes in the beliefs and rituals of Inca religion.[176]

The huge tumblers of the Middle Horizon 1B offerings are the forerunners of the smaller tumblers employed as offerings in Middle Horizon Epoch 2 and later. The decline in size of the offering pottery is one of the reflections of the less awe-inspiring, less extraordinary character of the offerings of the later Huari Empire and after the fall of Huari. For comparison, see the tumblers from the offering platform of the Pyramid of the Sun at Moche (figs. 92, 93).

It is impossible to overstress the importance of the discovery of the sacred offerings of Nasca, Ayacucho and Huari, for they are the clearest and most complete expressions of the religion that formed the focus and basis for the existence of the Huari Empire. The long shadow it cast on later cultures is reflected in its persistence to the time of the Incas, and in the crucial part it came to play once more in the conquests of the Inca Empire.

Huari religion also manifested itself in extraordinarily fine textiles, like some that were part of the offering deposit of the southern platform of the Pyramid of the Sun at Moche (fig. 89), or that were among the accompaniments of burials on the platforms of the temple of Chimu Capac (figs. 75-77). Uhle collected very fine examples of religious textiles in the valleys of Nasca and Ica.

The textile in figure 124 is a fine tapestry tunic in the Huari style of Middle Horizon Epoch 2A. This tunic was found by Uhle somewhere on the grounds of the large Hacienda Las Trancas in the upper part of the ravine of Tunga, the southernmost ravine in the Nasca drainage. No other information on the circumstances of its discovery is given. It is the short, broad, sleeveless style of tunic that presupposes the wearing of a loin cloth with an apron, or a hip cloth, below it. The tunic is only 53 cm. (21 inches) long, with a 4 cm. (1½ inch) long fringe at the bottom. By contrast, the width of the tunic is 128 cm. (50 inches). It means that though sleeveless, the garment would have covered a part of the upper arms, somewhat in the manner in which it is depicted on the god of the Middle Horizon 1B offerings (figs. 122, 123, left).

One side of the tunic is still sewn together, with only the arm hole left open, but on the other side the seam has come unstitched, and the garment can be seen unfolded, in its entire web. It is made of fine tapestry in at least seven contrasting colors. In keeping with customary Huari design techniques, the background is a wine red, and the design outlines are black. The designs are woven in gold, pink, a tan with a greenish tinge, cream, blue, and possibly some other shades. Tapestry, as noted, is the textile technique used for the finest, most honored textiles in ancient Andean tradition.

The designs are religious, of a kind that suggests that the garment was the property of a very important man closely connected with the state religion. This does not mean that he was a priest, though he could have been. Since religion formed the nucleus of the expansion movement of the Huari Empire, and was conspicuously represented at major government centers, it is probable that all important administrators of the empire, as well as other socially prominent persons, had a close connection with the state religion.

The religious depictions on the tunic are particularly informative. The front and back sides of the garment were each decorated with meticulously executed representations of two Feline Star Animals, seen face to face. The design details of these figures are another example of religious syncretism, this time between the Feline Star Animal of Huari religion and a mythical being of late Nasca religion, the "Humped Animal."

Each principal Star Animal on the tunic has depicted in its body three similar smaller Star Animals. The heads of all these mythical animals have only Huari features, including the circle nose which designates a feline. Middle Horizon 1B forms of these mythical animals are painted on small vessels in the sacrificial offering deposit of Pacheco (fig. 125). The bodies of the larger animals have no feet, and are entirely enclosed by a "halo" of step-block designs, similar to the halo of triangles around mythical animals of Epoch 1B in the Pacheco offerings. The halo effect is of Nasca origin, where it appears in association with the Humped Animal design beginning with Early Intermediate Period Epoch 7.

The body halo of the smaller mythical animals in the tunic design consists of short rays with recurved tips, a design also used as an alternative to the triangle halo in the Middle Horizon 1B offerings. These are Huari adaptations of the halo rays enclosing Nasca Humped Animal designs of Early Intermediate Period Epoch 7. A Nasca-style example of Middle Horizon Epoch 1B is shown in

figure 126. The small mythical animals in the tunic have another distinctive feature in the head ornament, which consists of a set of three angular rays, the central one with a plain tip, the side ones with recurved tips. This trait is characteristic of many of the Humped Animal depictions of late Nasca religion, and is unrelated to Huari religion. In the tunic designs the rays are red, except that the central ray has a white tip. A ray tip in a contrasting color is a loan feature from a Huari appendage design not of Nasca origin (fig. 127).

The clearest indication that the tunic depictions represent Huari Star Animals is in the tail feather designs, especially of the smaller mythical animals within the body of the large ones. Four tail appendages terminate in circles with central dots, a design that also characterizes the Star Animal depictions in Huari offering pottery of Epoch 1A in the highlands (fig. 63). This Huari feature also has parallels in religious depictions of Tiahuanaco and is unrelated to Nasca religion. In the larger mythical animals on the tunic the circle and dot designs of the tail are elaborated into faces. The smaller Star Animals have claw-like feet, like the corresponding mythical animals in the Middle Horizon 1A offering depictions of the highlands, and like some of the Star Animals in the religious art of Tiahuanaco.

Another version of a mythical feline appears on a particularly fine, though torn, tapestry pouch from the Nasca region (fig. 127). This piece may be contemporary with the tunic, or of slightly later date. This mythical feline depiction has no features of Nasca origin. Although the tapestry weave is much finer than that of the tunic, the colors employed in the principal design area are the same ones. This form of the depiction of this mythical feline has not been recorded from sacred offerings. It has been found painted on pottery in the burial of a person of distinction.[177]

Another example of the close ties that bound all parts of the Huari Empire is a small carving only 4 cm. (1½ inches) long, which appears to be a miniature version of the carved wooden tube, probably a lime container, from Chimu Capac (fig. 128; for comparison, see fig. 74). All carvings of this kind have a larger hole at the bottom end and a smaller hole at the top. The larger holes were plugged with various kinds of inlays, including stone, shell or, in one example, gold.[178] The smaller holes were open. In the large tubes, a shelf-like recess is carved around the top hole. This shelf may have been designed to catch spillage of the contents of the tube. The larger, plugged hole at the bottom may have been the opening through which the container was filled. (For a further discussion of lime containers, see chapter 6).

In the side of the Middle Horizon tubes, nearer the

top, a human figure was carved. All these figures represent a man with a highly dignified mien. Carvings of this kind have been reported from Nasca, Ica, Pachacamac, and as far north as Ecuador. The style and sometimes the associations of the carved wooden tubes indicate a close relationship with the Huari tradition. They are remarkably similar over the entire area of their occurrence.

The miniature tube found by Uhle in the Nasca drainage consists only of the head and body of the figure. The head is carved of wood, while the body is a simple bone tube. The bone ''body'' is ornamented on the front and back with a design of blackened grooves depicting a very stylized, round head. Identical designs constitute body markings on many examples of the Feline-headed Floating Angels painted on sacred Huari offering urns of Middle Horizon Epoch 1A. These body markings on the miniature from Nasca indicate most clearly its close association with the religious cult of Huari. The stylistic conservatism of the design suggests that this small container dates either to the beginnings of the Huari Empire in Epoch 1B or, at the latest, to Epoch 2A. It may have been part of an offering.

The human head of the tube is carved of hard wood, and is very similar in detail to the carving from Chimu Capac. The shell inlays of the eyes are still preserved, as is the black pupil of one eye. The carved heads on both tubes resemble the wooden mummy mask heads and the heads of the carved wooden offering figures from the north coast and Chimu Capac, all also datable to the Middle Horizon (figs. 45, 96). Like all these carvings, the face of the miniature from Nasca is painted with red ocher.

The carving from Nasca is probably the earliest recorded example of this class of wooden carvings of the Huari tradition. It is a particularly realistic portrayal, rich in individual detail, with a stern, fierce expression. Such realism is characteristic of modeled features of sacred Huari offering pottery of Middle Horizon Epoch 1B (fig. 129).

Uhle excavated two small Middle Horizon cemeteries on the southwestern desert border of an oasis in the lower Ica Valley.[179] Although there was considerable disturbance by treasure seekers, he found intact graves dating to Middle Horizon Epochs 3 and 4.[180] A few pottery fragments from these sites date to Epoch 2B, after the pervasive intrusion of Pachacamac influence. Uhle also published illustrations of two textiles which were not included in the collection deposited at the University of California. One of them is in the geometric style of textile designs typical of the Middle Horizon 2B stratum uncovered by Uhle in front of the oldest part of the temple of Pachacamac.[181] The other piece depicts the Pachacamac Griffin.[182]

At one of these small cemeteries Uhle found the fragmentary remainder of a Huari textile, datable on stylistic grounds to Epoch 1B or 2A under the empire. It is part of a very large cloth of the finest tapestry, nearly as fine as the small pouch from Nasca shown in figure 127.[183] Uhle found it tied to a three meter (nearly 10 foot) long pole. Uhle notes that the entire cloth had been found by treasure seekers, fastened to the pole, but they had evidently torn off pieces and abandoned the pole with the remaining fragment. This fragment is preserved in the Lowie Museum collection.

This remarkable tapestry is ornamented with highly religious depictions (fig. 130). Its attachment to the pole suggests that it had a special function, probably not as an ordinary garment. The find may not have been part of a burial, but possibly an offering deposit. The design shows segments of two large deity or angel figures, each holding in his hand a human victim by a hair strand. This is also the manner of showing human victims of the deity and Feline-headed Angel on the sacred Huari offering pottery of Epoch 1A in the highlands (figs. 62, 67). Trophy head depictions fill the spaces around the deity or angel figures on the textile, and ornament one figure's garment. The position of one finished edge of the cloth shows that the deity or angel figures were headless. Perhaps this cloth was used to cover a cult object that had a fully formed head, with the cloth designed to represent the body.

In the space between the arm and the top row of trophy heads a mythical eagle head with a gaping beak is depicted. Mythical eagle heads with gaping beaks are characteristic of only two kinds of mythical beings in Huari religion. One is the Eagle-headed Floating Angel of the original Huari cult of the highlands (fig. 91, right), and the other is the Pachacamac Griffin, both in its full-bodied and in its bodiless form. The position and appearance of the bodiless eagle head on the Ica tapestry make its identity ambiguous. If it should reflect an early form of the Pachacamac Griffin, it is a unique, and possibly the earliest, manifestation of it on record.

The fall of the Huari Empire brought disturbances, and a deepening cultural and economic decline to the peoples of the south coast, especially to the Nasca drainage. This decline stands in contrast to the apparent continued flourishing of the great centers of the north coast, where native religion had been stimulated into innovation and a new independent flowering under the impact of Huari influence. Toward the end of Middle Horizon Epoch 4 an archaizing movement began on the south coast, with its main center in the Ica Valley, which sought a cultural renewal. Unlike the flourishing of north coast religion, the Ica revival was inspired entirely by the great religion and art of the Huari Empire. Both angel and griffin figures of Nasca-Huari and Pachacamac-Huari religion were revived in Epoch 1 of the Late Intermediate Period. However, these depictions are not exactly like those of the Huari Empire some 170 to 360 years before. The Ica Griffin of the Late Intermediate Period partly recalls the griffin of the highland Huari Star Animals of Epoch 1A, partly the Ica-Pachacamac Griffin, and has partly new features (figs. 131, 132). Some of the stylistic innovations suggest that the Late Intermediate Period figures were copies of designs of the Huari Empire of which the original meaning was no longer clearly understood.[184]

The innovative movement of Ica in the Late Intermediate Period also included a flourishing revival in textile art, with original innovation. In this revival, Middle Horizon 2B textiles of Ica were imitated. Much of all Late Intermediate Period art of Ica consists of intricate geometric patterns used primarily for textiles of Middle Horizon Epoch 2B at Ica and Pachacamac. The elegance of Late Intermediate Period geometric art of Ica was widely admired abroad, and imported as far north as the valleys of the Rimac and Chillón and the Necropolis of Ancón.

Figure 133 shows a typical example of a finely preserved pouch from a burial datable to about the middle of Late Intermediate Period Epoch 3, one of the epochs during which Ica art enjoyed particular acclaim abroad. The method of its manufacture was an unusual kind of tapestry technique, an "underfloat weft tapestry," probably unique to Ica textiles and their imitations.[185]

The character of the archaizing movement of the Ica tradition in pottery is particularly apparent in a unique double-chambered vessel, found as an offering in the upper part of a tomb of a very distinguished man of Late Intermediate Period Epoch 3A or B (fig. 134). The vessel is composed of the modeled figure of a feline, joined by a short tube to a tumbler. This is a conservative revival of a category of Huari offering vessel of Middle Horizon Epoch 1B (for comparison, see fig. 135). The Ica 3 feline figure is ornamented with body spots similar to those found on the Middle Horizon 1B feline, though both modeled and painted features differ in detail. The tumbler, on the other hand, is ornamented entirely in a standard Ica 3 design pattern adapted from designs originating in Middle Horizon 2B textile decoration, quite unlike any that are found on Huari offering pottery of the Middle Horizon.

The artistic innovations in the Ica tradition inspired by the imitations of the art of the Huari Empire caused sufficient enthusiasm to lead the Ica artists away from imitation to innovation. Ica art of Late Intermediate Period Epoch 6 and the Late Horizon, discussed earlier, represents late forms of this independent development (figs. 32, 33). The innovative quality and high artistic standards of this art created the widespread prestige mentioned, especially during Late Intermediate Period Epoch 3 and Epoch 6.

During the early half of the Late Intermediate Period, the people of Chincha copied the art of Ica to a very large extent. However, some time thereafter copies of Ica art diminished in number, and artistic traits of the coast to the north appeared in most of the pottery art of Chincha.[186] We do not know how early these influences were present at Chincha, but they evidently began to dominate the Chincha style late in Late Intermediate Period Epoch 5.

Uhle is the only archaeologist who has ever made a good collection of Chincha-style remains. Since his collection is unique, a fine example of the distinctive Chincha-style pottery of Late Intermediate Period Epoch 8 is shown here (fig. 136). Chincha-style pottery ornamentation of this epoch is distinguished by a matte, off-white base color, ornamented with designs in a very dark purple outlined with black. Before the designs were painted on the white ground, the vessels were dipped in a second white-pigmented clay solution, probably to give the surface a smoother appearance. As in the Teatino style of Chancay and Ancón, some areas of the vessel bodies remained undipped, either by accident or design, leaving ornamental lenses in slightly contrasting shades of ground color on the surfaces of some of these vessels, as in the one shown in figure 136.

6

Before the Huari Empire: Some Moche
Antecedents to "Chimu" Culture

Uhle writes that at the site of Moche he uncovered 37 intact graves directly in front of the Pyramid of the Moon (cf. chapter 4C).[187] Objects from 34 burials from this excavation were deposited in the collection of the Lowie Museum. These graves belong to the Moche culture of Early Intermediate Period Epochs 5 to 8 (at one estimate about 100 to 540 A.D.).

Moche culture was distinctive and imposing. Its art and other archaeological remains indicate that Moche society was very hierarchical, with great differences in rank and wealth among its people. A complex religion and much ritual and ceremony are in evidence. There was also a high degree of development of technology in fields such as metallurgy, textiles, pottery, architecture, irrigation, and other areas of endeavor.

In later times Moche traditions came to have a profound impact on Andean culture history everywhere, through the agency of two empires, that of Huari and that of the Incas. We have seen that Moche traditions were not extinguished in the time of the Huari Empire, but only became mingled to some extent with Huari ideas. Moreover, under the stimulation of Huari ideas, particularly in the realms of religion and aggrandizement of power, north coast culture appears to have undergone a new flowering in slightly altered form, a form in which it was spread far more widely than before.

Before the time of the Huari Empire the home area of Moche culture was bounded by the Lambayeque River system and the upper Piura Valley in the north, and by the Nepeña Valley in the south, with the main seats of power in the Moche and Chicama Valleys. In the time of the Huari Empire, and for some time after its fall, the main seats of power and influence were in the Lambayeque River system. During this time north coast ideas of art, religion and technology appear strongly as far south as Pachacamac, and, through the agency of Pachacamac, to some extent at Ica and even Nasca on the south coast. In the time of the Huari Empire the north coast centers also entered into a long-lasting relationship, something like an alliance perhaps, with a strong, distinguished neighboring culture center at Cajamarca and Huamachuco in the north highlands.

North coast cultural vigor survived the fall of the Huari Empire in a way that no other recorded Andean culture did, well into the early part of the Late Intermediate Period. Its traditions persisted even through a period of apparent decline thereafter, into the time of the great renewal under the Kingdom of Chimor, the incorporation of this kingdom into the Inca Empire, and, to some extent, into the present time.[188]

In a 1948 publication, the Peruvian archaeologist Rafael Larco Hoyle subdivided the pottery art of the Moche culture into five subdivisions on the basis of style differences in the contents of different burials.[189] He felt that these subdivisions represented change through time, each subdivision or "phase" having been the style variant of a different epoch. These observations of changes in style through time are the necessary prerequisite for reconstructing the history of Moche culture.

Larco never published the evidence of associations on which he based his conclusions, with the result that his conclusions were generally ignored. Uhle's 34 burials provided a singular opportunity to test Larco's generalizations on style changes in Moche art, and John H. Rowe did so in 1949. He was able to verify Larco's observations. Since then generations of Rowe's students have tested and elaborated the sequence on the basis of Uhle's collection and additional field work. One of Rowe's former students, Christopher B. Donnan, has built an important archive of slides and other records on the subject of Moche art and culture at the University of California at Los Angeles, and he and his students in turn continue to conduct active research on the subject.[190]

The latest of Larco's Moche style phases, Phase V, dates to Middle Horizon Epoch 1B, the earliest epoch in the time of the Huari Empire. This temporal placement is indicated by the association of Moche V and Huari-style features on some objects, and the associations of Moche V and Huari-style objects in the same burials.[191]

Uhle's burials from the plain in front of the Pyramid of the Moon contained pottery in Larco's Phases II, III and IV, and one burial dating to a phase transitional between Larco's Phases I and II. Thus, they all predate the Huari Empire. Studies by Rowe and his students have made it possible to subdivide Larco's Phase III into sub-phases A, B and C, which are also presumed to date to different periods of time. The sequence from Phase I-II to Phase IIIC appears to represent a more or less continuous span of time of about 200 to 250 years in which gradual changes can be observed in the art. Between Uhle's Phase IIIC and Phase IV burials there is a stylistic gap in the pottery art which presumably represents an interval of time for which Uhle failed to uncover burials.

Uhle found one vessel in front of the Pyramid of the Moon which combines Moche V and Huari-style features of Middle Horizon Epoch 1B (4-2688). No associations are recorded for this piece, and Uhle does not give its precise location or depth at which it was found. Neither Uhle nor Donnan found burials of Moche Phase V at the site of Moche, though Uhle found fragments in this style phase on the offering platform of the Pyramid of the Sun (chapter 4C). Donnan also failed to uncover Moche V refuse on the site of the settlement on the plain between the pyramids. While this need not mean that none was there, it suggests that not many people were living at the site in the time of the Huari Empire.

It appears, then, that with the beginning of the Huari Empire the site of Moche changed in character, and the main seat of power in the Moche Valley was transferred to another site. Perhaps this site transfer was a device by the new authorities to neutralize the ancient seat of power of Moche culture, since its ancient traditions and the importance attached to this seat may have been obstacles to the new order. The religious importance of the great shrines of Moche evidently was not as easily dealt with, since the Pyramid of the Sun continued to function as an important offering and burial site. New religious murals were also painted at this time on the walls of the old Pyramid of the Moon.[192]

The Moche cemetery uncovered by Uhle extended 14 meters (46 feet) from the base of the front wall of the Pyramid of the Moon into the plain. The area of his excavation was 28 meters (92 feet) wide, in central position in front of the pyramid wall.[193] The graves lay 4 to 5 meters (13 to 16 feet) below the surface of the plain. The upper 2 to 3 meters (6.5 to 12 feet) of soil of the plain in front of the pyramid consisted of an upward sloping accumulation of later refuse, probably accumulated in the Late Intermediate Period and Late Horizon, after the Pyramid of the Moon was no longer in use.[194] The Moche graves thus lay 2 to 3 meters below the surface of the Early Intermediate Period occupation refuse.

The burials Uhle describes are different from other recorded Moche burials. In other Moche burials the dead are described as lying in extended position, while Uhle states that the individuals in the graves he found were in seated position.[195] Most of the burials were unstructured interments in the sand, but some seven were made in irregularly rectangular adobe chambers which Uhle describes as ''sarcophagi'' 3 meters (12 feet) long, 1 to 1½ meter (3.28 to 5 feet) wide, and 1 meter (3.28 feet) high.[196] Such sarcophagi, lined with adobes or cane, are also described by other excavators. However, Uhle's burials were also distinctive in that some, at least, contained several complete dead, including men, women and children, as well as individual skulls without bodies and the bones of sacrificial llamas. Perhaps the burial pattern described by Uhle reflects a special character of burials that had some particular connection with ritual functions.

The base of the foundation wall of the Pyramid of the Moon, which was at least 5 meters below the surface, projected slightly forward. Uhle found a rectangular chamber built against this wall base, and in it a number of pottery rattles, whistles and figurines.[197] None of these objects is included in the collection at the Lowie Museum. Uhle illustrates two, neither of which is ornamented.[198] However, the rattle he illustrates (pl. IVB) is like one found in one of the Moche IV graves (F-25, 4-3253). This cache was evidently an offering, one that may have been made some time after the construction of the pyramid, as Uhle notes. While it is not possible to compare the style of these offerings with the fragmentary musical instruments Uhle found among the offerings on the southern platform of the Pyramid of the Sun, it is evident that such offerings were a Moche practice before the time of the Huari Empire.

In his field catalog Uhle mentions another offering cache adjoining the front wall of the Pyramid of the Moon. This cache contained a plain, fragmentary trumpet and two whistles with press-molded mythical representations on the front (4-2775-2777). The three objects were placed in a row in the sand, and were inclined toward the wall.[199] Uhle does not state at what depth they were found. The objects are in the style of Moche IV examples (see below).

It is fortunate for the study of Moche culture history that Moche artists specialized in pictorial representations, both in the form of painting and sculpture. Because the preservation conditions of perishable objects such as textiles and food are relatively poor on the north coast compared with the coast to the south, archaeologists must rely heavily on artists' depictions for a reconstruction of Moche culture. Moche artists showed many aspects of their daily life, their religion and their complex society in extraordinarily clear and graphic form. Christopher B. Donnan has pointed out, however, that in general the depictions by Moche artists were selections of special aspects of life which had ceremonial significance, or were singled out for some other reason.

Ordinary scenes of daily activities, such as farming and most regular household routines, were not shown unless they had some connection with ritual or myth.

Only a few pieces of Moche art are illustrated here. They are selected for the bearing they have on later Andean culture history as it is unfolded by Uhle's field work and collections.

Since the expansion of the Huari Empire was centered around a great religion with a profound impact on Andean societies, we need to look at examples of Moche religion which have a bearing on the later events. The mythical beings of Moche religion were not dissimilar to those of Huari religion, but there were important differences in the organization of the religious concepts. The similarities between particular mythical beings provided the basis for the rapid but selective syncretism between Huari and north coast religion. This factor also appears to lie behind the instantaneous stimulation of north coast culture into a new flowering, and an expansion of independent north coast power in the time of the Huari Empire and later.

Moche religion, as reflected in Moche art, appears to be much more complex in the diversity of concepts of mythical beings than Huari religion. In Huari religion one can easily distinguish principal gods, secondary mythical beings that can be described as "angels" or "winged spirit men," and lesser mythical beings that can be described as "star animals," as noted in chapters 4 and 5. In Moche religious art a much greater variety of mythical beings falls into several general categories and a great variety of particular categories, with some overlap between them.

One general category of mythical being in Moche religious art may be called "Lords." Lords are distinguished by having a human body and human head, though they are endowed with some mythical features. The most consistent of these mythical features is a special broad mouth with protruding fangs and extended angular or curved mouth corners, "grimly grinning," as it were (figs. 137, 138). Many Lords also are distinguished by ear pendants in the form of serpent heads. Other features vary.

Mythical Moche Lords occur in many different contexts, with different kinds of meanings, despite their common characteristics. Their position can perhaps best be described as that of Lord of only the particular object, being, or activity with which each figure is associated. Moche Lords are found in scenes referring to abundance in agriculture and fishing, warfare, sacrifice, and some other activities. For example, Lords appear over modeled forms of agricultural staples like the tuber "yuca" or ears of the cereal corn (maize).[200] Lords are also shown with attributes of the crab, crayfish, octopus, a spiral shell and other sea creatures, sometimes only as portraits, other times engaged in fishing or warfare, as in figure 138. In all these contexts the Lords appear to represent the mythical being in charge, who can grant or deny petitions. The Lords are evidently capable of controlling the abundance of particular foods, success in warfare, or the effectiveness of tribute and sacrifice, all at their pleasure. Sometimes two different Lords are seen in combat, or a Lord fights another kind of mythical being, in evident contests for power.

The Moche concept of different Lords for various important aspects of life differs fundamentally from the concept of the Huari and Inca sky deities (Thunder, Sun and Moon) who appear alone, in sky scenes or, sometimes, with sacrificed humans, but in no other activities. The concept of a Sky Lord is not excluded from Moche religion, for in one scene a Moche Lord is seen supporting the Sky Serpent above his head.[201] However, in Moche art Lords are shown much more commonly in other contexts.

In most contexts Moche Lords are shown with a special bulging eye, usually round and lidless, in a wide-eyed stare or glare (fig. 138). However, one Moche Lord representation differs consistently from the rest, and belongs in a category by himself. He is shown as a modeled head without a body, alone, not engaged in any activity, and without features that might indicate a special function. In his Moche III and presumably later manifestations this Lord has a unique eye form, not shared by any other Moche being. The eye is rectangular or lunate, with hooded lids. This Lord always has a mythical form of ear, shown as a double curve or double fret (fig. 137). Other Lords have either a mythical ear or a normal human ear.

The unique eyes of this Lord, and his isolation from all other contexts, show him to represent a unique concept in Moche religion, one that may come closest to representing the more general deity concept of Inca and Huari religion. In the Middle Horizon, under the influence of Huari religion, the concept of an isolated Moche Lord evidently became merged to some extent with the Moche "Sky Lord" concept into a north coast version of a single male Huari deity. The manner in which this syncretism may have come about can be traced in part by the following examples.

The "Aloof Lord" with the hooded eyes is most commonly shown either without a head ornament, unlike other Moche Lords, or he is shown with a forehead band representing the pelt of a feline, its head in front and its tail in back.[202] A forehead band with a feline head, but usually without other details of the pelt markings, is a common head ornament for other Moche Lords as well as for some ordinary mortals. Other kinds of Lords usually have an additional head ornament above the forehead band, consisting of a large disk in the form of an oval or circle (fig. 138). The disk ornament is also shared by a special category of mortals, men who wear nose rings.[203] The head disk ornaments are usually framed by a band of rectangular or circular segments, as in figures 80 and 138.

One modeled depiction of the Aloof Lord in Uhle's collection is illustrated in figure 137. Its head ornament illustrates particularly clearly the special distinction of this Lord. The disk of the head ornament differs from those of other Lords in being enclosed by six rays with curled tips. Head disks enclosed by such rays appear to be confined to special, highly religious contexts (see also figs. 86, 142). The forehead band is concealed from front view by the disk, but the small head in the center of the disk represents the head that should be at the front of the forehead band. This head is human instead of the usual feline head. The human head ornament in this position appears to be confined to association with the curled-ray head disk. Heavily lined faces like that in this depiction of the Aloof Lord are used occasionally for a variety of mythical beings. They represent very old age. It is evident that the concept of "ancient" had a special value attached to it in Moche culture, a value especially applicable to mythical beings.

When the concept of Moche Lords becomes merged with that of the single male Huari deity, the image stops being a Moche Lord and becomes the "Chimu God." The term "Chimu" is here used for the tradition that originates in the time of the Huari Empire, long before the time of the Kingdom of Chimor. The Chimu God appears most commonly as sculptured pottery of smoked blackware (fig. 81). During the Middle Horizon and the early Late Intermediate Period, images of the Chimu God had their main centers of occurrence in the Lambayeque-Pacasmayo River system.

The incised eye of the Chimu God, with its elongated projection at the outer corner, is a modification of the painted Moche eye form of mythical beings and some humans appearing in religious scenes. For a Moche example of the painted eye, see figure 140. The vertical bands below the eyes of the Chimu God are a Huari trait. Perhaps the most notable difference between depictions of Moche Lords and the Chimu God is the absence of projecting fangs in the latter.

The Chimu God representations are shown either in sky scenes, or alone like the Aloof Lord of Moche culture. The Chimu God is also sometimes seen accompanied by smaller depictions of humans or animals, who appear in supportive or reverential attitudes. The variety of Moche Lords, each with his own domain, evidently disappeared under the impact of Huari influence. A scene involving a Moche Lord in a specialized context is illustrated here for comparison (fig. 138).

Like the Aloof Lord image, the Moche Lord depiction shown in figure 138 appears on a "stirrup-spout bottle." This is a bottle with a stirrup-like spout base, a form characteristic of prestige vessels of the north coast tradition. The top of the bottle body is ornamented with a sculptured representation of a Moche Lord. The back of the Lord's human body is covered with the body of a crab, and the Lord is seen as a mythical fisherman, fishing with hook and line. A mythical fish, represented by a large depiction in press-molded low relief on the front of the bottle body, has been caught and is in the process of being hauled in, an indication of success in harvest of a sea product. All around this mythical fish are simply painted representations of ordinary, non-mythical sea animals, including a variety of fish, molluscs and sea birds. These painted designs are much smaller than the mythical fish. Both their small size and lack of modeling emphasize the difference between the supernatural and natural creatures. The natural sea creatures are crowded onto the design surface in an eloquent depiction of abundance.

There could be no clearer indication than this mythical scene to bring out what appears to be the most important function of the Moche Lords, as mythical beings capable of granting abundance. As we have seen, the same theme appears just as clearly in north coast religious depictions of the Middle Horizon, though the context is altered and confined in major part to sky scenes.

There are other categories of mythical beings in Moche culture, some of them with a bearing on religious depictions of the Middle Horizon. Chief among these is the Moon Animal, which came to be treated interchangeably with the Feline Star Animal of Huari religion.

The Moon Animal originates very early in the Early Intermediate Period or even earlier, before the time of the Moche culture. It is prominently recorded in the "Recuay" culture of the northern highlands (at one estimate between 200 and 100 B.C.), and is incorporated into north coast religion as a foreign import.

One of Uhle's Moche II graves contained a good early Moche example of a painted representation of the Moon Animal (fig. 139). The painting appears on the side of a stirrup-spout bottle. One of the features that identifies the Moon Animal is an ornament projecting from the top of the head. The ornament has an upright linear base with a linear appendage toward the back.

Other marks of the Moon Animal are a long, curved or angular tail, a gaping mouth, four or five claws on each foot, and sometimes body spots. In later phases the Moon Animal is commonly shown with a solid red or white body, sometimes marked with a narrow stripe in the contrasting color over the top of the back.[204]

Moon Animal representations with the stripe across the top of the back are identifiable as the native desert fox, *Canis azarae*.[205] Ordinary foxes with these markings, in desert scenes or in ordinary or mythical hunting scenes, are also depicted in Moche art.[206] However, the Moon Animal representations do not always suggest a fox quite as clearly, as when they are shown with spotted body markings suggestive of the pelt markings of a feline (fig. 139). Thus, while the fox identity is the clearest and most consistent, the Moon Animal may have been thought of as a composite of various animal attributes.

The Moche Moon Animal is sometimes shown within the sickle of a young crescent moon, surrounded by stars, in an unmistakeable sky scene.[207] This is also the context in which it is consistently found in the Middle Horizon. In one Moche example Sky Serpent appendages are attached to each end of the moon sickle, an association that furnishes an additional link with the Middle Horizon sky scenes.[208] Although the Moche Moon Animal is shown most commonly in painted form, it also occurs as a press-molded design.[209] From the Middle Horizon on the Moon Animal ordinarily appears as a press-molded design, although occasional painted examples survive under the Huari Empire.[210]

Like the Huari Star Animals, the Moche Moon Animal is a sky spirit in animal form. There is another manifestation of this mythical being, however, which is endowed with more human features. A Moon Animal head appears on a human body in profile position (fig. 140). The human body and other features endow this mythical being with some of the attributes of Moche Lords. These features include the mythical ear composed of two frets. In some of the depictions the garments worn by this figure are unambiguously male. This "Moon Spirit Man" is further distinguished by two appendages emerging from the top of the head, and a long loin cloth tie cord in the form of a mythical serpent. The serpent-head tie cord is also a feature of other figures appearing in mythical Moche sky scenes. The appendages emerging from the head of the Moon Spirit Man are sectioned into parallel bands. The Moon Spirit Man regularly has a knife in one hand and a trophy head in the other, evidently in token of his connection with human sacrifice.

The Moon Spirit Man of Moche religion is very similar to the Feline-headed Angel of Huari religion (fig. 67). Disregarding stylistic detail, the principal difference is that the Moon Spirit Man does not appear in running position, and in the depiction shown in figure 140 does not have wings. However, the same mythical being is also represented in modeled form and as a press-molded design in Moche art. In these forms it is shown as a winged figure. A modeled example of the winged Moon Spirit Man appears in figure 141. In addition to the mythical ear, he is wearing the serpent head ear pendants that also mark most Moche Lords.

Like the Huari Feline-headed Angel, the Moche Moon Spirit Man wears a broad collar, an item of apparel that also appears on representations of some mythical and non-mythical Moche soldiers. In the painted example he also wears the short, sleeved north coast tunic, which allows part of the loin cloth to show below it (fig. 140). The tunic is ornamented with one of the designs regularly used for tunic decoration, a checkerboard with pairs of dots near one border of each check.

The concept of the Moon Spirit Man is perpetuated in the new Middle Horizon religion of the north coast, in which he plays a major part. Pairs of Moon Spirit Men in a combination of north coast and Huari features appear on painted cloths and in press-molded pottery designs in Middle Horizon 3 sky scenes (fig. 65). Despite stylistic innovations, the link of the Middle Horizon figures to the Moche Moon Spirit Man is perfectly clear in their attributes.

An unusual manifestation of the Moon Spirit Man is illustrated in figure 142. This is a small (12.5 cm. or 4⅞ inch high) figure which forms the front of a whistle. It is the kind of object that is used in religious offerings, such as in the offerings adjoining the front wall of the Pyramid of the Moon, those on the southern terrace of the Pyramid of the Sun, and one at a site in the Santa Valley.[211] The example shown here is from one of the special burials found in front of the Pyramid of the Moon.

Like the offering figures, this depiction is press-molded in low relief on a matte, unpainted orange-tan surface. This technique forms the antecedent for north coast press-molded pottery decoration in the Middle Horizon, which is also primarily centered around religious art (cf. chapter 4B, C). The design area was once covered with a coating of white paint applied after firing. Only some residue of this paint remains.

The manifestation of the Moon Spirit Man on the whistle is unusual for several reasons. He is shown in a special guise, as a musician, instead of his usual manifestation as a taker of trophy heads. Instead of the trophy head and hafted knife, he holds a mythical trumpet ending in a serpent head, which he is seen playing. It is clear that as in Huari religion, so in Moche religion, music played an important part in sacred ritual. The Moon Spirit Man identity of this figure is apparent from the form of the snout and the pair of banded ray-like appendages which emerges from the top of the head (for comparison, see fig. 140). The special distinction of the Moon Spirit Man in this guise is brought out by the head ornament, a disk composed of six curled rays, the same head disk that appears on the head of the Aloof Lord in figure 137.

In the offering cache in the sand in front of the wall of the Pyramid of the Moon, Uhle found two whistles each ornamented with similar mythical trumpeters, except that these figures had entirely human heads, lacking the animal snout. One of these whistles was illustrated by Kroeber, and has subsequently been lost.[212] The other is still in the collection (fig. 143). These spirit men share with the Moon Spirit Man the paired banded ray appendages emanating from the top of the head, a peculiar eye form, and traces of white resin paint. The eye form of all these figures resembles a normal human eye in Moche art, except that the eyeball is more bulging, and the outer corners of the eye have a slight elongation, a feature associated with mythical beings in painted decoration, as noted.

The spirit men lacking animal features are adorned with head ornaments normally associated with Moche Lords and some ordinary mortals. The resemblance of these human spirit men to those appearing on most of the offering instruments from the southern platform of the Pyramid of the Sun is very strong in most features that are not related to innovations of Huari inspiration. Some differences in stylistic detail of traditional Moche features also serve to distinguish the spirit men of the time of Huari from the pre-Huari ones. The representations associated with Huari influence differ slightly in details of the eye form and the tunic, they lack the shoulder cape, and they are not seen playing the mythical trumpet.

In summary, while the musical instruments associated with Moche IV offerings are antecedents to offerings datable to the Middle Horizon, there are significant differences. Huari influence transformed the principal figures on these instruments from Moche spirit men to a Huari deity figure.

The other Moche vessels illustrated here show secular aspects of Moche culture which illustrate customary clothing and other items that have a bearing on discussions in the preceding chapters.

Figure 144 illustrates an ordinary Moche man of respectable social status in informal dress, not engaged in any activity. He is not seen wearing the shoulder mantle or headdress normally shown on people engaged in the various activities depicted in Moche art. The man is seated. His arms are apparently folded over his knees beneath his tunic, to judge by the bulge in the middle front of the garment and the absence of arm depictions on the outside.

The respectable social status of the man is suggested by his ear ornaments and by the fine ornamentation of his tunic. He wears round disk pendants in his lower lobes, one of the standard ear ornaments of Moche men who show various attributes of respectability. This individual has two additional smaller pendants attached to each upper ear lobe, a rarer form of ear ornament. The tunic is the short, sleeved garment of the north coast, allowing the loin cloth to be seen below it.

The designs painted on the tunic are standard Moche textile designs. One kind of design is used for the border bands of the sleeves and bottom of the garment, and another for the rest of the tunic. This is the same general arrangement also used for the sleeved Middle Horizon tunics from Chimu Capac (figs. 76, 77). Moche tunic designs are of particular interest, for they form the antecedents for some of the textile designs first appearing on Middle Horizon 2B textiles from Chimu Capac and Pachacamac (fig. 77).[213] These textiles, like some of the pottery and other kinds of remains, illustrate the expansion of traits of the north coast culture through the agency of the Huari Empire.

The absence of any kind of head ornament on the Moche figure shown here reveals his hair style. The hair is cut in a short bang above the forehead and is long in back, the long hair pushed or cut back to leave the ears free.

A coppery reddish-brown pigment covers the face. This pigment could represent the natural complexion of the man, but since it does not cover the ears and neck it may represent face paint instead. The features of the face have the qualities of an individual portrait. The form of the eyes is that used for ordinary mortals, in contrast to mythical beings. They are almond shaped, with naturally modeled eyelids in low relief. The hooked nose is typical of the native peoples of the Andes.

The woman with the baby shown in figure 145 is from the same burial, and appears to be a companion piece to the vessel shown in figure 144. Like the latter figure, she is shown in informal dress, and is not engaged in a special activity. She is also seated, and wears only her wrap-around dress and no shoulder mantle. The woman's garment is most clearly recognizable by the pins with large heads which hold the wrap-around cloth together at each shoulder. The garment covers her from neck to feet. This kind of wrap-around was in wide use as a woman's garment in the Andean area, and continued in use into the time of the Incas. At the back of the Moche figure there is painted the indication of a belt at the waist, which is concealed at the front by the baby and arms of the woman. Ladies in Moche society are regularly shown wearing the kind of necklace this woman is wearing. In this example the necklace includes an explicit representation of a section of pendants in front, presumably shell.

The woman's hair is dressed much like the man's, but it differs from the latter in that the long hair covers the sides of the head, including the ears. This is a regular distinction between men's and women's hair in Moche culture. The lady also has coppery brown pigment on her face, but this pigment covers only the cheeks and top of the nose. Most of the area around the mouth, the forehead, and the sides of the face near the hair are not painted. A similar pattern of partial pigmentation of the face is seen on the imitation north coast-style representation of a woman found in a Middle Horizon 2 burial at the ruins of Chimu Capac, Supe Valley (fig. 53). This partial painting again suggests the possibility that the pigmentation may represent face paint rather than the natural complexion.

The portrayal of a man similar to that shown in figure 144 and from the same burial, is shown in figure 146. The vessel is only slightly larger and has a jar rather than a bottle neck. This man is dressed more simply, without ear ornaments and without ornamentation of the tunic, except for a border band at the bottom. On the other hand, he has his mantle tied casually over one shoulder, and carries the modeled depiction of a bulging pouch suspended by a strap around his neck, hanging down his back. Pouches of this kind are standard apparel of the fully dressed man, and usually represent containers for coca leaves. In this instance the man appears to be in the process of taking coca, for he is seen in the act of withdrawing lime from a lime container held in his left hand with the pointed implement in his right. Representations of Moche lime containers have a characteristic shape, with a sack-like bulging bottom and a shelf-like top. The top is recessed in the center around a small aperture.

As noted, the chewing of the anaesthetic coca has an ancient history in the Andean area, its use going back to Preceramic or Initial Period times and persisting to the present. The lime was necessary as a solvent for the medicinal chemical in the coca leaves. Under the Inca Empire, coca was used a great deal in religious ritual and as an offering. This use evidently also goes back to ancient times. A ritual centered around the use of coca is painted on a Moche vase in a German collection.[214] In this scene a man is seen addressing prayers to the sky,

which is represented by the Sky Serpent and stars. A huge coca bag and two lime containers with their sticks float in the space beside the praying man. Before him sit three other men engaged in drawing lime from containers, with coca pouches at their sides. All the men in this scene wear elaborate headdresses, finely ornamented tunics, and the pendant ear disks also worn by the man in figure 144. Another ritual scene evidently representing prayers for the abundance of coca is painted on a Moche-style bottle from the Chicama Valley.[215]

Uhle found a particularly fine sculptured portrait vessel at the site of Moche, in a looted cemetery that extended on both sides and in back of the Pyramid of the Moon on the slopes of the Cerro Blanco (fig. 147). This vessel is a medium-sized jar with a regular jar body, on which the garments and arms of the man are only sketchily indicated by shallow incised grooves and contrasting color areas. His feet are modeled at the base of the jar. Like the man in the preceding portrayal, this one is engaged in coca taking, for he is holding his coca pouch in his right hand and his lime container, with its stick in place, in his left. The extraordinarily fine sculpture of the portrait head appears on the jar neck.

This portrayal probably represents a traveler, for his mantle covers his head as well as his "shoulders" and the back of his entire body. Such attire is characteristic of weary-looking travelers, the sick, and the very old, evidently as special protection for people in need of it. Like most Moche portrait heads, this one has an expression of serious, stoic dignity, but there appears to be a special emphasis on sadness or pain in the mobile contours of his mouth. Today, as in former times, one of the uses of coca is as protection against sensations of cold, hunger and pain, especially in use by foot travelers on long journeys and by underfed, overworked laborers.

The man in this portrayal appears to be of a different social affiliation than the man in figure 144. His ear ornaments are small tubular plugs rather than disk pendants. He also wears a special, relatively rare head ornament beneath the mantle cover. A forehead band holds a two-pronged plume with a knotted base at the front above the band, and a narrow fringe covers the forehead below the band. The man in this portrayal has no attributes that signify high status.

The vessel in figure 148 shows more explicitly the theme of the weary traveler. A modeled figure of the traveler is seen seated on top of the body of the stirrup-spout bottle. He is seen nursing one sore foot. His mantle covers his entire back and upper body in front, and a scarf-like cloth is draped over the chest and shoulders, hanging down the back. The head is enveloped in a scarf tied with a band over the top of the head and under the chin. The forehead band covers this cloth. The drooping corners of the mouth betray discomfort.

Upon sitting down to rest and nurse his sore foot, the traveler is seen to have discarded various items which are depicted strewn about him. These depictions are painted on the top of the vessel body, all about the modeled figure. They include a coca bag with its carrying strap and a lime container beside it, below the undamaged foot of the traveler, a rectangular object that may represent a large pouch, cloth or mat to his left, two pottery vessels to his right, and, toward the back, a club on his right and a sling on his left.

The vessel shown in figure 149 is an unusual and most illuminating modeled depiction of a minor mythical being. We see an ancient individual with a deeply lined face, his lips pursed in whistling position, holding a sick-looking child with closed eyes in his left arm. The figure seems to represent a man, for he is seen wearing a man's tunic and not a woman's wrap-around. A mantle covers his head, back and shoulders, down to the ground, as befits the very old. The figure is seated.

The form of the eyes and the pursed whistling mouth show this personage to be a mythical being. The eyes are the lidless, round, staring eyes characteristic of some classes of mythical beings (cf. fig. 138). Mythical individuals similar to the one shown here are often shown whistling, an act that evidently had mythical significance. At the present time, curers of the north coast, who combine physicians' skills with religious powers, use whistling at various times during rituals to invoke guardian spirits.[216]

In their illuminating study of the paraphernalia, beliefs and activities of a north coast curer, Sharon and Donnan describe an important spirit associated with curing ritual, the Single Woman. This spirit is conceived as an ancient spinster, "a sort of wise old lady whom Eduardo [the curer] associates with the traditional herbal lore and wisdom of the pre-Columbian peoples."[217] The Single Woman spirit always wears a shawl covering head and body, and governs sacred lagoons in the northern Andes where the most powerful magical herbs used in healing are to be found.

Except for the man's tunic, the modeled depiction shown here matches the description of the Single Woman. The appearance of illness in the child suggests that the child is in need of curing. Perhaps, if the Moche figure was thought of as a spinster, her single condition, combined with her great age and mythical character, may have caused her to have been regarded as partly unsexed, thus enabling her to wear a man's tunic. On the other hand, it is equally possible that in the time of the Moche culture a spirit of this kind was thought of as a man.

In Moche art, various kinds of mythical beings are sometimes shown as ancients with heavily lined faces, like that of the "Single Woman" or "Single Man." Occasionally, the Single Woman or Single Man spirit is represented with an owl's head instead of a human head.[218] According to the modern curer of the north coast, "the owl is considered to be a symbol of wisdom and vision because of its capacity to see in the dark, and it is used to invoke the spirits of the ancients inhabiting *huacas* [pre-Columbian ruins] in order to cure witchcraft."[219] The modern curer sees a close relationship between these attributes of the Owl Spirit and the Single Woman Spirit. The same association was made in Moche times.

Epilogue

The foregoing discussion is organized to bring out a few important aspects of Andean archaeology, as exemplified by the record of Uhle's work.

Some Andean cultures had a carefully ordered social structure, with distinguished upper classes. In the archaeological record, differences in social standing are revealed by differences in settlements, in the structure and contents of buildings and graves, in artistic depictions, and in several other ways. Technology and art played important parts in the Andean past. Many of these achievements were accomplished to glorify a religion, a powerful government, a distinguished and autocratic nobility, or all three.

To most Andean peoples, who were profoundly religious, correct religious behavior was a central concern. In many different ways they prayed to be ''given this day their daily bread,'' and they sought by all means, both religious and worldly, to guard against pain, illness, death and other misfortunes. In addition to prayers, religious ceremonies and sacrifice, they used a great variety of ingenious technical, practical, and disciplined means of achieving their goals in life. As for their pursuit of happiness, the greatest pleasures of many peoples were congenial company and social gatherings, respect and self-esteem gained through achievement in farming, fighting, in some regions perhaps fishing, and in art and technical skills of various kinds, especially weaving. From historical and modern records we know that some peoples also had and still have great skills in poetic expression and music.

Some Andean peoples set a high value on their liberty, some to the extent that no price was too great to pay for it.

Before the Spanish conquest two empires effected profound changes in the course of Andean culture history, and took their toll of peoples who valued their liberty. Even when peoples survived the conquests and eventually regained their freedom, they did not do so unchanged.

The Huari Empire brought a new and differently structured religion to its conquered peoples. The effect of this new religion can be appreciated particularly clearly by comparing north coast religious art before and after the Huari Empire. It is possible that the complex, intricate structure of Moche religion before the Huari Empire may be a reflection of Moche social structure. Scenes in Moche art depict earthly lords and lesser persons in a manner similar to the relationships between depictions of mythical Lords and lesser mythical beings. After the Huari conquest, Moche religious structure was partly transformed to resemble the much simpler structure of Huari religion. This need not mean, however, that the social structure of society on earth was significantly altered in the homeland of Moche (now ''Chimu'') culture.

Huari religion found greater acceptance on the south coast, which had traditional ties with the people of the Huari region. Nevertheless, Nasca religion before the Huari Empire was also structured very differently. The important difference between the reaction of north and south coast peoples to the Huari conquest was that the people of Nasca evidently chose to identify with Huari culture, while the people of the Moche region maintained a high degree of independent power, as well as many of their traditional ways.

The central coast centers accepted the Huari religion and then proceeded to compete with the Huari capital in power, probably by various means. One of these means was the emphasis on one minor mythical being in Huari religion, the Griffin, as a rival spirit symbolizing the competing power of the great religious center of Pachacamac.

The greatest danger to the continued dominance of the Huari capital lay in a possible merger between the power center of the north coast and the rival Huari center of Pachacamac. This danger became apparent at the outset of the Huari conquest, when north coast influences first appeared in the archaeological record of the central coast. It must have been apparent enough at the time so that the Huari capital established a guardian outpost at the northern border of the cultural community of the central coast, at Chimu Capac in the Supe Valley. The archaeological record shows that this device was effective for a time.

As we begin to unravel the cultural relationships between the different power centers under the Huari Empire, we see that rival powers of the coast threatened the cohesion of the empire from the outset, and that there is a good degree of likelihood that these rivalries contributed to the eventual fall of the empire.

The fall of the Huari Empire freed the different regions to give expression to their sentiments, and the aftermath of the empire revealed more clearly the differences in relationships between the Huari capital and its respective provinces. Only the center with the greatest cultural independence and power under the empire, the north coast, survived the fall of the empire more or less unscathed, and even managed to flourish for a time. Even here, however, Huari religion and the Huari conquest left their inevitable marks in the form of considerable changes.

New prestige and power centers developed eventually. The first to rise from the ashes were the people of Ica, with an archaizing movement that attempted a return to the dimly remembered days of glory under the Huari Empire. Other kinds of renewals followed, such as at the culture center of Chancay and the religious center of Pachacamac. After a period of decline, north coast culture rose once more with the beginnings of the Kingdom of Chimor. With the beginning of Late Intermediate Period Epoch 6 a whole new cycle of activity by rival powers was in full motion.

The effects of the Inca Empire were in many ways as devastating as those of the Huari Empire. However, these effects were more pronounced in the areas of social structure, economics and nationalism than of religion. Despite local survivals of aspects of pre-Huari religions, the entire Andean area was joined in a dominance of Huari religious concepts derived from the time of the Huari Empire, at the time the Incas began their conquests. In terms of religious concepts, the Incas brought no profound changes in orientation to the conquered peoples, unlike the Huari conquerors. Thus, one of the worst problems of imperial control of divergent nations facing the Huari Empire did not face the Incas.

The policies of the Inca government bore their own seeds of destruction, principally in the areas of nationalistic sentiments of conquered nations, social hierarchy, and land control. It is easily possible that the Inca government might have succeeded in dealing with its problems of control much more successfully and for a much longer time than the Huari government. The inopportune arrival of the Spaniards prevented the Incas from bringing their ingenuity to this test.

Endnotes

Acknowledgments. This study was carried out with the help of extensive discussions with John H. Rowe, and many of his ideas are incorporated in it, with or without special acknowledgment. It has also benefited from information and editorial suggestions furnished by Karen O. Bruhns, Lawrence E. Dawson, and Christopher B. Donnan. Particular thanks go to Christopher B. Donnan for supplying important data on north coast archaeology. The manuscript was completed December, 1974.

The maps and chronological table were drawn by Catherine T. Brandel. The line drawings in figures 62, 63, 66, 67 and 91 were traced to scale by Catherine T. Brandel and Brian Shekeloff from color slides and original tracings by D. Menzel. Unless otherwise indicated, photographs were made by Eugene R. Prince.

1. Rowe, John, 1954, pp. 6-7.
2. Rowe, John, 1954, pp. 1-6.
3. Rowe, John, 1961b.
4. Richard Burger, personal communication.
5. Rowe, John, 1966; Rowe and Menzel, 1967, chronological table.
6. Rowe, John, 1962a.
7. Rowe, John, 1945, pp. 277-282; 1947, pp. 203-208; Cabello Valboa, 1951, pt. 3, caps. 14-24, pp. 296-396.
8. Rowe, John, 1954, p. 11.
9. Rowe, John, 1967.
10. Rowe, John, 1967, pl. XXXIV; 1944.
11. Rowe, John, 1967; Morris, 1973; Menzel, 1959.
12. Rowe, John, 1947, pp. 263-269.
13. Rowe, John, 1944, shapes a, b, p. 48, fig. 8.
14. Morris, ms.; Rowe, John, personal communication.
15. Rowe, John, 1961a.
16. Rowe, John, ms.
17. Lyon, 1966.
18. Rowe, John, 1945, pp. 270, 279; Cieza de León, 1946, cap. LXXIV, p. 380.
19. Cieza de León, 1946, cap. LXI, p. 346. For a reconstruction of such a villa at Puruchucu, Lima Valley, see Rowe 1974, pl. 341.
20. Cieza de León, 1946, cap. LXI, pp. 346-347.
21. Cieza de León, 1946, cap. LXIII, pp. 352-354.
22. Cieza de León, 1946, cap. LXII, pp. 347-351.
23. Uhle, ms., vol. III, p. 60b.
24. Tombs Tc, Td-8, Ti-5, Tl-2.
25. Guaman Poma de Ayala, 1936, p. 451 [458]. Research done by John H. Rowe.
26. Rowe, John, 1947, pp. 260-264.
27. Rowe, John, 1947, p. 263.
28. Cieza de León, 1946, cap. LXIII, p. 352.
29. Guaman Poma de Ayala, 1936, pp. 11066 [1162], 11056 [1156]. Research on digging boards done by John H. Rowe.
30. Information collected by Oscar Núñez del Prado, told to John H. Rowe in 1954.
31. Cieza de León, 1946, cap. LXXIII, p. 375.
32. Rowe, John, 1947, p. 216.
33. Schmidt, 1929, figs. 426-433.
34. Mead, 1924, p. 340 and fig. 6.
35. For illustrations of complete examples, see Schmidt, 1929, fig. 444-11, 12, 13.
36. For intact examples of necklaces of such pendants, see Uhle's collection, 4-5076, and Schmidt, 1929, fig. 468-2.
37. Tombs Ti-5, Th-1, Tg.
38. Tomb Th-1.
39. Burial Tb and tomb Ta.
40. "Brocade" is a method of supplementary weft patterning in weaving.
41. There are eight brocade stripes, each 3/4 of an inch (2 cm.) to 7/8 of an inch (2.3 cm.) wide, separated by 1 (2.5 cm.) to 1-1/2 inch (3.8 cm.) wide stripes of cotton gauze weave. Each brocade stripe has a design in two colors. Either red or gold colored yarn is found in each stripe. Four of the stripes have designs in red and gold. Each of the other four has a different color combination, these being red and white, red and dark brown, red and medium brown, and gold and gray-green.

Symmetry is maintained in the ornamentation of the cloth, except for slight deviations. For example, the division by colors in the brocade stripes follows a symmetrical canon in which half the stripes are in red and gold, and the rest are each in a different color combination in which either red or gold is used with another color that occurs only once. The basic symmetry of this canon of color patterning is slightly modified by the introduction of deliberate irregularities in arrangement which dispel the monotony of absolute symmetry.

There is a slight deviation in the symmetry of stripe alternation. Instead of an alternation of one red/gold stripe and one of the singularly colored ones, one red/gold stripe is alternated with two singularly colored ones. As a result, one red/gold stripe is left over at one end, bordering the cloth next to another red/gold stripe. A plain cotton weave border counterbalances the spare red/gold stripe on the opposite side of the cloth. Further, while the obvious symmetry would have been to pattern the singularly colored brocade stripes so that two would contain red and two would contain gold as one of their colors, in fact three contain red and only one gold.

A further complexity in arrangement is introduced by the use of dual symmetry, in which a second, independent patterning of designs cuts across the patterning of colors. Two alternate designs are used in the brocade stripes. In one, elongate diamond figures are created by diagonal crosshatching, and a stylized bird figure is placed in the center of each diamond. The second design consists of a pattern of stylized fish figures which resemble elongate diamonds, except that each figure has two triangular appendages in front to represent the head of the fish. In contrast to the pattern of alternation by color, the decoration is arranged so that one stripe with bird designs always alternates with one stripe with fish designs, except for the last red/gold stripe, which is again a duplicate of its neighbor. If one disregards this last asymmetrically placed stripe, the rest are arranged so that the two outermost red/gold stripes have bird designs while the central red/gold stripe has a fish design. The two singularly colored stripes adjoining the central red/gold one in turn have bird designs, while their singularly colored neighbors have fish designs.

Distinctive aspects of the patterning do not stop with the dual striping arrangement. For example, in the singularly colored stripes, the bird designs are both done in red and brown, though the shades of brown differ, while the fish designs appear in the bands that contain lighter hues. Furthermore, despite the variety of color combinations, red and gold are consistently emphasized. Wherever red appears, it is used to form the design figures, while the other color is seen as the background. In the one stripe where red does not appear, the gold is used for the design.

42. Uhle, 1903, p. 90, pl. 19, fig. 1.

43. Jiménez de la Espada, 1965, vol. 183, pp. 207, 232, 243; sections 15 in the descriptions of the provinces of Vilcas Guaman [1586], San Francisco de Atunrucana y Laramati [1586], and Rucanas Antamarcas [1586].

44. Rowe, John, 1947, p. 235.

45. Uhle, 1903, pl. 19, fig. 1 and p. 90.

46. The resin paint disintegrated upon exposure to the dry air, so that at best only traces remain. Uhle describes the rapidity with which this disintegration took place when speaking of one vessel: "When fresh taken from the grave, its colors were splendid like red and gold, but when dry they faded." (Uhle, ms., vol. III, p. 84b, 5028).

47. A more detailed discussion of this group of figurines can be found in Menzel, 1967.

48. Rowe, John, 1948.

49. Cieza de León, 1946, cap. LXVII, p. 362.

50. Rowe, John, 1948, p. 32; Calancha, 1639, Libro III, cap. 2, p. 550.

51. Kosok, 1959; 1965, pp. 87, 115, 119, 135-146.

52. Cieza de León, 1946, caps. LVII, LXVII, LXVIII, pp. 340, 362-364.

53. Schaedel, 1951a, p. 237.

54. Schaedel, 1951a, pp. 234-235; Kosok, 1965, pp. 86-87, 94, 105-106; Keatinge and Day, 1973, fig. 1, pp. 276-278; Keatinge, 1974, fig. 19, p. 68.

55. Kosok, 1965, p. 110, fig. 36; Schaedel, 1967, p. 384.

56. Kosok, 1965, pp. 87-88.

57. Estete, 1946, p. 95. Estete does not mention Supe by name, but gives its location.

58. Estete, 1946, pp. 95-96.

59. Rowe, John, 1948, p. 33; Calancha, 1639, Libro III, cap. 2, p. 550; Libro III, cap. 14, p. 606.

60. Cobo, 1956, cap. 7, p. 301.

61. Moseley and Mackey, 1973, p. 318; Keatinge and Day, 1973, p. 278; 1974, p. 229, Keatinge, 1974, p. 66; Horkheimer, 1944, p. 62; Kosok, 1965, p. 85, fig. 19.

62. Moseley and Mackey, 1973, p. 324; Keatinge, 1974, p. 66; Keatinge and Day, 1974, p. 229.

63. West, 1970, Keatinge and Day, 1974, p. 229.

64. Moseley and Mackey, 1973, p. 318; Keatinge and Day, 1973, p. 282; 1974, p. 229; Keatinge, 1974, p. 66; Kosok, 1965, pp. 71 ff., figs. 1-4, 6-10, 12, 15-18.

65. Moseley and Mackey, 1973, pp. 338, 341, 344; Donnan and Mackey, ms.; Keatinge and Day, 1973, pp. 278-285.

66. Donnan and Mackey, ms.

67. Donnan and Mackey, ms.

68. Keatinge and Day, 1973, pp. 278-279; West, 1970.

69. Moseley and Mackey, 1973, p. 344.

70. Moseley and Mackey, 1973.

71. Schaedel, 1951a, pp. 237-238.

72. Ubbelohde-Doering, 1966, pp. 19, 81, fig. 53.

73. Willey, 1953, pp. 307-310, 324-329; Collier, 1955, pp. 35-46, 96-98, sites V-124, V-269.

74. Collier, 1955, p. 98; Schaedel, 1951a, pp. 241-242.

75. Schaedel, 1951a, p. 238.

76. Menzel, 1959.

77. Kroeber, 1926a, pp. 15-17.

78. Schaedel, 1967; 1951c, pp. 16-22; 1949, pp. 73-77; Kosok, 1965, pp. 14-15, 87-89, figs. 1-5; Horkheimer, 1944, figs. 60-62.

79. Rowe, John, 1948, pp. 39-40.

80. Rowe, John, 1948, p. 42.

81. Bonavia, 1962; Lothrop and Mahler, 1957.

82. Menzel, 1966, pp. 107-108.

83. Jérez, 1946, p. 98; Menzel and Rowe, 1966, p. 68.

84. Rowe, John, 1948, pp. 40-41; Calancha, 1639, Libro III, cap. 4, p. 562.

85. Rowe, John, 1948, pp. 45-46.

86. Menzel and Rowe, 1966, p. 64; Menzel, 1966.

87. The Inca pronunciation of Chimor was Chimu. In the archaeological literature the term "Chimu" is used not only for the style phases of Chimor, but also for much earlier style phases (cf. chronological table).

88. Rowe, John, 1948, p. 47; Calancha, 1639, Libro III, cap. 2, pp. 553-554.

89. Moseley and Mackey, 1973, pp. 338, 341, 344.

90. Cabello Valboa, 1951, pt. 3, cap. 13, pp. 332, 333.

91. A publication now in press furnishes archaeological records of burials, but none is datable to the time of the Kingdom of Chimor before the later Inca occupation period (Donnan and Mackey, ms.).

92. Uhle, 1913b, p. 97, fig. 1; Kroeber, 1925a, p. 197.

93. Regal, 1936, p. 113, Salaverry.

94. Uhle, 1925, p. 258.

95. Regal, 1936, lám. III, p. 37.

96. Uhle, 1903, Cemetery VI.

97. Burial E-13, 4-5041.

98. Double-chambered bottle, 4-2497.

99. Kosok, 1965, pp. 217-220.

100. Uhle, 1925; Kroeber, 1925b.

101. Schmidt, 1929, fig. 550-2.

102. Reiss and Stübel, 1880-1887, vol. I, pls. 16, 17, 21a-1, 2.

103. Kroeber, 1925b, pl. 72f, g.

104. Carrión Cachot, 1959.

105. Sharon and Donnan, 1974, p. 56.

106. Rowe, John, 1947, pp. 294-295.

107. Rowe, John, 1947, p. 295. The observations on the relationship between Inca and Middle Horizon Star Animals were made by Rowe.

108. Carrión Cachot, 1959, pp. 31-38.

109. Carrión Cachot, 1959, pp. 15-28.

110. Carrión Cachot, 1959, pp. 59-66.

111. Sharon and Donnan, 1974, pp. 52, 54.

112. Kosok, 1965, p. 39, fig. 2.

113. Donnan and Mackey, ms.

114. The names of the pyramids are arbitrary and of recent origin, and do not necessarily reflect associations with the Moon and Sun.

115. See also Donnan and Mackey, ms.

116. Uhle, 1913b, p. 110.

117. Christopher B. Donnan reports that excavations made on this platform in 1972 turned up some habitation refuse (personal communication). There is no record on when this refuse was accumulated.

118. Uhle, 1913b, pp. 110-111.

119. Uhle, 1913b, p. 112, fig. 16-2, p. 114.

120. Donnan, 1973, figs. 202-207, 219-221, pl. 6.

121. Donnan, 1973, figs. 219-221.

122. Uhle, 1913b, pl. V-d; fig. 81, right.

123. Uhle, 1913b, p. 115, fig. 19, second row center, bottom row.

124. Ravines, 1968.

125. Uhle, 1913b, p. 114.

126. Uhle, 1913b, p. 113, figs. 16-1, 17.

127. For the other example, see Conklin, 1971.

128. Uhle, 1913b, fig. 16-5.

129. Schaedel, 1949; 1951c; 1967; Kosok, 1965, pp. 14-15, 87-89. Rowe, John, 1974, pl. 318a.

130. For comparison, see textile designs from a stratum in front of the temple of Pachacamac, where Uhle found burials datable to Middle Horizon Epoch 4 and the early epochs of the Late Intermediate Period (Uhle, 1903, pl. 8, figs. 17, 18).

131. Schaedel, 1951c.

132. Schaedel, 1951c, p. 21, fig. 17, left.

133. The identifications of the human remains were made by Theodore D. McCown.

134. Reiss and Stübel, 1880-1887.

135. Rowe, John, 1954, p. 2.

136. Willey, 1943.

137. Huapaya Manco, 1948.

138. Chumpitaz C., 1973.

139. Uhle, 1913a.

140. Strong, 1925.

141. Johnson, 1930, figs. 75, 76; Lanning, 1965, p. 69.

142. Huapaya Manco, 1948, p. 97.

143. Uhle recorded the remains of only one adult in this tomb, identified by Theodore D. McCown as those of a man. However, Uhle's records were not always complete, and recording errors occurred occasionally. He did not usually mention nor record human or other remains if they were too decayed to be preserved. Since many of the tombs contained more than one dead, a woman could also have been buried in tomb P-17. A skull of a child is also recorded for this grave, but Uhle does not always make it clear whether a body accompanied the skulls he collected. A bodiless skull would be an offering, but complete children's burials also sometimes accompanied the dead and were not necessarily sacrificial. While children's burials in graves with adults were most commonly placed with women, some could have accompanied men. The record is not clear on this point.

144. Reiss and Stübel, 1880-1887, vol. I, pl. 10, fig. 7; Chumpitaz C., 1973, pp. 434-435, tombs T.739, 637, 494.

145. Reiss and Stübel, 1880-1887, vol. I, pl. 10, fig. 2.

146. Reiss and Stübel, 1880-1887, vol. I, pl. 16, fig. 1.

147. Huapaya Manco, 1948, p. 98.

148. Reiss and Stübel, 1880-1887, vol. I, pl. 10, fig. 1.

149. Uhle, 1913a, fig. 5a, P-15, P-17, P-21.

150. Uhle, 1913a, fig. 5a, P-18, P-19, fig. 5b; Huapaya Manco, 1948, fig. 2, p. 95.

151. Reiss and Stübel, 1880-1887, vol. I, pl. 10-4; Uhle, 1913a, fig. 6, Z-2, fig. 7, T-7, T-14, T-5, T-3, T-10, T-1.

152. Reiss and Stübel, 1880-1887, vol. I, pl. 14, fig. 1, Middle Horizon 3.

153. Bonavia, 1962.

154. Menzel and Rowe, 1966, p. 68; data collected by John H. Rowe.

155. Schmidt, 1929, figs. 548, 549.

156. Reiss and Stübel, 1880-1887, vol. I, pl. 33.

157. Chumpitaz C., 1973, p. 434, T.734.

158. Reiss and Stübel, 1880-1887, vol. III, pl. 83-11. A complete balance with its net bags is illustrated in Bennett, 1954, fig. 134, p. 117.

159. Gayton, 1961; Murra, 1962.

160. Patterson, 1971. In this article Patterson publishes the metallurgical analysis of the Moche-style ornament, which was found in a Moche II burial from the site of Moche (association recorded by John H. Rowe). The bronze of this ornament contains 2% arsenic. Patterson has reported verbally to John H. Rowe that the bronze club head from the late Middle Horizon 2B tomb P-21 (4-6306) was deliberately made arsenic bronze containing 1.5% arsenic.

161. Kosok, 1965, chapter VI.

162. Uhle, 1906; 1913c. The spelling ''Nazca'' crept into common use through error, and is historically and linguistically

incorrect, as noted by John H. Rowe (Menzel, Rowe and Dawson, 1964, p. 8).

163. Menzel, Rowe and Dawson, 1964.

164. Ica Valley, Ocucaje Basin, Site A, burial 1.

165. Menzel, 1964, pp. 4, 5, 8-10; Benavides Calle, 1972, Huarpa Tricolor.

166. Menzel, 1964; 1968.

167. The later branch oracle may have been established in much later times, in Late Intermediate Period Epoch 5 or 6 (Menzel and Rowe, 1966).

168. Lyon, 1966.

169. Ravines, 1968; Menzel, 1968.

170. Menzel, 1964, pp. 6, 23-28, 35-36, footnote 196.

171. Yakovleff, 1932, figs. 17, 18, p. 110; Yakovleff and Herrera, 1934-35, tomo III, p. 258, fig. 4r, p. 306, fig. 27, p. 308, fig. 28.

172. Ravines, 1968, fig. 84.

173. Uhle, 1903, pl. 6, fig. 8; Van Stan, 1967, figs. 27, 28.

174. Rowe, John, 1947, pp. 293-295.

175. Rowe, John, 1960.

176. Rowe, John, 1947, pp. 293-314.

177. Menzel, 1968, figs. 19a, b.

178. Schmidt, 1929, p. 32, fig. 421-1, 2, 3, 4.

179. Uhle, 1913c, pp. 347-349; Ocucaje, Site E, Kroeber and Strong, 1924b.

180. Lyon, 1966.

181. Uhle, 1913c, p. 350, fig. 5-10; for comparison, see Uhle, 1903, pl. 6, particularly figs. 8, 9, 12, 13.

183. Uhle, 1913c, p. 348, fig. 4

184. Lyon, 1966.

185. Rowe, Ann, ms., pp. 31-56, 79, pls. II, III, IV.

186. Menzel and Rowe, 1966; Menzel, 1966.

187. Uhle, 1913b, pp. 104-109.

188. cf. Sharon and Donnan, 1974.

189. Larco Hoyle, 1948.

190. Donnan, 1965; 1973; Donnan and Mackey, ms.; Sharon and Donnan, 1974.

191. Ubbelohde-Doering, 1966, Pacatnamú, H-31, burial E-1, pls. 62-66, 68-80; 1957; Donnan, 1973, pl. 7; Rowe, John, 1942; Muelle, 1942, pp. 276-278; Schaedel, 1957, fig. 4C; Stumer, 1959, fig. 5.

192. Oral presentation by Carol J. Mackey.

193. Uhle, 1913b, p. 106, fig. 11.

194. Uhle, 1913b, pp. 105-106, fig. 10.

195. Uhle, 1913b, p. 107.

196. Uhle, 1913b, figs. 11, 12, pp. 106-107.

197. Uhle, 1913b, p. 106.

198. Uhle, 1913b, pl. IVB, upper left, pl. Ve.

199. Uhle, ms., catalogue vol. I, pp. 69-70.

200. Kroeber, 1925a, pl. 55b; Schmidt, 1929, fig. 176-4.

201. Schmidt, 1929, fig. 164-2.

202. Kroeber, 1925a, pl. 54j, 1; Schmidt, 1929, fig. 160.

203. For example, Ubbelohde-Doering, 1952, figs. 184-185.

204. Kutscher, 1954, figs. 45, 46A; 1950, fig. 1.

205. Kutscher, 1954, fig. 1A, pp. 12, 47.

206. Kutscher, 1954, figs. 1A, 1B, 13, 38; 1950, fig. 1.

207. Kutscher, 1954, figs. 44-47.

208. Kutscher, 1954, fig. 47, right.

209. Kutscher, 1954, fig. 48A.

210. Kutscher, 1954, fig. 49A, D.

211. Donnan, 1973, p. 134, PV28-97, Cache 1.

212. Kroeber, 1944, pl. 48E.

213. Uhle, 1903, pl. 6, figs. 7-9, 12.

214. Kutscher, 1950, fig. 5.

215. Ubbelohde-Doering, 1952, figs. 172, 173.

216. Sharon and Donnan, 1974, p. 59.

217. Sharon and Donnan, 1974, pp. 52-53.

218. Schmidt, 1929, fig. 173-2; Sharon and Donnan, 1974, pl. 6A.

219. Sharon and Donnan, 1974, p. 52.

Bibliography

Baughman, James Wallace

ms. *Ancient Peruvian painted textiles.* Thesis submitted in partial satisfaction of the requirements for the degree of Master of Arts in Decorative Art in the Graduate Division of the University of California, Berkeley, January, 1953.

Benavides Calle, Mario

1972. *Análisis de la cerámica Huarpa.* Actas y Memorias del XXXIX Congreso Internacional de Americanistas, Lima, 2-9 agosto, 1970, vol. 3, Proceso y Cultura en la Sierra Central del Perú, eds. Rosalía Avalos de Matos, Rogger Ravines, pp. 63-88. Instituto de Estudios Peruanos, Lima.

Bennett, Wendell Clark

1939. *Archaeology of the north coast of Peru; an account of exploration and excavation in Viru and Lambayeque Valleys.* Anthropological Papers of The American Museum of Natural History, vol. XXXVII, part I. New York.

1954 *Ancient arts of the Andes; with an introduction by René D'Harnoncourt.* The Museum of Modern Art, New York. Distributed by Simon and Schuster, New York.

Bonavia Berber, Duccio

1959 *Cerámica de Puerto Viejo (Chilca).* Actas y Trabajos del II Congreso Nacional de Historia del Perú, Epoca Pre-Hispánica, 4-9 de agosto de 1958, vol. I, pp. 137-168. Lima.

1962. *Sobre el estilo Teatino.* Revista del Museo Nacional, tomo XXXI, pp. 43-94. Lima.

Bonavia Berber, Duccio, and Ravines Sánchez, Rogger H.

1971 *Influence inca sur la côte nord du Pérou.* Traduction de Georges Lobsiger. Bulletin de la Société Suisse des Américanistes, no. 35, pp. 3-18. Genève. Original presented at the Premier Symposium d'Archéologie de Lambayeque, Jan. 20, 1967.

Cabello Valboa, Miguel

1951 [1586].*Miscelánea Antártica; una historia del Perú antiguo. Con prólogo, notas é indices a cargo del Instituto de Etnología, Facultad de Letras, Universidad Nacional Mayor de San Marcos, Lima.* Imprenta López, Buenos Aires.

Calancha, Antonio de la

1639 *Coronica moralizada del orden de San Avgvstin en el Perv, con sucesos egenplares de esta monarqvia.* Pedro Lacavalleria, Barcelona.

Carrión Cachot de Girard, Rebeca

1959 *La religión en el antiguo Perú (norte y centro de la costa, período post-clásico).* Tipografía Peruana, S.A., Lima.

Chumpitaz C., E.

1973 *Tipos de tumbas y fardos en los diferentes estratos, estudiados en una area de 130 m. de largo por 16 m. de ancho a partir de la falda Este del montículo "K." hacia el lado Sur. Ancón, julio de 1952. In* Manual de arqueología peruana, by Federico Kauffmann Doig, pp. 434-435. Ediciones Peisa, Lima. Published earlier in Revista del Museo Regional de Ica, año IV, no. 5, 1952, following p. 36. Ica.

Cieza de León, Pedro de

1946 [1550]. *La crónica del Perú. In* Crónicas de la Conquista del Perú, Julio Le Riverend, ed., pp. 127-497. Colección Atenea, Editorial Nueva España, S.A., México.

Cobo, Bernabé

1956 [1639]. *Fundación de Lima.* Biblioteca de Autores Españoles, vol. 92, Obras del P. Bernabé Cobo . . . II. Estudio preliminar y edición del P. Francisco Mateos . . . Ediciones Atlas, Madrid.

Collier, Donald

1955 *Cultural chronology and change as reflected in the ceramics of the Virú Valley, Peru.* Fieldiana: Anthropology, vol. 43. Chicago Natural History Museum, Chicago.

Conklin, William J.

1971 *Peruvian textile fragment from the beginning of the Middle Horizon.* Textile Museum Journal, vol. III, no. 1, December 1970, pp. 15-24. Washington.

Day, Kent C.

1972 *Urban planning at Chan Chan, Peru. Man, Settlement and Urbanism,* edit. by P.J. Ucko, R. Tringham and G.W. Dimbleby, pp. 927-930. Gerald Duckworth, London.

Donnan, Christopher Bruce

1965 *Moche ceramic technology.* Ñawpa Pacha 3, pp. 115-134. Berkeley.

1973 *Moche occupation of the Santa Valley, Peru.* University of California Publications in Anthropology, vol. 8. University of California Press, Berkeley, Los Angeles, London.

Donnan, Christopher Bruce, and Mackey, Carol J.

ms   *Ancient burial patterns of the Moche Valley, Peru*. In press.

Estete, Miguel de

1946   [1534]. *La relación del viaje que hizo el señor capitán Hernando Pizarro por mandado del señor Gobernador, su hermano, desde el pueblo de Caxamalca a Parcama, y de allí a Jauja. In* Jérez, Francisco de, Conquista del Perú y provincia del Cuzco. Crónicas de la Conquista del Perú, Julio Le Riverend, ed., pp. 90-108. Colección Atenea, Editorial Nueva España, S.A., México.

Gayton, Anna Hadwick

1927   *The Uhle collections from Nievería*. University of California Publications in American Archaeology and Ethnology, vol. 21, no. 8, pp. i-ii, 305-329. Berkeley.

1961   *The cultural significance of Peruvian textiles: production, function, aesthetics.* Kroeber Anthropological Society Papers, no. 25, pp. 111-128. Berkeley. Reprinted in Rowe and Menzel, 1967, pp. 275-292.

Gayton, Anna Hadwick, and Kroeber, Alfred Louis

1927   *The Uhle pottery collections from Nazca.* University of California Publications in American Archaeology and Ethnology, vol. 24, no. 1, pp. i-ii, 1-46. Berkeley.

Guaman Poma de Ayala, Felipe

1936   [1615]. *Nueva corónica y buen gobierno (codex péruvien illustré).* Travaux et Mémoires de l'Institut d'Ethnologie, XXIII. Paris.

Horkheimer, Hans

1944   *Vistas arqueológicas del noroeste del Perú.* Instituto Arqueológico de la Universidad Nacional de Trujillo. Librería e Imprenta Moreno, Trujillo.

1965   *Identificación y biografía de importantes sitios prehispánicos del Perú.* Arqueológicas, no. 8. Museo Nacional de Antropología y Arqueología, Lima.

Huapaya Manco, Cirilo

1948   *Nuevo tipo de tumba descubierto en las Necropolis de Ancón.* Revista del Museo Nacional de Antropología y Arqueología, vol. II, no. 1, primer semestre, pp. 93-98. Lima.

Jérez, Francisco de

1946   [1534]. *Conquista del Perú y provincia del Cuzco. In* Crónicas de la Conquista del Perú, Julio Le Riverend, ed., pp. 29-118. Colección Atenea, Editorial Nueva España, S.A., México.

Jiménez de la Espada, Don Marcos

1965   *Relaciones Geográficas de Indias.—Perú.* Edición y estudio preliminar por José Urbano Martínez Carreras. *In* Biblioteca de Autores Españoles, vols. 183-185. Ediciones Atlas, Madrid.

Johnson, Lieutenant George R.

1930   *Peru from the air.* With text and notes by Raye R. Platt. American Geographical Society, Special Publication No. 12. New York.

Kauffmann Doig, Federico

1973   *Manual de arqueología peruana* Ediciones Peisa, Lima.

Keatinge, Richard W.

1974   *Chimu rural administrative centres in the Moche Valley, Peru. World Archaeology, vol. 6, no. 1, June, pp. 66-82. London.*

Keatinge, Richard W., and Day, Kent C.

1973   *Socio-economic organization of the Moche Valley, Peru, during the Chimu occupation of Chanchan.* Journal of Anthropological Research, vol. 29, no. 4, winter, pp. 275-295. Albuquerque.

1974   *Chan Chan; a study of precolumbian urbanism and the management of land and water resources in Peru.* Archaeology, vol. 27, no. 4, October, pp. 228-235. New York.

Kosok, Paul

1959   *El valle de Lambayeque; 1ra sección, costa norte.* Actas y Trabajos del II Congreso Nacional de Historia del Perú, 4-9 de agosto de 1958, vol. I, Epoca Pre-Hispánica, pp. 49-66. Lima.

1965   *Life, land and water in ancient Peru.* Long Island University Press, New York.

Kroeber, Alfred Louis

1925a   *The Uhle pottery collections from Moche.* University of California Publications in American Archaeology and Ethnology, vol. 21, no. 5, pp. i-ii, 191-234. Berkeley.

1925b   *The Uhle pottery collections from Supe.* University of California Publications in American Archaeology and Ethnology, vol. 21, no. 6, pp. i-ii, 235-264. Berkeley.

1926a   *Archaeological explorations in Peru, Part I; ancient pottery from Trujillo.* First Captain Marshall Field Archaeological Expedition to Peru. Field Museum of Natural History, Anthropology, Memoirs, vol. II, no. 1. Chicago.

1926b   *The Uhle pottery collections from Chancay.* University of California Publications in American Archaeology and Ethnology, vol. 21, no. 7, pp. i-ii, 265-292. Berkeley.

1930   *Archaeological explorations in Peru, Part II; the northern coast.* First Marshall Field Archaeological Expedition to Peru. Field Museum of Natural History, Anthropology, Memoirs, vol. II, no. 2. Chicago.

1944   *Peruvian archeology in 1942.* Viking Fund Publications in Anthropology, no. 4. New York.

Kroeber, Alfred Louis, and Strong, William Duncan

1924a   *The Uhle collections from Chincha.* University of California Publications in American Archaeology and Ehtnology, vol. 21, no. 1, pp. i-ii, 1-54. Berkeley.

1924b   *The Uhle pottery collections from Ica.* University of California Publications in American Archaeology and Ethnology, vol. 21, no. 3, pp. i-ii, 95-120. Berkeley.

Kutscher, Gerdt

1950   *Iconographic studies as an aid in the reconstruction of Early Chimu civilization.* Transactions of the New York Academy of Sciences, Series II, vol. 12, no. 6, pp. 194-203. Reprinted in Rowe and Menzel, 1967, pp. 115-124.

1954   *Cerámica del Perú septentrional; nordperuanische Keramik.* Monumenta Americana I, Ibero-Amerikanische Bibliothek zu Berlin, Schriftleitung Gerdt Kutscher. Verlag Gebr. Mann, Berlin.

Lanning, Edward Putnam

1965   *Early Man in Peru.* Scientific American, vol. 213, no. 4, October, pp. 68-76. New York.

Larco Hoyle, Rafael

1948   *Cronología arqueológica del norte del Perú.* Biblioteca del Museo de Arqueología "Rafael Larco Herrera," Hacienda Chiclín-Trujillo. Sociedad Geográfica Americana, Buenos Aires.

Lothrop, Samuel Kirkland, and Mahler, Joy

1957   *A Chancay-style grave at Zapallan, Peru; an analysis of its textiles, pottery and other furnishings.* Papers of the Peabody Museum of Archaeology and Ethnology, Harvard University, vol. L, no. 1. Cambridge.

Lyon, Patricia Jean

1966   *Innovation through archaism; the origins of the Ica pottery style.* Ñawpa Pacha 4, pp. 31-61. Berkeley. Reprinted in part in Rowe and Menzel, 1967, pp. 177-209.

Mead, Charles W.

1924   *The musical instruments of the Incas.* Anthropological Papers of The American Museum of Natural History, vol. XV, part III, pp. i-ii, 313-347. American Museum Press, New York.

Menzel, Dorothy

1959   *The Inca occupation of the south coast of Peru.* Southwestern Journal of Anthropology, vol. 15, no. 2, pp. 125-142. Albuquerque. Reprinted in Rowe and Menzel, 1967, pp. 217-234.

1964   *Style and time in the Middle Horizon.* Ñawpa Pacha 2, pp. 1-105. Berkeley.

1966   *The pottery of Chincha.* Ñawpa Pacha 4, pp. 77-144. Berkeley.

1967   *Late Ica figurines in the Uhle collection.* Ñawpa Pacha 5, pp. 15-38. Berkeley.

1968   *New data on the Huari Empire in Middle Horizon Epoch 2A.* Ñawpa Pacha 6, pp. 47-114. Berkeley.

Menzel, Dorothy, and Rowe, John Howland

1966   *The role of Chincha in late pre-Spanish Peru.* Ñawpa Pacha 4, pp. 63-76. Berkeley.

Menzel, Dorothy, Rowe, John Howland, and Dawson, Lawrence Emmett

1964   *The Paracas pottery of Ica; a study in style and time.* University of California Publications in American Archaeology and Ethnology, vol. 50. University of California Press, Berkeley and Los Angeles.

Morris, Craig

1973   *Establecimientos estatales en el Tawantinsuyu: una estrategia de urbanismo obligado.* Revista del Museo Nacional, tomo XXXIX, pp. 127-141. Lima.

ms   *Storage in Tawantinsuyu.* A dissertation submitted to the Faculty of the Division of the Social Sciences in Candidacy for the Degree of Doctor of Philosophy, Department of Anthropology, The University of Chicago, December, 1967.

Moseley, Michael E., and Mackey, Carol J.

1973   *Chan Chan, Peru's ancient city of kings.* National Geographic, vol. 143, no. 3, March, pp. 318-345. National Geographic Society, Washington.

Muelle, Jorge Clemente

1942   *Notas bibliográficas.* Rowe, John Howland.— A new pottery style from the Department of Piura, Perú . . . Revista del Museo Nacional, tomo XI, no. 2, II semestre, pp. 276-278. Lima.

Murra, John Victor

1962   *Cloth and its function in the Inca state.* American Anthropologist, vol. 64, no. 4, August, pp. 710-728. Menasha.

O'Neale, Lila M., and Kroeber, Alfred Louis

1930   *Textile periods in ancient Peru.* University of California Publications in American Archaeology and Ethnology, vol. 28, no. 2, pp. 23-56. University of California Press, Berkeley.

Patterson, Clair C.

1971   *Native copper, silver and gold accessible to early metallurgists.* American Antiquity, vol. 36, no. 3, July, pp. 286-321. Washington.

Ravines Sánchez, Rogger H.

1968   *Un depósito de ofrendas del Horizonte Medio en la sierra central del Perú.* Ñawpa Pacha 6, pp. 19-45. Berkeley.

Regal, Alberto

1936   *Los caminos del Inca en el antiguo Perú.* Sanmarti y Cía., S.A., Lima.

Reiss, Johann Wilhelm, and Stübel, Moritz Alphons

1880-   *The Necropolis of Ancon in Peru; a contribution to our*
1887   *knowledge of the culture and industries of the empire of the Incas, being the results of excavations made on the spot.* Translated by Professor A.H. Keane. A. Asher & Co., Berlin. 3 vols.

Rowe, Ann Pollard

ms   *A group of Late Intermediate Period textiles from Ica, Peru.* Thesis submitted in partial satisfaction of the requirements for the degree of Master of Arts in Design in the Graduate Division of the University of California, Berkeley, June, 1970.

Rowe, John Howland

1942   *A new pottery style from the Department of Piura, Peru.* Carnegie Institution of Washington, Division of Historical Research, Notes on Middle American Archaeology and Ethnology, vol. I, no. 8, pp. 30-34. Cambridge.

1944   *An introduction to the archaeology of Cuzco.* Papers of the Peabody Museum of American Archaeology and Ethnology, vol. XXVII, no. 2. Cambridge.

1945   *Absolute chronology in the Andean area.* American Antiquity, vol. X, no. 3, January, pp. 265-284. Menasha.

1947   *Inca culture at the time of the Spanish conquest. In* Handbook of South American Indians, Julian H. Steward, ed.; Smithsonian Institution, Bureau of American Ethnology, Bulletin 143, vol. 2, pp. 183-330, pls. 77-84. Washington, D.C.

1948   *The kindgom of Chimor.* Acta Americana, vol. VI, no. 1-2, January-June. Mexico.

1954   *Max Uhle, 1856-1944; a memoir of the father of Peruvian archaeology.* University of California Publications in American Archaeology and Ethnology, vol. 46, no. 1. Berkeley and Los Angeles.

1960   *The origins of Creator worship among the Incas. In* Culture in History: Essays in Honor of Paul Radin, Stanley Diamond, ed., pp. 408-429. Columbia University Press, New York.

1961a   *The chronology of Inca wooden cups. In* Essays in pre-Columbian art and archaeology, by Samuel K. Lothrop and others, pp. 317-341, 473-475, 498-500. Harvard University Press, Cambridge.

1961b   *Stratigraphy and seriation.* American Antiquity, vol. 26, no. 3, January, pp. 324-330. Salt Lake City.

1962a   *Stages and periods in archaeological interpretation.* Southwestern Journal of Anthropology, vol. 18, no. 1, pp. 40-54. Albuquerque. Reprinted in Rowe and Menzel, 1967, pp. 1-15.

1962b   *Worsaae's Law and the use of grave lots for archaeological dating.* American Antiquity, vol. 28, no. 2, October, pp. 129-137. Salt Lake City.

1966   *An interpretation of radiocarbon measurements on archaeological samples from Peru.* Proceedings of the Sixth International Conference, Radiocarbon and Tritium Dating, Washington State University, Pullman, Washington, June 7-11, 1965, pp. 187-198. U.S. Atomic Energy Commission, Division of Technical Information, CONF-650652 Chemistry (TID-4500). Springfield, Virginia. Reprinted in Rowe and Menzel, 1967, pp. 16-30.

Rowe, John Howland

1967   *What kind of a settlement was Inca Cuzco?* Ñawpa Pacha 5, pp. 59-76. Berkeley.

1974   *Kunst in Peru und Bolivien. In* Propyläen Kunstgeschichte, Band XVIII: Das alte Amerika, Gordon R. Willey, ed. Propyläen Verlag, Berlin.

ms   *Standardization in Inca tapestry tunics.* In press.

Rowe, John Howland, and Menzel, Dorothy

1967   *Peruvian archaeology; selected readings.* Peek Publication, Palo Alto.

Schaedel, Richard Paul

1949   *Uncovering a frieze on the Peruvian coast.* Archaeology, vol. 2, no. 2, June, pp. 73-75. Archaeological Institute of America, Cambridge, Massachusetts.

1951a   *Major ceremonial and population centers in northern Peru.* The Civilizations of Ancient America, pp. 232-243. Selected Papers of the XXIXth International Congress of Americanists, New York, Sept. 5-12, 1949, Sol Tax, ed., with an introduction by Wendell C. Bennett. University of Chicago Press, Chicago.

1951b   *Mochica murals at Pañamarca.* Archaeology, vol. 4, no. 3, September, pp. 145-154. Archaeological Institute of America, Cambridge.

1951c   *Wooden idols from Peru.* Archaeology, vol. 4, no. 1, March, pp. 16-22. Archaeological Institute of America, Cambridge.

1957   *Highlights of Andean archaeology, 1954-1956.* Archaeology, vol. 10, no. 2, June, pp. 93-99. Brattleboro.

1967   *The huaca El Dragón.* Journal de la Société des Américanistes, tome LV-2, pp. 383-471. Paris.

Schmidt, Max

1929   *Kunst und Kultur von Peru.* Propyläen-Verlag, Berlin.

Sharon, Douglas, and Donnan, Christopher Bruce

1974   *Shamanism in Moche iconography.* Ethnoarchaeology, Monograph IV, Christopher B. Donnan and C. William Clewlow, Jr., eds., pp. 49-77. Institute of Archaeology, University of California, Los Angeles.

Strong, William Duncan

1925   *The Uhle pottery collections from Ancon.* University of California Publications in American Archaeology and Ethnology, vol. 21, no. 4, pp. i-ii, 135-190. Berkeley.

Stumer, Louis Michael

1959   *Contactos foráneos en la arquitectura [sic: arqueología] de la costa central.* Revista del Museo Nacional, tomo XXVII, 1958, pp. 11-30. Lima.

Ubbelohde-Doering, Heinrich

1951   *Ceramic comparisons of two north coast Peruvian valleys.* The Civilizations of Ancient America, pp. 224-231. Selected Papers of the XXIXth International Congress of Americanists, New York, Sept. 5-12, 1949; Sol Tax, editor, with an introduction by Wendell C. Bennett. The University of Chicago Press, Chicago.

1952   *The art of ancient Peru.* Frederick A. Praeger, New York.

1957   *Der Gallinazo-Stil und die Chronologie der altperuanischen Frühkulturen.* Bayerische Akademie der Wissenschaften, Philosophisch-Historische Klasse, Sitzungsberichte, Heft 9. München.

1959   *Bericht über archäologische Feldarbeiten in Peru.* II. Ethnos, 1-2, pp. 1-32. The Ethnographical Museum of Sweden, Stockholm.

1960   *Bericht über archäologische Feldarbeiten in Peru.* III. Ethnos, 3-4, pp. 153-182. The Ethnographical Museum of Sweden, Stockholm.

1966   *Kulturen Alt-Perus; Reisen und archäologische Forschungen in den Anden Südamerikas.* Verlag Ernst Wasmuth, Tübingen.

Uhle, Max

1903   *Pachacamac; report of the William Pepper, M.D., LL.D. Peruvian Expedition of 1896.* University of Pennsylvania, Philadelphia.

1906   *Aus meinem Bericht über die Ergebnisse meiner Reise nach Südamerika 1899-1901. Ueber die historische Stellung der feinen bunten Gefässe von Ica unter den übrigen prähistorischen Resten von Peru.* Internationaler Amerikanisten-Kongress, Vierzehnte Tagung, Stuttgart 1904, zweite Hälfte, pp. 581-592. Stuttgart, Berlin, Leipzig.

1910   *Ueber die Frühkulturen in der Umgebung von Lima.* Verhandlungen des XVI. Internationalen Amerikanisten-Kongresses, Wien, 9. bis 14. September, 1908. Zweite Hälfte, pp. 347-370. Wien und Leipzig.

1913a   *Die Muschelhügel von Ancon, Peru.* International Congress of Americanists. Proceedings of the XVIII. Session, London, 1912. Part I, pp. 22-45. London.

1913b   *Die Ruinen von Moche.* Journal de la Société des Américanistes, n.s., tome X, fasc. I, pp. 95-117. Paris.

1913c   *Zur Chronologie der alten Culturen von Ica.* Journal de la Société des Américanistes, n.s., tome X, fasc. II, pp. 341-367. Paris.

Uhle, Max

1924a   *Explorations at Chincha.* Edited by A.L. Kroeber. University of California Publications in American Archaeology and Ethnology, vol. 21, no. 2, pp. 57-94. Berkeley.

1924b   *Notes on Ica valley.* Edited by A.L. Kroeber and W.D. Strong. University of California Publications in American Archaeology and Ethnology, vol. 21, no. 3, Appendix A, pp. 121-123. Berkeley.

1924c   *Notes on sites and graves excavated, extracted from catalog [on Ica] of Max Uhle.* "Condensed from comments in the excavator's specimen catalogue." by A.L. Kroeber and W.D. Strong. University of California Publications in American Archaeology and Ethnology, vol. 21, no. 3, Appendix B, pp. 123-127. Berkeley.

1924d   *Ancient civilizations of Ica valley.* Edited by A.L. Kroeber and W.D. Strong. University of California Publications in American Archaeology and Ethnology, vol. 21, no. 3, Appendix C, pp. 128-132. Berkeley.

1925   *Report on explorations at Supe.* [Appendix to A.L. Kroeber, *the Uhle pottery collections from Supe.*] University of California Publications in American Archaeology and Ethnology, vol. 21, no. 6, pp. 257-263. Berkeley.

1926   *Report on explorations at Chancay.* [Appendix to A.L. Kroeber, *The Uhle pottery collections from Chancay.*] University of California Publications in American Archaeology and Ethnology, vol. 21, no. 7, pp. 293-303. Berkeley.

ms   *Field catalogs of Uhle's collections from Peru, made between 1899 and 1905, deposited at the Robert H. Lowie Museum of Anthropology,* University of California, Berkeley. 10 vols.

Van Stan, Ina

1967   *Textiles from beneath the Temple of Pachacamac, Peru; a part of the Uhle collection of The University Museum, University of Pennsylvania.* Museum Monographs, the University of Pennsylvania, Philadelphia.

West, Michael

1970   *Community settlement patterns at Chan Chan, Peru.* American Antiquity, vol. 35, no. 1, January, pp. 74-86. Salt Lake City.

Willey, Gordon Randolph

1943   *A supplement to the pottery sequence at Ancon.* Columbia Studies in Archeology and Ethnology, vol. I, no. 4, pp. i-iv, 201-211. Columbia University Press, New York.

Willey, Gordon Randolph

1947   *Archaeology. A Middle Period cemetery in the Virú Valley, northern Peru.* Journal of the Washington Academy of

Sciences, vol. 37, no. 2, February 15, pp. 41-47. Washington.

1953   *Prehistoric settlement patterns in the Virú Valley, Perú.* Smithsonian Institution, Bureau of American Ethnology, Bulletin 155. Washington.

Yacovleff, Eugenio Nicándrevich

1932   *Las falcónidas en el arte y en las creencias de los antiguos peruanos.* Revista del Museo Nacional, tomo I, no. 1, pp. 33-111. Lima.

Yacovleff, Eugenio Nicándrevich, and Herrera, Fortunato Luciano

1934-   *El mundo vegetal de los antiguos peruanos.* Revista del
1935   Museo Nacional, tomo III, no. 3, pp. 241-322; tomo IV, no. 1, I semestre 1935, pp. 29-102. Lima.

Maps and Chronological Table

Chronological Table: Peruvian Archaeology (shaded areas indicate time ranges represented by Uhle specimens in Lowie Museum collections)

Key to Illustrations

Unless otherwise indicated, specimens are from the collections of the Robert H. Lowie Museum of Anthropology, Berkeley (RHLMA). A few pieces are from the Museo Nacional de Antropología y Arqueología, Lima, Peru (MNAA) and the American Museum of Natural History, New York (AMNH). The period and epoch designations are abbreviated as follows: Late Horizon (LH), Late Intermediate Period (LIP #), Middle Horizon (MH #) and Early Intermediate Period (EIP #).

Chapter 2

Fig. 1. 4-7993. Imperial Inca style, high-necked jar; Cuzco; LH. 1 m. high (see also Rowe, 1974, pl. 432a).

Fig. 2. 4-7995. Imperial Inca style, wide-mouthed jar; Cuzco; LH. 57 cm. high (see also Rowe, 1974, pl. 432b).

Fig. 3A. 4-5369. Imperial Inca style, faceneck jar; Ica Valley, Old Ica, Site T, Bur. Tk; LH. 17.6 cm. high (see also Rowe, 1974, pl. 430).

Fig. 3B. 4-5387. Imperial Inca style, bottle; Ica Valley, Old Ica, Site T, Bur. Tk; LH. 13.7 cm. high.

Fig. 4. 4-5096. Imperial Inca style, wooden drinking cup (tumbler); Ica Valley, Old Ica, Site T, Bur. Tf; LH. 20.4 cm. high.

Fig. 5. 4-8325. Imperial Inca style, man's tunic; Acarí Valley, Chaviña; LH. 83.8 cm. x 71 cm.

Fig. 6. 4-4348. Pottery vessel representing a man wearing an Inca tunic, drinking from a cup; Ica Valley, Old Ica, Site M, from disturbed burial above Ica 3A tomb M-1; LH. 15.3 cm. high.

Chapter 3

Fig. 7. 4-5010. Inca style, wooden stool, seat of a nobleman; Ica Valley, Old Ica, Site T, Tomb Td-8; LH. Supports and central part of the seat 10 cm. high, rim of seat 11.8 cm. high.

Fig. 8A. 4-5016. Painted wooden figures that ornamented the top of a ceremonial digging board; Ica Valley, Old Ica, Site T, Tomb Td-8; LH. 24 cm. wide.

Fig. 8B. 4-5013. Gold sheathing of wooden bird (wood decayed) that ornamented the top of a ceremonial digging board; Ica Valley, Old Ica, Site T, Tomb Td-8; LH. 16.5 cm. long.

Fig. 9. 4-4663. Ceremonial wooden digging board; Ica Valley, Ullujaya; LH. 1.69 m. high.

Fig. 10. 4-5382. Ceremonial wooden digging board; Ica Valley, Old Ica, Site T, Bur. Tk; LH. 2.02 m. high.

Fig. 11. 4-5047. Gold plume holder; Ica Valley, Old Ica, Site T, Tomb Td-8; LH. 7.1 cm. high.

Fig. 12. Pottery ocarinas; Ica Valley, Old Ica, Site T; LH. A. 4-5048. Tomb Td-8. 11 cm. long. B. 4-5335. Tomb Ti-5. 11 cm. long.

Fig. 13. AMNH 41.0-1625. Pottery flute; Ica Valley; LH. ca. 22 cm. long. Photo courtesy of the American Museum of Natural History.

Fig. 14. 4-5051. Set of wooden gaming sticks; Ica Valley, Old Ica, Site T, Tomb Td-8; LH. Longest pieces 14.6 cm.

Fig. 15. 4-4991. "Container" or "purse" cloth; Ica Valley, Old Ica, Site T, retainer bur. Td-1; LH. 59 cm. x 51.5 cm. (see also O'Neale and Kroeber, 1930, pl. 35c).

Fig. 16. 4-4990. Woman's belt *(mamachumpi);* Ica Valley, Old Ica, Site T, retainer bur. Td-1; LH. Length of broad section without end cords, 67 cm.

Fig. 17. Provincial Inca A style, high-necked jars; Ica Valley, Old Ica, Site T, Tomb Td-8; LH. A. 4-5019, 47.5 cm. high; B. 4-5024, 16.5 cm. high.

Fig. 18. 4-5370. Provincial Inca A style, plate; Ica Valley, Old Ica, Site T, Bur. Tk; LH. 19 cm. diam. Two nearly identical plates, less well preserved, were found in tomb Td-8.

Fig. 19. 4-5043b. Provincial Inca A style, cooking pot; Ica Valley, Old Ica, Site T, Tomb Td-8; LH. 8 cm. high.

Fig. 20. 4-4998. Provincial Inca style, wide-mouthed jar; Ica Valley, Old Ica, Site T, retainer bur. Td-1; LH. 12.5 cm. high.

Fig. 21. 4-5041. Imitation Provincial Inca A style, plate; Ica Valley, Old Ica, Site T, Tomb Td-8; LH. 12.7 cm. diam.

Fig. 22. 4-4977b. Ica 9, "Angular-Rim Bowl;" Ica Valley, Old Ica, Site T, sacrificial bur. Tb; LH. 10.5 cm. high.

Fig. 23. 4-5028. Ica-Inca A style, "Lamp Bottle;" Ica Valley, Old Ica Site T, Tomb Td-8; LH. 11.75 cm. high.

Fig. 24. 4-5027. Ica-Inca A style, "Drum Bottle;" Ica Valley, Old Ica, Site T, Tomb Td-8; LH. 13.5 cm. high.

Fig. 25A. 4-5011. Ica 9, incised blackware, "Angular-Rim Dish;" Ica Valley, Old Ica, Site T, Tomb Td-8; LH. 6.4 cm. high.

Fig. 25B. 4-4997. Ica 9, incised blackware, "Angular-Rim Bowl;" Ica Valley, Old Ica, Site T, retainer bur. Td-1; LH. 10.9 cm. high.

Fig. 26. 4-4984. Gold mask for the dead; Ica Valley, Old Ica, Site T, Tomb Tc; LH. 14 cm. high.

Fig. 27A, B. 4-4982, 4983. Gold beakers; Ica Valley, Old Ica, Site T, Tomb Tc; LH. A. 15 cm. high; B. 16.5 cm. high (see also Rowe, 1974, pl. LIII right, color).

Fig. 28. 4-4985. Gold dish; Ica Valley, Old Ica, Site T, Tomb Tc; LH. 13.3 cm. rim diam.

Fig. 29. 4-5252. Ica 6, gold mask for the dead; Ica Valley, Old Ica, Site T, Tomb Th-1; LIP 6. 16.3 cm. high.

Fig. 30. 4-5254. Ica 6, gold beaker; Ica Valley, Old Ica, Site T, Tomb Th-1; LIP 6. 19 cm. high (see also Rowe, 1974, pl. LIII left, color).

Fig. 31A. 4-5255. Ica 6, gold drinking cup (tumbler). 11.8 cm. high. Both this piece and the following, are from Ica Valley, Old Ica, Site 1, Tomb Th-1; LIP 6.

Fig. 31B. 4-5272. Ica 6, silver tumbler. 11.1 cm. high.

Fig. 32A, B. 4-5154, 5145. Ica 6, "Simple Bottles;" Ica Valley, Old Ica, Site T, Tomb Th-1; LIP 6. A. 15.7 cm. high; B. 24.4 cm. high.

Fig. 33. 4-5202. Ica 6, "Deep Open Dish;" Ica Valley, Old Ica, Site T, Tomb Th-1; LIP 6. 6.7 cm. high.

Fig. 34. 4-5320-21, 5323-29. Ica 6, family group portrayal, unbaked clay figurines; Ica Valley, Old Ica, Site T, Tomb Tg; LIP 6. Tallest figurine 12.75 cm. high.

Chapter 4

Fig. 35. Aerial view of Chanchan, capital of the Kingdom of Chimor; section of core of city, view from seaward side inland toward the southeast. Photo #334879 by Robert Shippee and Lt. George R. Johnson (Johnson, 1930).

Fig. 36. Provincial Inca jars, north coast style; Moche, Site B; LH. A. 4-6, 18 cm. high; B. 4-42, 22 cm. high.

Fig. 37. 4-9142. Provincial Inca jar, north coast style; coast north of Lima; LH. 19 cm. high.

Fig. 38. Chimu-Inca style, bottles with handles; LH. A. 4-110. Moche, Site B; 19 cm. high. B. 4-7585. Pativilca Valley, Olivar; 18.5 cm. high.

Fig. 39. 4-27. Chimu-Inca style, double-chambered whistling bottle, cream ware; Moche, Site B; LH. 17.6 cm. high.

Fig. 40. 4-5394. Chimu-Inca style, double-chambered whistling bottle, smoked blackware; Ica Valley, Old Ica, Site T, Bur. Tk; LH. 19.2 cm. high.

Fig. 41. Man carrying large fish. Photo taken by Lonnie Wilson, staff photographer of the Oakland Tribune, at the port of Belén, near Iquitos, upper Amazon, eastern Peru. Photo appeared in the Oakland Tribune, Thursday, July 4, 1974. Reproduced by permission of Lonnie Wilson.

Fig. 42. 4-109. Chimu style, double-chambered whistling bottle; Moche, Site B; LH. 17.7 cm. high to top of bird head.

Fig. 43. 4-2489. Chimu style, animal-head bottle; Moche, Site B; LH. 15.4 cm. diam.

Fig. 44. Chimu style, stirrup-spout bottles; Moche, Site B; LH. A. 4-11, 18 cm. high; B. 4-2499, 21.8 cm. high.

Fig. 45. 4-7412. False wooden mummy head; Supe Valley, Chimu Capac; MH. 17.5 cm. high, incl. neck.

Fig. 46A-C. Provincial Huari style, pottery tumblers; Supe Valley, Chimu Capac, Bur. 6; MH 2B. A. 4-7665, 17.5 cm. high; B. 4-7662, 17.8 cm. high; C. 4-7663, 15.5 cm. high.

Fig. 47. 4-7353. Provincial Huari style, pottery tumbler; Supe Valley, Chimu Capac; MH 2B. 12 cm. high.

Fig. 48A, B. Provincial Huari style, pottery tumblers; Supe Valley, Chimu Capac; MH 2B. A. 4-7664, Bur. 6, 13 cm. high; B. 4-7636, Bur. 5, 12 cm. high.

Fig. 49. 4-7378a. Provincial Huari style, cup; Supe Valley, Chimu Capac; MH 2B. 9.8 cm. high.

Fig. 50. 4-7632. Provincial Huari style, double-spout bottle; Supe Valley, Chimu Capac, Bur. 5; MH 2B. 14.7 cm. high.

Fig. 51. 4-7615. Provincial Huari style, double-spout bottle; Supe Valley, Chimu Capac; MH 2B. 18 cm. high.

Fig. 52. 4-2572a, b. Provincial Huari style, fragments of a double-spout bottle as in fig. 51; a. Small modeled head from top of bridge; b. Part of bridge; Moche, Site A; MH 2B. Head 5.2 cm. high.

Fig. 53. 4-7660. Provincial north coast style, jar depicting woman with child; Supe Valley, Chimu Capac, Bur. 6; MH 2B. 17.5 cm. high.

Fig. 54. 4-7742. Provincial Huari style, double-spout bottle; Supe Valley, Chimu Capac; MH 2B. 14.5 cm. high, 13 cm. diam.

Fig. 55. 4-7634. Provincial north coast style, jar; Supe Valley, Chimu Capac, Bur. 5; MH 2B. 12 cm. high.

Fig. 56. 4-7834. Painted cloth; Supe Valley, Chimu Capac; prob. MH 3. 1.10 m. x .74 m.

Fig. 57. 4-7221. Painted cloth; Supe Valley, Chimu Capac; prob. MH 3. 1.7 m. x .895 m.

Fig. 58. 4-7282. Painted cloth; Supe Valley, Chimu Capac; prob. MH 3. 1.38 m. x .56 m.

Fig. 59. 4-7138. Painted cloth; Supe Valley, Chimu Capac; prob. MH 3. 1.6 m. x .67 m.

Fig. 60. 4-7801. Jar, flask-shaped body; Supe Valley, Chimu Capac; MH 3. 26.3 cm. high.

Fig. 61. 4-7801. Same as fig. 60, opposite face.

Fig. 62. MNAA. Conchopata style, Huari Deity, traced from painting on fragments of rim of large offering urns; near city of Ayacucho, suburb of Conchopata; MH 1A. ½ size.

Fig. 63. MNAA. Conchopata style, Huari Star Animal, traced from painting on fragments of rim of large offering urns; near city of Ayacucho, suburb of Conchopata; MH 1A. ½ size.

Fig. 64. 4-7751. Jar representing house with deity couple; Supe Valley, Chimu Capac; MH 3. 25 cm. high.

Fig. 65. 4-7800. Jar, flask-shaped body; Supe Valley, Chimu Capac; MH 3. 22 cm. diam.

Fig. 66. MNAA. Conchopata style, Huari Walking Angel (Angel D), traced from painting on fragments of rim of large offering urns; near city of Ayacucho, suburb of Conchopata; MH 1A. ½ size.

Fig. 67. MNAA. Conchopata style, Huari Feline-headed Angel (Angel A), traced from painting on fragments of rim of large offering urns; near city of Ayacucho, suburb of Conchopata; MH 1A. ½ size.

Fig. 68. 4-7799. Faceneck jar, mythical figure; Supe Valley, Chimu Capac; MH 3. 34.5 cm. high.

Fig. 69A. 4-7850. Mythical serpent, wood carving; Supe Valley, Chimu Capac; prob. MH 3. 23 cm. long.

Fig. 69B. 4-7641. Mythical serpent, wood carving; Supe Valley, Chimu Capac, Bur. 5; MH 2B. 13.7 cm. long.

Fig. 70. 4-7414b. Pyro-engraved gourd, design in provincial Huari style; Supe Valley, Chimu Capac; MH 2A or 1B. 5.5 cm. high.

Fig. 71. 4-7067b. Pyro-engraved gourd; Supe Valley, Chimu Capac, Bur. 2; MH 4. 5 cm. high.

Fig. 72. 4-7638. Ceremonial club, Janus-headed, Supe Valley, Chimu Capac, Bur. 5; MH 2B. 74 cm. long.

Fig. 73. 4-7234. Ceremonial club; Supe Valley, Chimu Capac; prob. MH 3. 49 cm. long.

Fig. 74. 4-7770. Lime container, carved wood with inlays; Supe Valley, Chimu Capac; MH. 21.8 cm. long.

Fig. 75. 4-7771. Huari style, man's tunic; Supe Valley, Chimu Capac; prob. late MH 2B. 1.4 m. x .98 m.

Fig. 76. 4-7827. Sleeved man's tunic; Supe Valley, Chimu Capac; prob. late MH 2B. 1.73 m. x .955 m.

Fig. 76A. Detail from tapestry band across chest of tunic in fig. 76.

Fig. 76B. Detail from tapestry band at lower border, opposite side of tunic in fig. 76. The designs on this side are oriented in reverse direction to the other side. Note that the border figs. are in upside-down view.

Fig. 77. 4-7701c. Sleeve from tunic like that in fig. 76 in form; Supe Valley, Chimu Capac; MH 2. 22 cm. x 16 cm.

Fig. 78. Aerial view of the site of Moche, looking east. The Cerro Blanco ("White Hill") is in the background, with the "Pyramid of the Moon" at its base; the "Pyramid of the Sun" is in the foreground, near the Moche River. Shippee-Johnson photo # 334908 (Johnson, 1930).

Fig. 79. Aerial view of the site of Moche, looking northwest, showing the "Pyramid of the Sun," with the Moche River and cultivated river plain in the background. Shippee-Johnson photo # 334913 (Johnson, 1930).

Fig. 80. 4-2633b. Moche IV, modeled pottery head from the top of a bottle, depicting a Moche Lord; Moche, Site A; EIP 8-MH 1A. 8.95 cm. high.

Fig. 81A. 16-13778. Chimu style, deity figure; from "near Lambayeque;" MH. 15.4 cm. high (see also Rowe, 1974, pl. 419).

Fig. 81B. 4-2529. Chimu style, bottle, face-spout representing Chimu deity; Pacasmayo Valley; MH. 20.5 cm. high.

Fig. 82. 4-2580d. Whistle or trumpet fragment, showing body of Chimu deity; Moche, Site A; prob. MH 2. 7 cm. wide.

Fig. 83. 4-2580f. Trumpet fragment, showing Chimu deity head; Moche, Site A; prob. MH 2. 5.4 cm. wide.

Fig. 84. 4-2579d. Trumpet fragment, showing part of Chimu deity head; Moche, Site A; prob. MH 2. 13 cm. long.

Fig. 85. 4-2579a. Trumpet fragment, showing headdress of Chimu deity head; Moche, Site A; prob. MH 2. 13.5 cm. long.

Fig. 86. 4-2581a. Whistle fragment, showing Chimu deity head; Moche, Site A; prob. MH 2. Headdress 4 cm. wide.

Fig. 87. 4-2620. Gold clasp of necklace with blue stone inlay, prob. Moche IV; Moche, Site A, Cache 1; prob. EIP 8—MH 1A. 4.3 cm. high (see also Rowe, 1974, pl. XLVIa, color).

Fig. 88. 4-2621. Hollow gold figure with blue stone inlay, prob. Moche IV; Moche, Site A, Cache 1 (with fig. 87); prob. EIP 8—MH 1A. 4.5 cm. high.

Fig. 89. 4-2594. Provincial Huari style, fragmentary band depicting Huari Feline-headed Angel (Angel A); Moche, Site A; MH 1B. Band 8 cm. wide.

Fig. 90. 4-2603. Provincial Huari style, fragment of wooden tumbler, bottom to rim section complete, design prob. depicting part of a Huari Floating Angel (Angel B or C); Moche, Site A; MH 1B. 9.4 cm. high.

Fig. 91. MNAA. Conchopata style, Huari Floating Angels (Angels B and C), traced from painting on fragments of rim of large offering urns; near city of Ayacucho, suburb of Conchopata; MH 1A. ½ size.

Fig. 92. 4-2530. Provincial Huari style, reconstructed pottery tumbler; Moche, Site A; MH 2. 22.2 cm. high.

Fig. 93. 4-2552a. Provincial Huari style, fragment of pottery tumbler; Moche, Site A; MH 2. 9.3 cm. x 9 cm.

Fig. 94. 4-2538. Chimu style, jar, flask-shaped body; Moche, Site A; MH 2B or 3. 16 cm. high.

Fig. 95. 4-2537. Provincial Huari style, bottle shape; Moche, Site A; prob. MH 2. 17 cm. high.

Fig. 96. 4-2232. Carved wooden figure representing litter bearer, remnants of shell inlays; Moche, Site H; prob. MH 3. 56.5 cm. high.

Fig. 97. Map of the Ancón Necropolis. Copied with modifications from Strong, 1925, pl. 41. Strong's map is a slightly modified copy of Uhle's map in Uhle, 1913a, p. 24, fig. 2.

Fig. 98. Middle Horizon mummy bales from the Ancón Necropolis, from Reiss and Stübel, 1880-1887, vol. I, pl. 14-1.

Fig. 99. 4-5939. Pottery tumbler with a hole in the bottom, offering from upper level of Tomb P-5; Ancón Necropolis, Site P; MH 3. 15.5 cm. high.

Fig. 100. 4-6154. Teatino style, jar, flask-shaped body; Ancón Necropolis, Site P, Tomb P-21; prob. MH 2B. 19.5 cm. high.

Fig. 101. 4-6149. Teatino style, jar, tambourine-shaped body; Ancón Necropolis, Site P, Tomb P-21; prob. MH 2B. 20 cm. high.

Fig. 102. 4-6119. Teatino style, bowl; Ancón Necropolis, Site P, Tomb P-19; prob. very late MH 2B. 19.4 cm. diam.

Fig. 103. 4-5965. Provincial Nievería style, bowl with pouring spout and handle; Ancón Necropolis, Site P, Bur. P-7; MH 1B. 12 cm. high (for a Nievería-style vessel of the same shape from the Nievería cemetery in the Rimac Valley, see Rowe, 1974, pl. 400).

Fig. 104. 4-9304. Nievería style, handled bottle; Rimac Valley, Nievería cemetery; MH 1B. 16.6 cm. high.

Fig. 105. 4-9247. Nievería style, double-spout bottle; Rimac Valley, Nievería cemetery; MH 1B. 16.7 cm. high.

Fig. 106. 4-6035. Pachacamac-Huari style, faceneck jar; Ancón Necropolis, Site P, Tomb P-17; MH 2B. 20.3 cm. high.

Fig. 107. 4-6033. Pachacamac-Huari style, modeled figure bottle, depicting coca chewer; Ancón Necropolis, Site P, Tomb P-17; MH 2B. 17 cm. high.

Fig. 108. 4-6036. Derived Nievería style, handled bottle; Ancón Necropolis, Site P, Tomb P-17; MH 2B. 18.5 cm. high.

Fig. 109A. 4-6142. Provincial (north coast) Huari style, faceneck jar, body representing *Spondylus* shell; Ancón Necropolis, Site P, Bur. P-20; early MH 2B. 18.5 cm. diam.

Fig. 109B. 4-2356. *Spondylus* shell half; Moche, Site H; 10 cm. top to bottom.

Fig. 110. 4-6141. Provincial Huari style, jar, flask-shaped body, neck missing; Ancón Necropolis, Site P, Bur. P-20; early MH 2B. 17.3 cm. high.

Fig. 111. 4-6196. Jar, flask-shaped body; Ancón Necropolis, Site P, Tomb P-24; MH 3. 21 cm. high.

Fig. 112. 4-5710. White-slipped faceneck jar, modified *Spondylus* shell body; Ancón Necropolis, Site T, Tomb T-7; MH 4. 18.5 cm. body diam.

Fig. 113. Jars; Ancón Necropolis, Site T; MH 4. A. 4-5660, Tomb T-14, 18.8 cm. high; B. 4-5648, Tomb T-1, 23.5 cm. high.

Fig. 114. 4-5991a. Pachacamac-Inca style, part of modeled figure jar; Ancón Necropolis, Site P, surface; LH. 17.2 cm. high.

Fig. 115. 4-5810. Cloth painting on grave tablet; Ancón Necropolis, Site H, Bur. H-2; prob. MH 3 or 4. 22.5 cm. x 19.5 cm.

Fig. 116. 4-5718. Carved wooden ornament, front of ear plug; Ancón Necropolis, Site T, Tomb T-7; MH 4. 7.9 cm. diam.

Fig. 117. 4-5669a. Wooden balance beam; Ancón Necropolis, Site T, Tomb T-14; MH 4. 3.4 cm. high (see also Rowe, 1974, pl. 415).

Fig. 118. 4-5716. Hollow pottery figurine; Ancón Necropolis, Site T, Tomb T-7; MH 4. 19 cm. high.

Chapter 5

Fig. 119. 4-9015c, d. Modeled face fragments of large tumbler, sacred Huari offering ("Robles Moqo") style; from "cemetery near Soisongo" (Fundo Pacheco), ravine of Nasca; MH 1B. 17.5 cm. wide.

Fig. 120. MNAA. Robles Moqo style, large tumbler, Huari offering; Fundo Pacheco, Hacienda Soisongo, ravine of Nasca, from excavations directed by Julio C. Tello, 1927; MH 1B. 58 cm. high. From color slide by D. Menzel.

Fig. 121. 4-9015a, b. Robles Moqo style, fragments of large handled urns with plant designs, Huari offering; from "cemetery near Soisongo" (Fundo Pacheco), ravine of Nasca; MH 1B. 12.5 cm. and 13. cm., respectively.

Fig. 122. AMNH 41.0-5314. Robles Moqo style, large handled urn, Huari offering; Fundo Pacheco, Hacienda Soisongo, ravine of Nasca; MH 1B. 65 cm. high. Photo courtesy of The American Museum of Natural History, New York.

Fig. 123. AMNH 41.0-5314. Interior view of the urn shown in fig. 122. From color slide by D. Menzel.

Fig. 124. 4-9052. Short, sleeveless man's tunic, provincial Huari decoration; Hacienda Las Trancas, ravine of Tunga, Nasca drainage; MH 2A. 128 cm. wide.

Fig. 124a. 4-9052. Design detail of tunic shown in fig. 124.

Fig. 125. MNAA. Robles Moqo style, double-chambered vessel, Huari offering; Fundo Pacheco, Hacienda Soisongo, ravine of Nasca, from excavations directed by Julio C. Tello, 1927; MH 1B. 14 cm. high. From color slide by D. Menzel.

Fig. 126. 4-9017. Nasca 9B, jar; Nasca drainage; MH 1B. 15.7 cm. high.

Fig. 127. 4-8786. Pouch (seams torn), provincial Huari design; from "cemetery near Cahuachi" (hacienda), ravine of Nasca; MH 2A. Pouch sides 10.5 cm. x 18 cm.

Fig. 128. 4-9029. Provincial Huari style, miniature lime container of bone and wood; Nasca drainage; prob. MH 1B. 4 cm. long.

Fig. 129. MNAA. Robles Moqo style, portrait head from large faceneck jar, Huari offering; Fundo Pacheco, Hacienda Soisongo, ravine of Nasca, from excavations directed by Julio C. Tello, 1927; MH 1B. Face 10 cm. high. From color slide by D. Menzel.

Fig. 130. 4-4556. Provincial Huari style, large religious tapestry fragment; Ica Valley, Ocucaje, Site E; MH 1B or 2A. 92.5 cm. x 52 cm.

Fig. 131. 16-11053. Ica 1A, jar with flask-shaped body, archaizing shape and design; ravine of Tunga, Nasca drainage; LIP 1A. 17.8 cm. high (see also Rowe, 1974, pl. 422).

Fig. 132. 16-10064. Ica 1A, jar, archaizing design; Ica Valley; LIP 1A. 16 cm. body diam.

Fig. 133. 4-4866. Ica 3B, pouch; Ica Valley, Old Ica, Hacienda Galagarza, Site Z, Bur. Z-4; LIP 3B. 25.5 cm. x 27 cm.

Fig. 134. 4-4312. Ica 3A, double-chambered vessel, offering from upper level of a deep tomb; Ica Valley, Old Ica, Chulpaca, Site M, Tomb M-1; LIP 3A. Tumbler 12.2 cm. high.

Fig. 135. MNAA. Robles Moqo style, double-chambered vessel, Huari offering; Fundo Pacheco, Hacienda Soisongo, ravine of Nasca, from excavations directed by Julio C. Tello, 1927; MH 1B. 14.5 cm. high. From color slide by D. Menzel.

Fig. 136. 4-3913. Chincha style, jar; Chincha Valley, Old Chincha, Site E, Bur. E-3; LIP 8. 25 cm. body diam. (see also Rowe, 1974, pl. 427).

Chapter 6

Fig. 137. 4-2682. Moche IIIB, stirrup-spout bottle, depiction of Aloof Lord; Moche, Site F, Bur. F-3; ca. EIP 6. 24 cm. high to top of figure head.

Fig. 138. 4-2942. Moche IIIB, stirrup-spout bottle, depiction of Crab Lord; Moche, Site F, Bur. F-12; ca. EIP 6. 22 cm. high to top of figure head (see also Rowe, 1974, pl. 393).

Fig. 139. 4-2994. Moche II, stirrup-spout bottle, depiction of Moon Animal; Moche, Site F, Bur. F-14; ca. EIP 4-5. 21.5 cm. high.

Fig. 140. 4-3273. Moche IIIB, stirrup-spout bottle, depiction of Moon Spirit Man; Moche, Site F, Bur. F-26, ca. EIP 6. 21.5 cm. high.

Fig. 141. 4-2977. Moche IIIB, modeled pottery vessel of smoked blackware depicting winged Moon Spirit Man; Moche, Site F, Bur. F-12; ca. EIP 6. 19.7 cm. high.

Fig. 142. 4-3185. Moche IV, whistle, depiction of Moon Spirit Man as trumpeter; Moche, Site F, Bur. F-23; EIP8—MH 1A. 12.5 cm. high.

Fig. 143. 4-2776a, b. Prob. Moche IV, whistle, Spirit Man as trumpeter; Moche, Site F, cache in front of "Pyramid of the Moon;" prob. EIP 8—MH 1A. 16.8 cm. high.

Fig. 144. 4-2956. Moche IIIB, stirrup-spout bottle, seated man in informal dress; Moche, Site F, Bur. F-12; ca. EIP 6. 14.8 cm. height of figure.

Fig. 145. 4-2948. Moche IIIB, stirrup-spout bottle, woman with child, in informal dress; Moche, Site F, Bur. F-12; ca. EIP 6. 13 cm. height of figure.

Fig. 146. 4-2964. Moche IIIB, jar in form of man taking lime for coca chewing from a container; Moche, Site F, Bur. F-12; ca. EIP 6. 18.5 cm. high.

Fig. 147. 4-2837. Moche III, jar with portrait head, showing man with coca bag in one hand, lime container in the other; Moche, Site F; ca. EIP 6. 31 cm. high.

Fig. 148. 4-2693. Moche IIIC, stirrup-spout bottle depicting theme of weary traveler; Moche, Site F, Bur. F-5; ca. EIP 6-7. 26 cm. high.

Fig. 149. 4-2938. Moche IIIB, stirrup-spout bottle, "Single Man" or "Single Woman" spirit curer with sick child; Moche, Site F, Bur. F-12; ca. EIP 6. 18 cm. to top of figure.

Maps and Chronological Table

Scale 1:24,000,000

Map 1   The Extent of the Inca Empire, 1532

After Rowe, American Antiquity, Volume. X, No. 3 January 1945, p. 273, Menasha, Wisconsin.

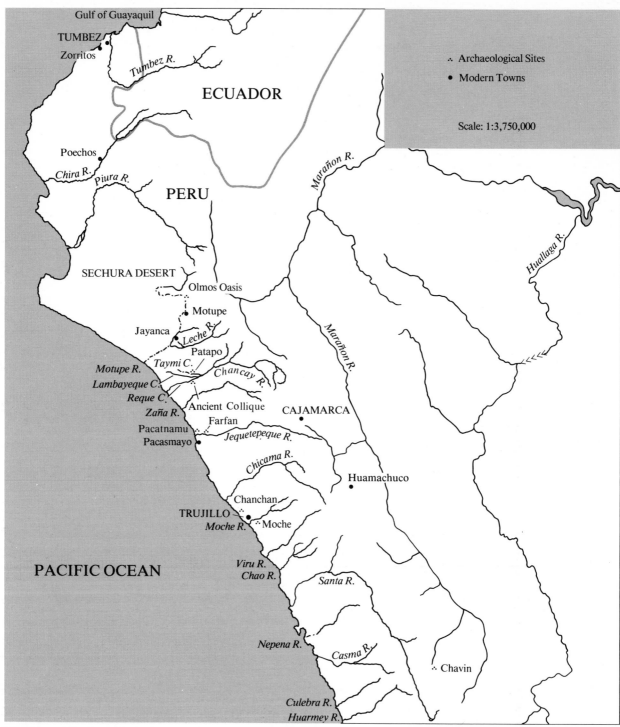

Map 2a The North Coast of Peru

86

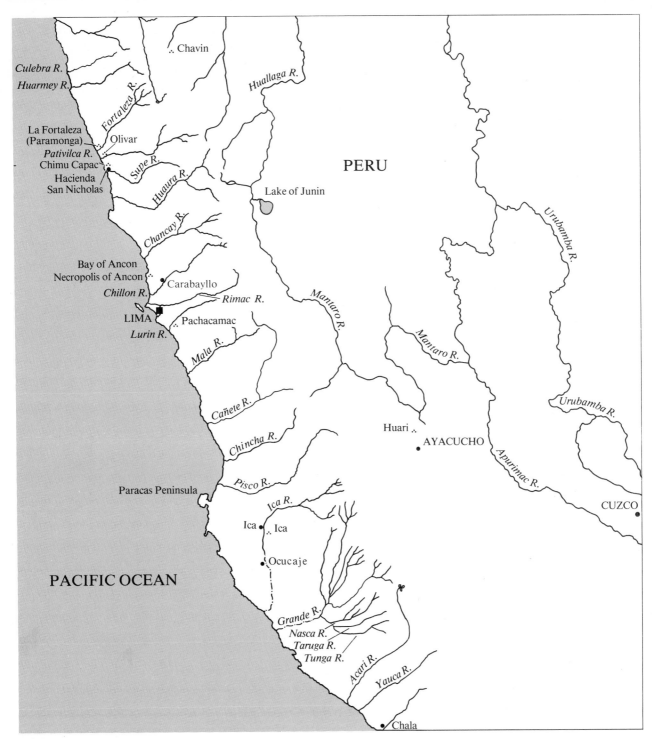

Map 2b   The Central and South Coast of Peru

87

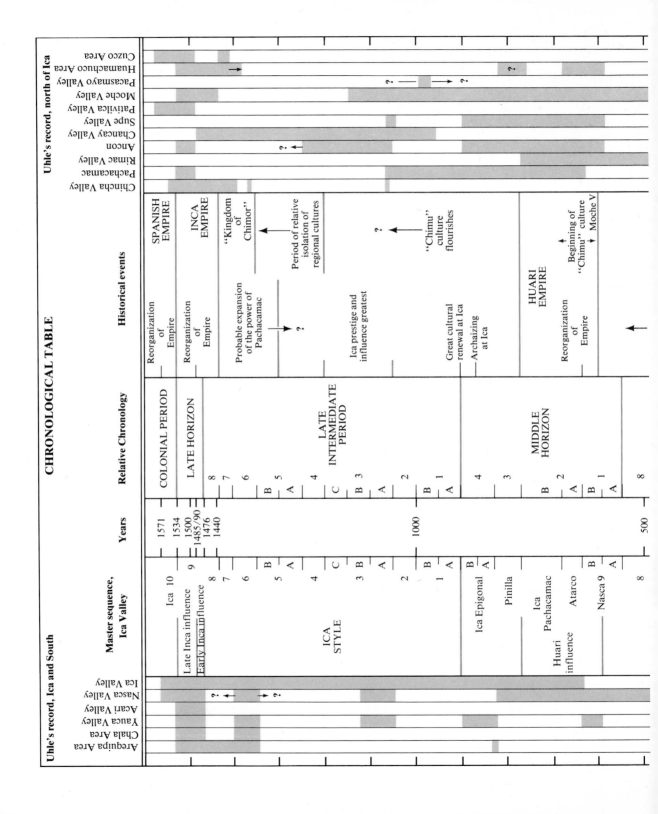

CHRONOLOGICAL TABLE

Illustrations

Fig. 1. Imperial Inca-style jar, Cuzco, LH.

Fig. 2. Imperial Inca-style jar, Cuzco, LH.

Fig. 3A. Imperial Inca-style jar, Ica, LH.

Fig. 3B. Imperial Inca-style bottle, Ica, LH.

Fig. 4. Imperial Inca-style tumbler, Ica, LH.

Fig. 6. Provincial Inca-style vessel, Ica, LH.

Fig. 5. Imperial Inca-style man's tunic, Acarí, LH.

Fig. 7. Imperial Inca-style wooden stool, Ica, LH.

Fig. 8A. Wooden ornaments of ceremonial digging board, Ica, LH.

Fig. 8B. Gold ornament of ceremonial digging board, Ica, LH.

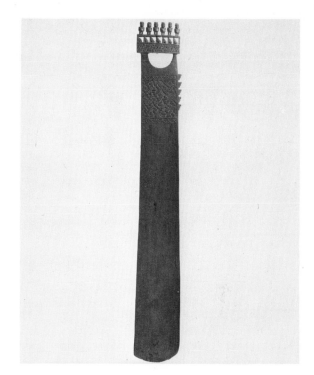

Fig. 9. Ceremonial digging board, Ica, LH.

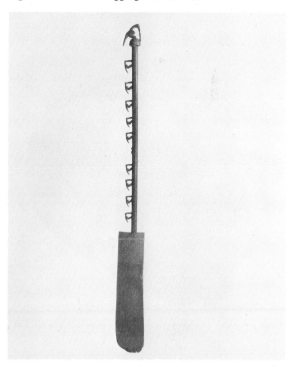

Fig. 10. Ceremonial digging board, Ica, LH.

93

Fig. 11. Gold plume holder, Ica, LH.

Fig. 13. Pottery flute, Ica, LH.

Fig. 12. Pottery ocarinas, Ica, LH.

Fig. 14. Gaming sticks, Ica, LH.

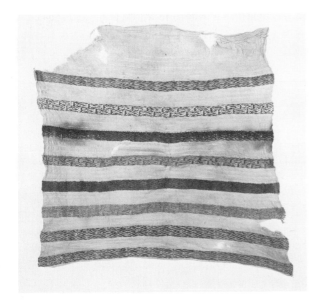

Fig. 15. ''Purse'' cloth, Ica, LH.

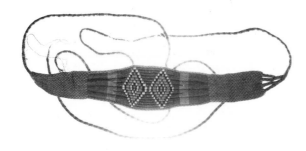

Fig. 16. Woman's belt, Ica, LH.

Fig. 17A. Provincial Inca-style jar, Ica, LH.

Fig. 17B. Provincial Inca-style jar, Ica, LH.

Fig. 18. Provincial Inca-style plate, Ica, LH.

Fig. 19. Provincial Inca-style cooking pot, Ica, LH.

Fig. 20. Provincial Inca-style jar, Ica, LH.

Fig. 21. Imitation provincial Inca-style plate, Ica, LH.

Fig. 22. Ica 9-style bowl, Ica, LH.

Fig. 23. Ica-Inca-style bottle, Ica, LH.

Fig. 24. Ica-Inca-style bottle, Ica, LH.

Fig. 26. Gold mask for the dead, Ica, LH.

Fig. 25A. Ica 9-style dish, incised blackware, Ica, LH.

Fig. 25B. Ica 9-style bowl, incised blackware, Ica, LH.

Fig. 27A,B. Gold beakers, Ica, LH.

Fig. 28. Gold dish, Ica, LH.

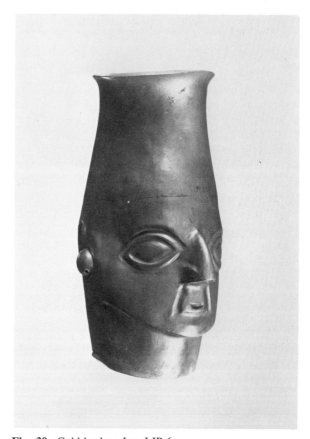

Fig. 30. Gold beaker, Ica, LIP 6.

Fig. 29. Gold mask for the dead, Ica, LIP 6.

Fig. 31A. Gold tumbler, Ica, LIP 6.

Fig. 32A. Ica 6-style bottle, Ica, LIP 6.

Fig. 31B. Silver tumbler, Ica, LIP 6.

Fig. 32B. Ica 6-style bottle, Ica, LIP 6.

Fig. 33. Ica 6-style dish, Ica, LIP 6.

Fig. 34. Family group of figurines, Ica, LIP 6.

Fig. 35. Part of ancient city of Chanchan, north coast.

Fig. 36A. Provincial Inca-style jar, Moche, LH.

Fig. 36B. Provincial Inca-style jar, Moche, LH.

100

Fig. 38A. Chimu-Inca-style bottle, Moche, LH.

Fig. 37. Provincial Inca-style jar, north coast, LH.

Fig. 38B. Chimu-Inca-style bottle, Pativilca, LH.

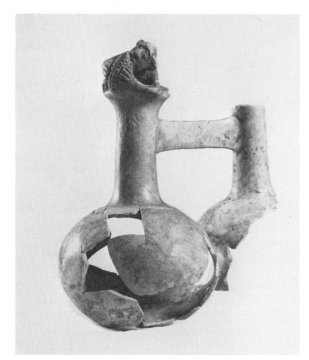

Fig. 39. Chimu-Inca-style bottle, Moche, LH.

Fig. 41. Photo by Lonnie Wilson, taken at Belén, eastern Peru.

Fig. 40. Chimu-Inca-style bottle, Ica, LH.

102

Fig. 42. Chimu-style bottle, Moche, LH.

Fig. 44A. Chimu-style bottle, Moche, LH.

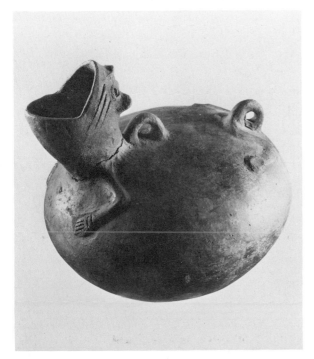

Fig. 43. Chimu-style bottle, Moche, LH.

Fig. 44B. Chimu-style bottle, Moche, LH.

Fig. 45. False mummy head, Chimu Capac, MH.

Fig. 47. Provincial Huari-style tumbler, Chimu Capac, MH 2B.

Fig. 46A, B, C. Provincial Huari-style tumblers, Chimu Capac, MH 2B.

Fig. 48A, B. Provincial Huari-style tumblers, Chimu Capac, MH 2B.

Fig. 50. Provincial Huari-style bottle, Chimu Capac, MH 2B.

Fig. 49. Provincial Huari-style cup, Chimu Capac, MH 2B.

Fig. 51. Provincial Huari-style bottle, Chimu Capac, MH 2B.

Fig. 52. Provincial Huari-style bottle frags., Moche, MH 2B.

Fig. 54. Provincial Huari-style bottle, Chimu Capac, MH 2B.

Fig. 53. Provincial north coast-style jar, Chimu Capac, MH 2B.

Fig. 55. Provincial north coast-style jar, Chimu Capac, MH 2B.

Fig. 56. Painted burial cloth, Chimu Capac, prob. MH 3.

Fig. 58. Painted burial cloth, Chimu Capac, prob. MH 3.

Fig. 57. Painted burial cloth, Chimu Capac, prob. MH 3.

Fig. 59. Painted burial cloth, Chimu Capac, prob. MH 3.

Fig. 60, 61. Jar, Chimu Capac, MH 3.

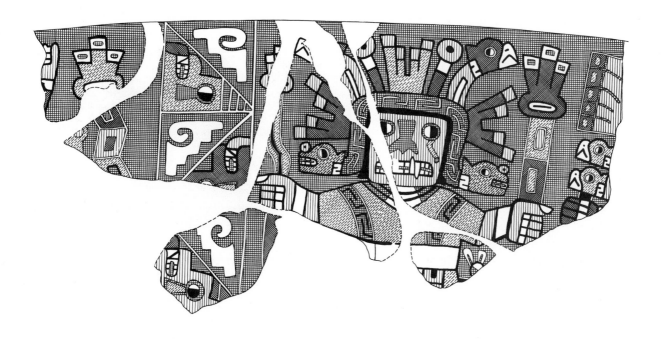

Fig. 62. Huari Deity, near Conchopata, MH 1A.

	Red		Flesh
	Purple		White
	Grey		Black
	Cream		Paste or worn surface
			Dark purple/grey

Red		Flesh	
Purple		White	
Grey		Black	
Cream		Paste or worn surface	
		Dark purple/grey	

Fig. 63. Huari Star Animal, near Conchopata, MH 1A.

Fig. 64. Jar, Chimu Capac, MH 3.

Fig. 65. Jar, Chimu Capac, MH 3.

Red		Flesh
Purple		White
Grey		Black
Cream		Paste or worn surface
		Dark purple/grey

Fig. 66. Huari Walking Angel, near Conchopata, MH 1A.

111

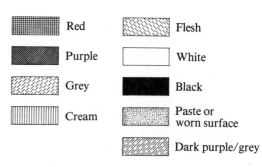

Red   Flesh
Purple   White
Grey   Black
Cream   Paste or
             worn surface
             Dark purple/grey

Fig. 67. Huari Feline-headed Angel, near Conchopata, MH 1A.

Fig. 69A. Mythical serpent, Chimu Capac, MH 3.

Fig. 69B. Mythical serpent, Chimu Capac, MH 2B.

Fig. 68. Jar, Chimu Capac, MH 3.

Fig. 70. Pyro-engraved gourd, Chimu Capac, MH 2A or 1B.

Fig. 71. Pyro-engraved gourd, Chimu Capac, MH 4.

Fig. 72. Ceremonial club, Chimu Capac, MH 2B.

Fig. 73. Ceremonial club, Chimu Capac, prob. MH 3.

Fig. 74. Lime container, Chimu Capac, MH.

Fig. 76. Man's tunic, provincial Huari-style design, Chimu Capac, prob. late MH 2B.

Fig. 75. Huari-style man's tunic, Chimu Capac, prob. late MH 2B.

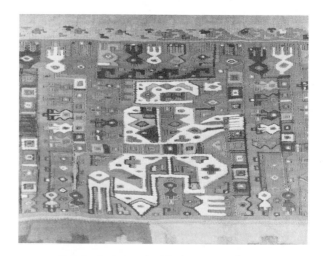

Fig. 76A, B. Details of tunic in fig. 76.

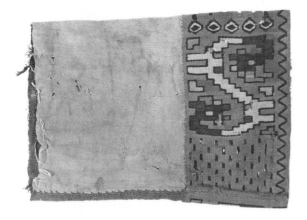

Fig. 77. Sleeve of man's tunic, Chimu Capac, MH 2.

Fig. 79. View of "Pyramid of the Sun," Moche.

Fig. 78. Site of Moche, north coast.

Fig. 80. Moche IV-style Lord head from top of bottle, Moche, EIP 8—MH 1A.

Fig. 82. Whistle frag., Moche, prob. MH 2.

Fig. 81A. Chimu-style deity, Lambayeque, MH.

Fig. 81B. Chimu-style deity bottle, Pacasmayo, MH.

Fig. 83. Trumpet frag., Moche, prob. MH 2.

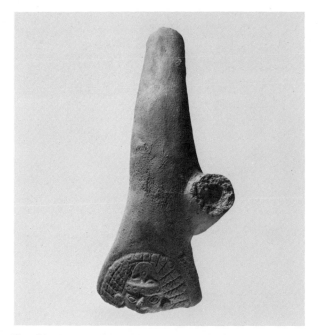

Fig. 84. Trumpet frag., Moche, prob. MH 2.

Fig. 86. Whistle frag., Moche, prob. MH 2.

Fig. 85. Trumpet frag., Moche, prob. MH 2.

Fig. 87. Moche IV-style gold ciasp of necklace, EIP 8-MH 1A.

117

Fig. 88. Moche IV-style hollow gold figure, part of necklace, EIP 8-MH 1A.

Fig. 90. Provincial Huari-style tumbler, Moche, MH 1B.

Fig. 89. Provincial Huari-style tapestry, Moche, MH 1B.

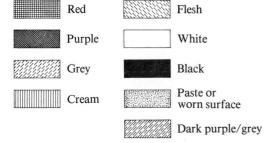

Red

Purple

Grey

Cream

Flesh

White

Black

Paste or
worn surface

Dark purple/grey

Fig. 91. Huari Floating Angels, near Conchopata, MH 1A.

Fig. 92. Provincial Huari-style tumbler, Moche, MH 2.

Fig. 93. Provincial Huari-style tumbler, Moche, MH 2.

Fig. 95. Provincial Huari-style bottle, Moche, MH 2.

Fig. 94. Chimu-style jar, Moche, MH 2B or 3.

Fig. 96. Litter bearer, Moche, prob. MH 3.

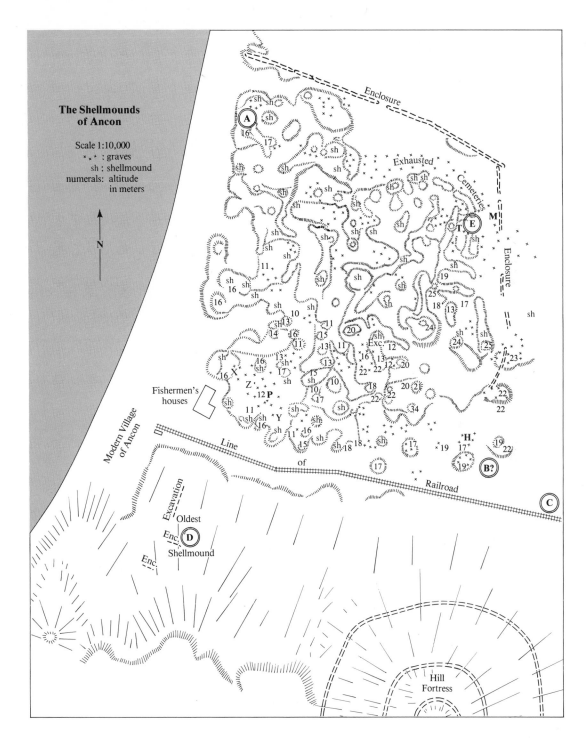

Fig. 97. Map of the Necropolis of Ancón.

Fig. 98. Mummy bales, Ancón, MH.

Fig. 100. Teatino-style jar, Ancón, prob. MH 2B.

Fig. 99. Offering tumbler, Ancón, MH 3.

Fig. 101. Teatino-style jar, Ancón, prob. MH 2B.

Fig. 102. Teatino-style bowl, Ancón, prob. MH 2B.

Fig. 104. Nievería-style bottle, Rimac, MH 1B.

Fig. 103. Provincial Nievería-style pouring bowl, Ancón, MH 1B.

Fig. 105. Nievería-style bottle, Rimac, MH 1B.

123

Fig. 106. Pachacamac-Huari-style jar, Ancón, MH 2B.

Fig. 108. Derived Nievería-style bottle, Ancón, MH 2B.

Fig. 109B. *Spondylus* shell, Moche.

Fig. 107. Pachacamac-Huari-style bottle, Ancón, MH 2B.

Fig. 109A. Provincial (north coast) Huari-style jar, Ancón, MH 2B.

Fig. 111. Jar, Ancón, MH 3.

Fig. 110. Provincial Huari-style jar, Ancón, MH 2B.

Fig. 112. Jar, Ancón, MH 4.

Fig. 114. Pachacamac-Inca-style vessel, Ancón, LH.

Fig. 113A, B. Jars, Ancón, MH 4.

Fig. 115. Grave tablet, Ancón, MH 3 or 4.

Fig. 116. Ear plug ornament, Ancón, MH 4.

Fig. 118. Figurine, Ancón, MH 4.

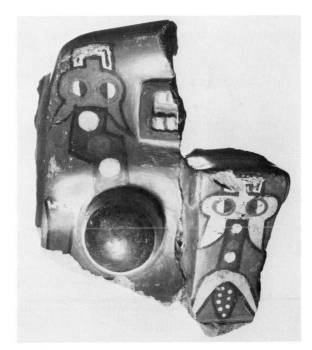

Fig. 119. Huari (Robles Moqo)-style tumbler frag., Nasca, MH 1B.

127

Fig. 120. Huari (Robles Moqo)-style tumbler, Nasca, MH 1B

Fig. 121. Huari (Robles Moqo)-style urn frags., Nasca, MH 1B.

Fig. 122, 123. Huari (Robles Moqo)-style urn, Nasca, MH 1B.

Fig. 124. Man's tunic, provincial Huari-style decoration, Nasca, MH 2A.

Fig. 125. Huari (Robles Moqo)-style offering vessel, Nasca, MH 1B.

Fig. 124a. Design detail of fig. 124.

Fig. 126. Nasca 9B-style jar, Nasca, MH 1B.

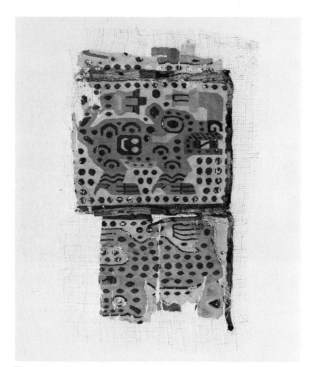

Fig. 127. Provincial Huari-style pouch, Nasca, MH 2A.

Fig. 129. Huari (Robles Moqo)-style jar frag., Nasca, MH 1B.

Fig. 128. Provincial Huari-style lime container, Nasca, prob. MH 1B.

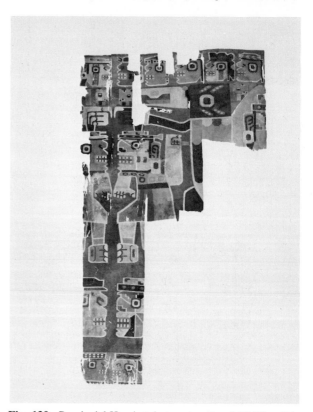

Fig. 130. Provincial Huari-style tapestry, Ica, MH 1B or 2A.

Fig. 131. Ica 1A-style jar, Nasca, LIP 1A.

Fig. 133. Ica 3B-style pouch, Ica, LIP 3B.

Fig. 132. Ica 1A-style jar, Ica, LIP 1A.

Fig. 134. Ica 3A-style offering vessel, Ica, LIP 3A.

Fig. 135. Huari (Robles Moqo)-style offering vessel, Nasca, MH 1B.

Fig. 136. Chincha-style jar, Chincha, LIP 8.

Fig. 137. Moche IIIB-style bottle, Aloof Lord, Moche, EIP, ca. 6.

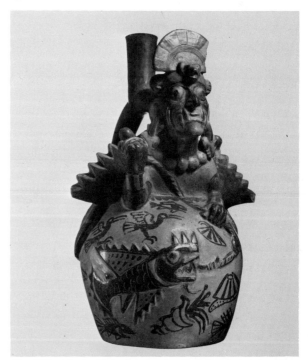

Fig. 138. Moche IIIB-style bottle, Crab Lord, Moche, EIP, ca. 6.

Fig. 139. Moche II-style bottle, Moon Animal, Moche, EIP, ca. 4-5.

Fig. 141. Moche IIIB-style vessel, Moon Spirit Man, Moche, EIP, ca. 6.

Fig. 140. Moche IIIB-style bottle, Moon Spirit Man, Moche, EIP, ca. 6.

Fig. 142. Moche IV-style whistle, Moche, EIP 8-MH 1A.

Fig. 143. Moche IV-style whistle, Moche, EIP 8-MH 1A.

Fig. 145. Moche IIIB-style bottle, woman and child, Moche, EIP, ca. 6.

Fig. 144. Moche IIIB-style bottle, man in informal dress, Moche, EIP, ca. 6.

Fig. 146. Moche IIIB-style jar, coca chewer, Moche, EIP, ca. 6.

Fig. 147. Moche III-style, jar with portrait head, Moche, EIP, ca. 6.

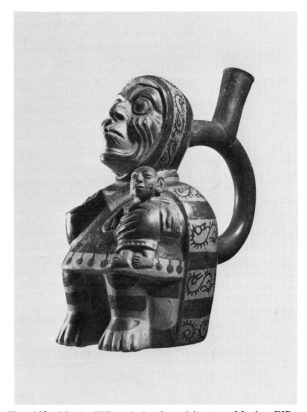

Fig. 149. Moche IIIB-style bottle, spirit curer, Moche, EIP, ca. 6.

Fig. 148. Moche IIIC-style bottle, "weary traveler," Moche, EIP, ca. 6-7.

135